Just The facts101 Textbook Key Facts

Textbook Outlines, Highlights, and Practice Quizzes

Molecular Biology of the Gene

by James D. Watson, 7th Edition

All "Just the Facts101" Material Written or Prepared by Cram101 Textbook Reviews

Title Page

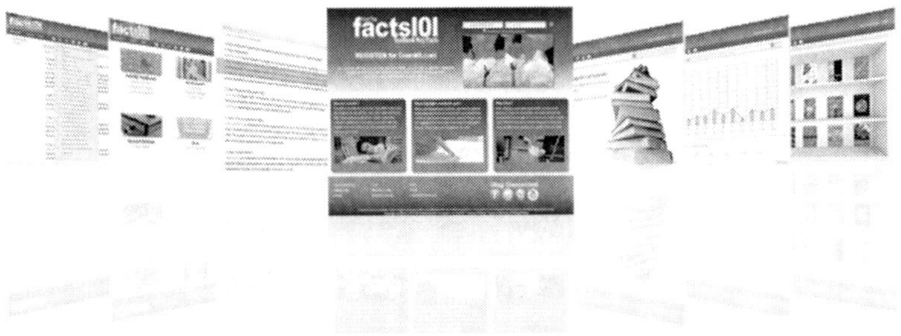

facts101
LEARNING SYSTEM

"Just the Facts101" is a Content Technologies publication and tool designed to give you all the facts from your textbooks. Visit JustTheFacts101.com for the full practice test for each of your chapters for virtually any of your textbooks.

Facts101 has built custom study tools specific to your textbook. We provide all of the factual testable information and unlike traditional study guides, we will never send you back to your textbook for more information.

YOU WILL NEVER HAVE TO HIGHLIGHT A BOOK AGAIN!

Facts101 StudyGuides

All of the information in this StudyGuide is written specifically for your textbook. We include the key terms, places, people, and concepts... the information you can expect on your next exam!

Want to take a practice test?

Throughout each chapter of this StudyGuide you will find links to JustTheFacts101.com where you can select specific chapters to take a complete test on, or you can subscribe and get practice tests for up to 12 of your textbooks, along with other exclusive Jtf101.com tools like problem solving labs and reference libraries.

JustTheFacts101.com

Only Jtf101.com gives you the outlines, highlights, and PRACTICE TESTS specific to your textbook. JustTheFacts101.com is an online application where you'll discover study tools designed to make the most of your limited study time.

By purchasing this book, you get 50% off the normal monthly subscription fee!. Just enter the promotional code **'DK73DW25017'** on the Jtf101.com registration screen.

www.JustTheFacts101.com

ISBN(s): 9781497008434. PUBI-5.2014529

facts101

Molecular Biology of the Gene
James D. Watson, 7th

CONTENTS

1. The Mendelian View of the World, ... 5
2. Nucleic Acids Convey Genetic Information, ... 15
3. The Importance of Weak and Strong Chemical Bonds, ... 25
4. The Structure of DNA, ... 34
5. The Structure and Versatility of RNA, 107 6 The Structure of Proteins, ... 56
6. Genome Structure, Chromatin, and the Nucleosome, ... 74
7. The Replication of DNA, ... 91
8. The Mutability and Repair of DNA, ... 105
9. Homologous Recombination at the Molecular Level, ... 119
10. Site-Specific Recombination and Transposition of DNA, ... 128
11. Mechanisms of Transcription, ... 141
12. RNA Splicing, ... 153
13. Translation, ... 163
14. The Genetic Code, ... 179
15. The Origin and Early Evolution of Life, ... 188
16. Transcriptional Regulation in Prokaryotes, ... 195
17. Transcriptional Regulation in Eukaryotes, ... 207
18. Regulatory RNAs, ... 221
19. Gene Regulation in Development and Evolution, ... 232
20. Systems Biology, ... 245

1. The Mendelian View of the World,

CHAPTER OUTLINE: KEY TERMS, PEOPLE, PLACES, CONCEPTS

- Insulin-like growth factor
- Chromosome
- Gene density
- Bacteriophage
- Darwin
- Recruitment
- Genotype
- Phenotype
- Color
- Flower
- Inheritance
- Theory
- Synapsis
- Gene
- Morgan
- X chromosome
- Barbara
- Homeotic gene
- Gene orders
- Order
- Genetics

1. The Mendelian View of the World,

CHAPTER OUTLINE: KEY TERMS, PEOPLE, PLACES, CONCEPTS

- Genetic variability
- Hot spot
- Mutation
- Origin
- Prediction
- Fisher
- George
- DNA damage
- Phenylalanine
- Rose

CHAPTER HIGHLIGHTS & NOTES: KEY TERMS, PEOPLE, PLACES, CONCEPTS

Insulin-like growth factor	The insulin-like growth factors are proteins with high sequence similarity to insulin. Insulin-like growth factors are part of a complex system that cells use to communicate with their physiologic environment. This complex system (often referred to as the Insulin-like growth factor 'axis') consists of two cell-surface receptors (Insulin-like growth factor1R and Insulin-like growth factor2R), two ligands (Insulin-like growth factor 1 (Insulin-like growth factor-I) and Insulin-like growth factor 2 (Insulin-like growth factor-2)), a family of six high-affinity Insulin-like growth factor-binding proteins (IGFBP-1 to IGFBP-6), as well as associated IGFBP degrading enzymes, referred to collectively as proteases.
Chromosome	A chromosome is an organized structure of DNA, protein, and RNA found in cells. It is a single piece of coiled DNA containing many genes, regulatory elements and other nucleotide sequences. Chromosomes also contain DNA-bound proteins, which serve to package the DNA and control its functions.

Gene density

In genetics, the gene density of an organism's genome is the ratio of the number of genes per number of base pairs, usually written in terms of a million base pairs, or megabase . The human genome has a gene density of 12-15 genes/Mb, while the genome of the C. elegans roundworm is estimated to have only 1 gene per 5000 base pairs.

Curiously, seemingly simple organisms such as bacteria and amoebas have a much higher gene density than humans.

Bacteriophage

A bacteriophage is a virus that infects and replicates within bacteria. The term is derived from 'bacteria' and the Greek fa?e?? phagein 'to devour'. Bacteriophages are composed of proteins that encapsulate a DNA or RNA genome, and may have relatively simple or elaborate structures.

Darwin

The darwin is a unit of evolutionary change, defined by J.B.S. Haldane in 1949. One darwin is defined to be an e-fold (about 2.718) change in a trait over one million years. Haldane named the unit after Charles Darwin.

Recruitment

In biology, recruitment occurs when juvenile organisms survive to be added to a population. The term is generally used to refer to a stage whereby the organisms are settled and able to be detected by an observer.

Genotype

The genotype is the genetic makeup of a cell, an organism, or an individual usually with reference to a specific characteristic under consideration. For instance, the human CFTR gene, which encodes a protein that transports chloride ions across cell membranes, can be dominant (A) as the normal version of the gene, or recessive (a) as a mutated version of the gene. Individuals receiving two recessive alleles will be diagnosed with Cystic fibrosis.

Phenotype

A phenotype is the composite of an organism's observable characteristics or traits, such as its morphology, development, biochemical or physiological properties, phenology, behavior, and products of behavior (such as a bird's nest). Phenotypes result from the expression of an organism's genes as well as the influence of environmental factors and the interactions between the two. When two or more clearly different phenotypes exist in the same population of a species, it is called polymorph.

Color

Color or colour is the visual perceptual property corresponding in humans to the categories called red, blue, yellow, green and others. Color derives from the spectrum of light (distribution of light power versus wavelength) interacting in the eye with the spectral sensitivities of the light receptors. Color categories and physical specifications of color are also associated with objects, materials, light sources, etc., based on their physical properties such as light absorption, reflection, or emission spectra.

Flower

A flower, sometimes known as a bloom or blossom, is the reproductive structure found in flowering plants .

1. The Mendelian View of the World,

CHAPTER HIGHLIGHTS & NOTES: KEY TERMS, PEOPLE, PLACES, CONCEPTS

	The biological function of a flower is to effect reproduction, usually by providing a mechanism for the union of sperm with eggs. Flowers may facilitate outcrossing (fusion of sperm and eggs from different individuals in a population) or allow selfing (fusion of sperm and egg from the same flower).
Inheritance	In genetic algorithms, inheritance is the ability of modelled objects to mate, mutate and propagate their problem solving genes to the next generation, in order to produce an evolved solution to a particular problem.
Theory	Theory is a contemplative and rational type of abstract or generalizing thinking, or the results of such thinking. Depending on the context, the results might for example include generalized explanations of how nature works. The word has its roots in ancient Greek, but in modern use it has taken on several different related meanings.
Synapsis	Synapsis is the pairing of two homologous chromosomes that occurs during meiosis. This is not to be confused with mitosis. Mitosis also has prophase, but does not do pairing of two homologous chromosomes.
Gene	A gene is a molecular unit of heredity of a living organism. It is widely accepted by the scientific community as a name given to some stretches of deoxyribonucleic acids (DNA) and ribonucleic acids (RNA) that code for a polypeptide or for an RNA chain that has a function in the organism, though there still are controversies about what plays the role of the genetic material. Living beings depend on genes, as they specify all proteins and functional RNA chains.
Morgan	Morgan is a lone female orca that was rescued in the Wadden Sea, off the northwestern coast of the Netherlands in June 2010. She lived several months in the Dolfinarium Harderwijk in the Netherlands. After a legal battle she was transported to the Loro Parque in Spain.
X chromosome	The X chromosome is one of the two sex-determining chromosomes in many animal species, including mammals (the other is the Y chromosome), and is found in both males and females. It is a part of the XY sex-determination system and X0 sex-determination system. The X chromosome was named for its unique properties by early researchers, which resulted in the naming of its counterpart Y chromosome, for the next letter in the alphabet, after it was discovered later.
Barbara	Barbara, also referred to as Bilad al-Barbar, was an ancient region on the northern coast of the Somalia. The area was inhabited by the Eastern Baribah or Barbaroi (Berbers), as the ancestors of the Somalis were referred to by medieval Arab and ancient Greek geographers, respectively. Along with the neighboring Habash (Abyssinians) of al-Habash, the Barbaroi are recorded in the 1st century Greek document the Periplus of the Erythraean Sea as engaging in extensive commercial exchanges with Egypt and pre-Islamic Arabia.
Homeotic gene	Homeotic genes cause the development of specific structures in plants and animals.

They include many of the Hox and ParaHox genes which are important for segmentation, They also include the MADS-box-containing genes involved the ABC model of flower development. It is important to note that not all homeotic genes are Hox genes; the MADS- box genes are homeotic but not Hox genes.

Gene orders

Gene orders is the permutation of genome arrangement. So far a fair amount of work trying to describe whether gene orders evolve according to a molecular clock (molecular clock hypothesis) or in jumps (punctuated equilibrium).

Some research on Gene orders in animals' mitochondrial gemone reveal that the mutation rate of gene orders is not a constant in some degrees.

Order

In scientific classification used in biology, the order is•a taxonomic rank used in the classification of organisms. Other well-known ranks are life, domain, kingdom, phylum, class, family, genus, and species, with order fitting in between class and family. An immediately higher rank, superorder, may be added directly above order, while suborder would be a lower rank.•a taxonomic unit, a taxon, in that rank.

Genetics

Genetics, a discipline of biology, is the science of genes, heredity, and variation in living organisms.

Genetics concerns the process of trait inheritance from parents to offspring, including the molecular structure and function of genes, gene behavior in the context of a cell or organism (e.g. dominance and epigenetics), gene distribution, and variation and change in populations (such as through Genome-Wide Association Studies). Given that genes are universal to living organisms, genetics can be applied to the study of all living systems; including bacteria, plants, animals, and humans.

Genetic variability

Genetic variability is a measure of the tendency of individual genotypes in a population to vary from one another. Variability is different from genetic diversity, which is the amount of variation seen in a particular population. The variability of a trait describes how much that trait tends to vary in response to environmental and genetic influences.

Hot spot

In veterinary medicine, a 'hot spot' (or acute pyoderma, acute moist pyotraumatic dermatitis) is one of the many names for a raw, painful, irritated skin lesion that results in and worsens from a pet (such as a dog or a cat) constantly biting, scratching, chewing, and licking an area of its skin that is irritated or itchy. If it is covered by the dog's hair, the hair holds in the moisture and further irritates it.

It is a patch that appears suddenly and is often bright red, hairless, and scaly looking.

Mutation

In genetics, a mutation is a change of the nucleotide sequence of the genome of an organism, virus, or extrachromosomal genetic element.

Mutations result from unrepaired damage to DNA or to RNA genomes (typically caused by radiation or chemical mutagens), errors in the process of replication, or from the insertion or deletion of segments of DNA by mobile genetic elements. Mutations may or may not produce discernible changes in the observable characteristics (phenotype) of an organism.

Origin

The anatomical origin is a concept used when describing muscles, tendons, ligaments, nerves, and blood and lymph vessels. While it often has a slightly different meaning depending on which kind of origin is referred to, it is generally used to explain the relative location of the anatomical structure in question. It is not to be understood in a temporal/ontogenetical sense.

Prediction

A prediction or forecast is a statement about the way things will happen in the future, often but not always based on experience or knowledge. While there is much overlap between prediction and forecast, a prediction may be a statement that some outcome is expected, while a forecast is more specific, and may cover a range of possible outcomes.

Although guaranteed information about the future is in many cases impossible, prediction is necessary to allow plans to be made about possible developments; Howard H. Stevenson writes that prediction in business '... is at least two things: Important and hard.'

Fisher

The fisher is a medium-sized mammal native to North America. It is a member of the mustelid family, commonly referred to as the weasel family. The fisher is closely related to but larger than the American Marten (Martes americana). The fisher is a forest-dwelling creature whose range covers much of the boreal forest in Canada to the northern fringes of the United States.

George

George was a Jack Russell Terrier from New Zealand who was posthumously awarded a PDSA Gold Medal in February 2009. He defended children from an attack by two Pit Bulls but subsequently died of his injuries.

DNA damage

DNA damage is an alteration in the chemical structure of DNA, such as a break in a strand of DNA, a base missing from the backbone of DNA, or a chemically changed base such as 8-OHdG. Damage to DNA that occurs naturally can result from metabolic or hydrolytic processes. Metabolism releases compounds that damage DNA including reactive oxygen species, reactive nitrogen species, reactive carbonyl species, lipid peroxidation products and alkylating agents, among others, while hydrolysis cleaves chemical bonds in DNA. Naturally occurring DNA damages arise about 10,000 to 100,000 times per day per mammalian cell.

DNA damage is distinctly different from mutation, although both are types of error in DNA. DNA damage is an abnormal chemical structure in DNA, while a mutation is a change in the sequence of standard base pairs.

Phenylalanine

Phenylalanine is an a-amino acid with the formula $C_6H_5CH_2CH(NH_2)COOH$. This essential amino acid is classified as nonpolar because of the hydrophobic nature of the benzyl side chain.

CHAPTER HIGHLIGHTS & NOTES: KEY TERMS, PEOPLE, PLACES, CONCEPTS

-Phenylalanine is an electrically neutral amino acid, one of the twenty common amino acids used to biochemically form proteins, coded for by DNA. The codons for -phenylalanine are UUU and UUC. Phenylalanine is a precursor for tyrosine, the monoamine signaling molecules dopamine, norepinephrine (noradrenaline), and epinephrine (adrenaline), and the skin pigment melanin.

Phenylalanine is found naturally in the breast milk of mammals.

Rose

A rose is a woody perennial of the genus Rosa, within the family Rosaceae. There are over 100 species. They form a group of plants that can be erect shrubs, climbing or trailing with stems that are often armed with sharp prickles.

CHAPTER QUIZ: KEY TERMS, PEOPLE, PLACES, CONCEPTS

1. The _________s are proteins with high sequence similarity to insulin. _________s are part of a complex system that cells use to communicate with their physiologic environment. This complex system (often referred to as the _________ 'axis') consists of two cell-surface receptors (Insulin-like growth factor1R and Insulin-like growth factor2R), two ligands (_________ 1 (_________-I) and _________ 2 (_________-2)), a family of six high-affinity _________-binding proteins (IGFBP-1 to IGFBP-6), as well as associated IGFBP degrading enzymes, referred to collectively as proteases.

   a. Blood sugar regulation
   b. Bovine somatotropin
   c. Chromatophobe
   d. Insulin-like growth factor

2. In veterinary medicine, a '_________' (or acute pyoderma, acute moist pyotraumatic dermatitis) is one of the many names for a raw, painful, irritated skin lesion that results in and worsens from a pet (such as a dog or a cat) constantly biting, scratching, chewing, and licking an area of its skin that is irritated or itchy. If it is covered by the dog's hair, the hair holds in the moisture and further irritates it.

   It is a patch that appears suddenly and is often bright red, hairless, and scaly looking.

   a. Botswana Wild Dog Research Project
   b. Cadaver dog
   c. Hot spot
   d. Cropping

3. . A _________ is a virus that infects and replicates within bacteria. The term is derived from 'bacteria' and the Greek fa?e?? phagein 'to devour'.

_________s are composed of proteins that encapsulate a DNA or RNA genome, and may have relatively simple or elaborate structures.

a. Bacterial conjugation
b. Horizontal gene transfer
c. Bacteriophage
d. Carbapenem resistant enterobacteriaceae

4. _________ was a Jack Russell Terrier from New Zealand who was posthumously awarded a PDSA Gold Medal in February 2009. He defended children from an attack by two Pit Bulls but subsequently died of his injuries.

a. Cairn Terrier
b. Chilean Fox Terrier
c. Sixth nerve palsy
d. George

5. A _________ is an organized structure of DNA, protein, and RNA found in cells. It is a single piece of coiled DNA containing many genes, regulatory elements and other nucleotide sequences. _________s also contain DNA-bound proteins, which serve to package the DNA and control its functions.

a. Dendrosome
b. Chromosome
c. Biodistribution
d. Biobank

ANSWER KEY
1. The Mendelian View of the World,

---

1. d
2. c
3. c
4. d
5. b

---

2. Nucleic Acids Convey Genetic Information,

CHAPTER OUTLINE: KEY TERMS, PEOPLE, PLACES, CONCEPTS

- George
- One gene-one enzyme hypothesis
- Martha
- Virulence
- Experiment
- Gene
- Genetics
- Nucleic acid
- Dosage compensation
- Adenine
- Bacteria
- Cytosine
- Discovery
- Guanine
- Kinase
- Marker gene
- Sequencing
- Thymine
- Amino acid
- Carbon
- Helix

2. Nucleic Acids Convey Genetic Information,

CHAPTER OUTLINE: KEY TERMS, PEOPLE, PLACES, CONCEPTS

Bacteriophage

Sequence

Cooperative binding

Cre recombinase

Deoxyribose

Ribose

Adaptor hypothesis

Transfer RNA

Hypothesis

Protein

Ligase ribozyme

Genetic code

Comparative genomics

Nonsense

George
George was a Jack Russell Terrier from New Zealand who was posthumously awarded a PDSA Gold Medal in February 2009. He defended children from an attack by two Pit Bulls but subsequently died of his injuries.

One gene-one enzyme hypothesis
The one gene-one enzyme hypothesis is the idea that genes act through the production of enzymes, with each gene responsible for producing a single enzyme that in turn affects a single step in a metabolic pathway. The concept was proposed by George Beadle and Edward Tatum in an influential 1941 paper on genetic mutations in the mold Neurospora crassa, and subsequently was dubbed the 'one gene-one enzyme hypothesis' by their collaborator Norman Horowitz. It is often considered the first significant result in what came to be called molecular biology.

Martha
Martha was the last known living Passenger Pigeon; she was named 'Martha' in honor of Martha Washington.

Virulence
Virulence is, by MeSH definition, the degree of pathogenicity within a group or species of parasites as indicated by case fatality rates and/or the ability of the organism to invade the tissues of the host. The pathogenicity of an organism - its ability to cause disease - is determined by its virulence factors. The noun virulence derives from the adjective virulent.

Experiment
The Experiment was an early nineteenth century boat powered by horses and incorporated the then novel idea of a screw propeller.

Gene
A gene is a molecular unit of heredity of a living organism. It is widely accepted by the scientific community as a name given to some stretches of deoxyribonucleic acids (DNA) and ribonucleic acids (RNA) that code for a polypeptide or for an RNA chain that has a function in the organism, though there still are controversies about what plays the role of the genetic material. Living beings depend on genes, as they specify all proteins and functional RNA chains.

Genetics
Genetics, a discipline of biology, is the science of genes, heredity, and variation in living organisms.

Genetics concerns the process of trait inheritance from parents to offspring, including the molecular structure and function of genes, gene behavior in the context of a cell or organism (e.g. dominance and epigenetics), gene distribution, and variation and change in populations (such as through Genome-Wide Association Studies). Given that genes are universal to living organisms, genetics can be applied to the study of all living systems; including bacteria, plants, animals, and humans.

Nucleic acid
The nucleic acids are polymeric macromolecules, or large biological molecules, essential for all known forms of life. Nucleic acids, which include DNA (deoxyribonucleic acid) and RNA (ribonucleic acid), are made from nucleotide monomers.

2. Nucleic Acids Convey Genetic Information,

CHAPTER HIGHLIGHTS & NOTES: KEY TERMS, PEOPLE, PLACES, CONCEPTS

Dosage compensation

Dosage compensation is a hypothetical genetic regulatory mechanism which operates to equalize the phenotypic expression of characteristics determined by genes on the X chromosome so that they are equally expressed in the human XY male and the XX female.

Dosage compensation may occur in other organisms like the fruit fly Drosophila melanogaster, the roundworm Caenorhabditis elegans and the plant White campion .

Species can have different mechanisms of dosage compensation.

Adenine

Adenine is a nucleobase (a purine derivative) with a variety of roles in biochemistry including cellular respiration, in the form of both the energy-rich adenosine triphosphate (ATP) and the cofactors nicotinamide adenine dinucleotide (NAD) and flavin adenine dinucleotide (FAD), and protein synthesis, as a chemical component of DNA and RNA. The shape of adenine is complementary to either thymine in DNA or uracil in RNA.

Bacteria

Bacteria constitute a large domain or kingdom of prokaryotic microorganisms. Typically a few micrometres in length, bacteria have a wide range of shapes, ranging from spheres to rods and spirals. Bacteria were among the first life forms to appear on Earth, and are present in most habitats on the planet.

Cytosine

Cytosine is one of the four main bases found in DNA and RNA, along with adenine, guanine, and thymine (uracil in RNA). It is a pyrimidine derivative, with a heterocyclic aromatic ring and two substituents attached (an amine group at position 4 and a keto group at position 2). The nucleoside of cytosine is cytidine.

Discovery

Discovery is the act of detecting something new, or something 'old' that had been unknown. With reference to science and academic disciplines, discovery is the observation of new phenomena, new actions, or new events and providing new reasoning to explain the knowledge gathered through such observations with previously acquired knowledge from abstract thought and everyday experiences. Visual discoveries are often called sightings.

Guanine

Guanine is one of the four main nucleobases found in the nucleic acids DNA and RNA, the others being adenine, cytosine, and thymine (uracil in RNA). In DNA, guanine is paired with cytosine. With the formula $C_5H_5N_5O$, guanine is a derivative of purine, consisting of a fused pyrimidine-imidazole ring system with conjugated double bonds.

Kinase

In enzymology, a [tyrosine 3-monooxygenase] kinase is an enzyme that catalyzes the chemical reactionATP + [tyrosine-3-monooxygenase] $\rightleftharpoons$ ADP + phospho-[tyrosine-3-monooxygenase]

Thus, the two substrates of this enzyme are ATP and tyrosine-3-monooxygenase, whereas its two products are ADP and [[phospho-[tyrosine-3-monooxygenase]]].

This enzyme belongs to the family of transferases, specifically those transferring a phosphate group to the sidechain oxygen atom of serine or threonine residues in proteins (protein-serine/threonine kinases). The systematic name of this enzyme class is ATP:[tyrosine-3-monoxygenase] phosphotransferase.

Marker gene

A marker gene is a gene used in nuclear biology to determine if a nucleic acid sequence has been successfully inserted into an organism's DNA. There are two types of marker genes: a selectable marker and a marker for screening.

Sequencing

In genetics and biochemistry, sequencing means to determine the primary structure of an unbranched biopolymer. Sequencing results in a symbolic linear depiction known as a sequence which succinctly summarizes much of the atomic-level structure of the sequenced molecule.

Thymine

Thymine is one of the four nucleobases in the nucleic acid of DNA that are represented by the letters G-C-A-T. The others are adenine, guanine, and cytosine. Thymine is also known as 5-methyluracil, a pyrimidine nucleobase.

Amino acid

Amino acids are biologically important organic compounds made from amine ($-NH_2$) and carboxylic acid (-COOH) functional groups, along with a side-chain specific to each amino acid. The key elements of an amino acid are carbon, hydrogen, oxygen, and nitrogen, though other elements are found in the side-chains of certain amino acids. About 500 amino acids are known and can be classified in many ways.

Carbon

Carbon is the chemical element with symbol C and atomic number 6. As a member of group 14 on the periodic table, it is nonmetallic and tetravalent--making four electrons available to form covalent chemical bonds. There are three naturally occurring isotopes, with ^{12}C and ^{13}C being stable, while ^{14}C is radioactive, decaying with a half-life of about 5,730 years. Carbon is one of the few elements known since antiquity.

Helix

The prominent rim of the auricula is called the helix. Where the helix turns downward behind, a small tubercle is frequently seen: the auricular tubercle of Darwin.

Bacteriophage

A bacteriophage is a virus that infects and replicates within bacteria. The term is derived from 'bacteria' and the Greek fa?e?? phagein 'to devour'. Bacteriophages are composed of proteins that encapsulate a DNA or RNA genome, and may have relatively simple or elaborate structures.

Sequence

In medicine, a sequence is a series of ordered consequences due to a single cause.

It differs from a syndrome in that seriality is more predictable: if A causes B, and B causes C, and C causes D, then D would not be seen if C is not seen.

2. Nucleic Acids Convey Genetic Information,

CHAPTER HIGHLIGHTS & NOTES: KEY TERMS, PEOPLE, PLACES, CONCEPTS

Cooperative binding	Molecular binding is an interaction between molecules that results in a stable association between those molecules. Cooperative binding occurs if the number of binding sites of a macromolecule that are occupied by a specific type of ligand is a non-linear function of this ligand's concentration. This can be due, for instance, to an affinity for the ligand that depends on the amount of ligand bound.
Cre recombinase	Cre Recombinase is a tyrosine recombinase enzyme derived from the P1 Bacteriophage. The enzyme uses a topoisomerase I like mechanism to carry out site specific recombination events. The enzyme (38kDa) is a member of the Integrase family of site specific recombinase and it is known to catalyse the site specific recombination event between two DNA recognition sites (loxP sites).
Deoxyribose	Deoxyribose, or more precisely 2-deoxyribose, is a monosaccharide with idealized formula H--(CH_2)-$(CHOH)_3$-H. Its name indicates that it is a deoxy sugar, meaning that it is derived from the sugar ribose by loss of an oxygen atom. Since the pentose sugars arabinose and ribose only differ by the stereochemistry at C2', 2-deoxyribose and 2-deoxyarabinose are equivalent, although the latter term is rarely used because ribose, not arabinose, is the precursor to deoxyribose.
Ribose	Ribose is an organic compound with the formula $C_5H_{10}O_5$; specifically, a monosaccharide with linear form H-(C=O)-$(CHOH)_4$-H, which has all the hydroxyl groups on the same side in the Fischer projection. The term may refer to either of two enantiomers. The term usually indicates -ribose, which occurs widely in nature and is discussed here.
Adaptor hypothesis	The adaptor hypothesis is part of a scheme to explain how information encoded in DNA is used to specify the amino acid sequence of proteins. It was formulated by Francis Crick in the mid-1950s, together with the central dogma of molecular biology and the sequence hypothesis
Transfer RNA	A Transfer RNA is an adaptor molecule composed of RNA, typically 73 to 94 nucleotides in length, that serves as the physical link between the nucleotide sequence of nucleic acids (DNA and RNA) and the amino acid sequence of proteins. It does this by carrying an amino acid to the protein synthetic machinery of a cell (ribosome) as directed by a three-nucleotide sequence (codon) in a messenger RNA (mRNA). As such, tRNAs are a necessary component of protein translation, the biological synthesis of new proteins according to the genetic code.
Hypothesis	A hypothesis is a proposed explanation for a phenomenon. For a hypothesis to be a scientific hypothesis, the scientific method requires that one can test it. Scientists generally base scientific hypotheses on previous observations that cannot satisfactorily be explained with the available scientific theories.
Protein	Proteins are large biological molecules consisting of one or more chains of amino acids.

Proteins perform a vast array of functions within living organisms, including catalyzing metabolic reactions, replicating DNA, responding to stimuli, and transporting molecules from one location to another. Proteins differ from one another primarily in their sequence of amino acids, which is dictated by the nucleotide sequence of their genes, and which usually results in folding of the protein into a specific three-dimensional structure that determines its activity.

Ligase ribozyme

The RNA Ligase ribozyme was the first of several types of synthetic ribozymes produced by in vitro evolution and selection techniques. They are an important class of ribozymes because they catalyze the assembly of RNA fragments into phosphodiester RNA polymers, a reaction required of all extant nucleic acid polymerases and thought to be required for any self-replicating molecule. Ideas that the origin of life may have involved the first self-replicating molecules being ribozymes are called RNA World hypotheses.

Genetic code

The genetic code is the set of rules by which information encoded within genetic material is translated into proteins by living cells. Biological decoding is accomplished by the ribosome, which links amino acids in an order specified by mRNA, using transfer RNA (tRNA) molecules to carry amino acids and to read the mRNA three nucleotides at a time. The genetic code is highly similar among all organisms and can be expressed in a simple table with 64 entries.

Comparative genomics

Definition

Comparative genomics is the study of the relationship of genome structure and function across different biological species or strains. Comparative genomics is an attempt to take advantage of the information provided by the signatures of selection to understand the function and evolutionary processes that act on genomes. While it is still a young field, it holds great promise to yield insights into many aspects of the evolution of modern species.

Nonsense

Nonsense is a communication, via speech, writing, or any other symbolic system, that lacks any coherent meaning. Sometimes in ordinary usage, nonsense is synonymous with absurdity or the ridiculous. Many poets, novelists and songwriters have used nonsense in their works, often creating entire works using it for reasons ranging from pure comic amusement or satire, to illustrating a point about language or reasoning.

2. Nucleic Acids Convey Genetic Information,

CHAPTER QUIZ: KEY TERMS, PEOPLE, PLACES, CONCEPTS

1. In enzymology, a [tyrosine 3-monooxygenase] _________ is an enzyme that catalyzes the chemical reactionATP + [tyrosine-3-monooxygenase] ⇌ ADP + phospho-[tyrosine-3-monooxygenase]

   Thus, the two substrates of this enzyme are ATP and tyrosine-3-monooxygenase, whereas its two products are ADP and [[phospho-[tyrosine-3-monooxygenase]]].

   This enzyme belongs to the family of transferases, specifically those transferring a phosphate group to the sidechain oxygen atom of serine or threonine residues in proteins (protein-serine/threonine _________s). The systematic name of this enzyme class is ATP:[tyrosine-3-monoxygenase] phosphotransferase.

   a. -1-benzyl-1,2,3,4-tetrahydroisoquinoline N-methyltransferase
   b. Kinase
   c. -2-methylmalate dehydratase
   d. -3-amino-2-methylpropionate transaminase

2. _________ is an organic compound with the formula $C_5H_{10}O_5$; specifically, a monosaccharide with linear form H-(C=O)-$(CHOH)_4$-H, which has all the hydroxyl groups on the same side in the Fischer projection.

   The term may refer to either of two enantiomers. The term usually indicates -_________, which occurs widely in nature and is discussed here.

   a. Lyxose
   b. Ribose
   c. John Martin Poyer
   d. RMS Tahiti

3. _________, a discipline of biology, is the science of genes, heredity, and variation in living organisms.

   _________ concerns the process of trait inheritance from parents to offspring, including the molecular structure and function of genes, gene behavior in the context of a cell or organism (e.g. dominance and epi_________), gene distribution, and variation and change in populations (such as through Genome-Wide Association Studies). Given that genes are universal to living organisms, _________ can be applied to the study of all living systems; including bacteria, plants, animals, and humans.

   a. Genetics
   b. Ham
   c. Laika
   d. Miss Baker

4. . The _________ is the set of rules by which information encoded within genetic material is translated into proteins by living cells. Biological decoding is accomplished by the ribosome, which links amino acids in an order specified by mRNA, using transfer RNA (tRNA) molecules to carry amino acids and to read the mRNA three nucleotides at a time. The _________ is highly similar among all organisms and can be expressed in a simple table with 64 entries.

a. Bacterial one-hybrid system
b. Baek Sung-hee
c. Biopolymer
d. Genetic code

5. In medicine, a _________ is a series of ordered con_________s due to a single cause.

It differs from a syndrome in that seriality is more predictable: if A causes B, and B causes C, and C causes D, then D would not be seen if C is not seen. However, in less formal contexts, the term 'syndrome' is sometimes used instead of _________.

a. 1q21.1 deletion syndrome
b. Bangstad syndrome
c. Barakat syndrome
d. Sequence

ANSWER KEY
2. Nucleic Acids Convey Genetic Information,

1. b
2. b
3. a
4. d
5. d

3. The Importance of Weak and Strong Chemical Bonds,

CHAPTER OUTLINE: KEY TERMS, PEOPLE, PLACES, CONCEPTS

Protein

Protein structure

RNA polymerase

Polymerase

Water

Alanine

Amino acid

Edman degradation

Environment

Cooperative binding

Hfq protein

Enzyme

Function

Plant

Acetylation

Photosynthesis

Biomolecule

Histone

Nucleosome

Symbol

DNA damage

3. The Importance of Weak and Strong Chemical Bonds,

CHAPTER OUTLINE: KEY TERMS, PEOPLE, PLACES, CONCEPTS

- Peptide
- Hydrolase
- Nucleic acid
- Nucleoside triphosphate
- Split

CHAPTER HIGHLIGHTS & NOTES: KEY TERMS, PEOPLE, PLACES, CONCEPTS

Protein	Proteins are large biological molecules consisting of one or more chains of amino acids. Proteins perform a vast array of functions within living organisms, including catalyzing metabolic reactions, replicating DNA, responding to stimuli, and transporting molecules from one location to another. Proteins differ from one another primarily in their sequence of amino acids, which is dictated by the nucleotide sequence of their genes, and which usually results in folding of the protein into a specific three-dimensional structure that determines its activity.
Protein structure	Protein structure is the biomolecular structure of a protein molecule. Each protein is a polymer - specifically a polypeptide - that is a sequence formed from various L-a-amino acids (also referred to as residues). By convention, a chain under 40 residues is often identified as a peptide, rather than a protein.
RNA polymerase	RNA polymerase, also known as DNA-dependent RNA polymerase, is an enzyme that produces RNA. In cells, RNAP is necessary for constructing RNA chains using DNA genes as templates, a process called transcription. RNA polymerase enzymes are essential to life and are found in all organisms and many viruses. In chemical terms, RNAP is a nucleotidyl transferase that polymerizes ribonucleotides at the 3' end of an RNA transcript.
Polymerase	A polymerase is an enzyme whose central biological function is the synthesis of polymers of nucleic acids. DNA polymerase and RNA polymerase are used to assemble DNA and RNA molecules, respectively, generally by copying a DNA or RNA template strand using base-pairing interactions.

Water	Water is a chemical compound with the chemical formula H2O. A water molecule contains one oxygen and two hydrogen atoms connected by covalent bonds. Water is a liquid at standard ambient temperature and pressure, but it often co-exists on Earth with its solid state, ice, and gaseous state, steam (water vapor).
Alanine	Alanine is an a-amino acid with the chemical formula $CH_3CH(NH_2)COOH$. The -isomer is one of the 20 amino acids encoded by the genetic code. Its codons are GCU, GCC, GCA, and GCG. It is classified as a nonpolar amino acid. -Alanine is second only to leucine in rate of occurrence, accounting for 7.8% of the primary structure in a sample of 1,150 proteins.
Amino acid	Amino acids are biologically important organic compounds made from amine ($-NH_2$) and carboxylic acid (-COOH) functional groups, along with a side-chain specific to each amino acid. The key elements of an amino acid are carbon, hydrogen, oxygen, and nitrogen, though other elements are found in the side-chains of certain amino acids. About 500 amino acids are known and can be classified in many ways.
Edman degradation	Edman degradation, developed by Pehr Edman, is a method of sequencing amino acids in a peptide. In this method, the amino-terminal residue is labeled and cleaved from the peptide without disrupting the peptide bonds between other amino acid residues.
Environment	The biophysical environment is the biotic and abiotic surrounding of an organism or population, and includes particularly the factors that have an influence in their survival, development and evolution. The naked term environment can make reference to different concepts, but it is often used as a short form for the biophysical environment. This practice is common, for instance, among governments, that usually name their departments and agencies dealing with the biophysical environment with denominations like Environment Agency.
Cooperative binding	Molecular binding is an interaction between molecules that results in a stable association between those molecules. Cooperative binding occurs if the number of binding sites of a macromolecule that are occupied by a specific type of ligand is a non-linear function of this ligand's concentration. This can be due, for instance, to an affinity for the ligand that depends on the amount of ligand bound.
Hfq protein	The Hfq protein encoded by the hfq gene was discovered in 1968 as an Escherichia. coli host factor that was essential for replication of the bacteriophage Qß. It is now clear that Hfq is an abundant bacterial RNA binding protein which has many important physiological roles.
Enzyme	Enzymes are large biological molecules responsible for the thousands of metabolic processes that sustain life. They are highly selective catalysts, greatly accelerating both the rate and specificity of metabolic reactions, from the digestion of food to the synthesis of DNA. Most enzymes are proteins, although some catalytic RNA molecules have been identified. Enzymes adopt a specific three-dimensional structure, and may employ organic (e.g. biotin) and inorganic (e.g.

3. The Importance of Weak and Strong Chemical Bonds,

CHAPTER HIGHLIGHTS & NOTES: KEY TERMS, PEOPLE, PLACES, CONCEPTS

Function	A function is the reason some object or process occurred in a system that evolved through a process of selection or Natural selection. Thus, function refers forward from the object or process, along some chain of causation, to the goal or success. Compare this to the mechanism of the object or process, which looks backward along some chain of causation, explaining how the feature occurred.
Plant	Plants, also called green plants (Viridiplantae in Latin), are living multicellular organisms of the kingdom Plantae. They form a clade that includes the flowering plants, conifers and other gymnosperms, ferns, clubmosses, hornworts, liverworts and mosses, as well as, depending on definition, the green algae. Plants exclude the red and brown seaweeds such as kelp, the fungi, Archaea and bacteria.
Acetylation	Acetylation describes a reaction that introduces an acetyl functional group into a chemical compound. (Deacetylation is the removal of the acetyl group). Specifically, acetylation refers to the process of introducing an acetyl group (resulting in an acetoxy group) into a compound, namely, the substitution of an acetyl group for an active hydrogen atom.
Photosynthesis	Photosynthesis is a process used by plants and other organisms to convert light energy, normally from the sun, into chemical energy that can be used to fuel the organisms' activities. Carbohydrates, such as sugars, are synthesized from carbon dioxide and water (hence the name photosynthesis, from the Greek f??, phos, 'light', and s???es??, synthesis, 'putting together'). Oxygen is also released, mostly as a waste product.
Biomolecule	A biomolecule is any molecule that is produced by a living organism, including large macromolecules such as proteins, polysaccharides, lipids, and nucleic acids, as well as small molecules such as primary metabolites, secondary metabolites, and natural products. A more general name for this class of molecules is biogenic substances.
Histone	In biology, histones are highly alkaline proteins found in eukaryotic cell nuclei that package and order the DNA into structural units called nucleosomes. They are the chief protein components of chromatin, acting as spools around which DNA winds, and play a role in gene regulation. Without histones, the unwound DNA in chromosomes would be very long (a length to width ratio of more than 10 million to 1 in human DNA).
Nucleosome	A nucleosome is the basic unit of DNA packaging in eukaryotes, consisting of a segment of DNA wound in sequence around eight histone protein cores. This structure is often compared to thread wrapped around a spool.

Symbol	For other uses see Symbol A logical symbol is a fundamental concept in logic, tokens of which may be marks or a configuration of marks which form a particular pattern. Although the term 'symbol' in common use refers at some times to the idea being symbolized, and at other times to the marks on a piece of paper or chalkboard which are being used to express that idea; in the formal languages studied in mathematics and logic, the term 'symbol' refers to the idea, and the marks are considered to be a token instance of the symbol. In logic, symbols build literal utility to illustrate ideas.
DNA damage	DNA damage is an alteration in the chemical structure of DNA, such as a break in a strand of DNA, a base missing from the backbone of DNA, or a chemically changed base such as 8-OHdG. Damage to DNA that occurs naturally can result from metabolic or hydrolytic processes. Metabolism releases compounds that damage DNA including reactive oxygen species, reactive nitrogen species, reactive carbonyl species, lipid peroxidation products and alkylating agents, among others, while hydrolysis cleaves chemical bonds in DNA. Naturally occurring DNA damages arise about 10,000 to 100,000 times per day per mammalian cell. DNA damage is distinctly different from mutation, although both are types of error in DNA. DNA damage is an abnormal chemical structure in DNA, while a mutation is a change in the sequence of standard base pairs.
Peptide	Peptides are short chains of amino acid monomers linked by peptide bonds. The covalent chemical bonds are formed when the carboxyl group of one amino acid reacts with the amino group of another. The shortest peptides are dipeptides, consisting of 2 amino acids joined by a single peptide bond, followed by tripeptides, tetrapeptides, etc.
Hydrolase	In biochemistry, a hydrolase is an enzyme that catalyzes the hydrolysis of a chemical bond. For example, an enzyme that catalyzed the following reaction is a hydrolase:A-B + H_2O ? A-OH + B-H.
Nucleic acid	The nucleic acids are polymeric macromolecules, or large biological molecules, essential for all known forms of life. Nucleic acids, which include DNA (deoxyribonucleic acid) and RNA (ribonucleic acid), are made from nucleotide monomers. Together with proteins, nucleic acids are the most important biological macromolecules; each is found in abundance in all living things, where they function in encoding, transmitting and expressing genetic information--in other words, information is conveyed through the nucleic acid sequence, or the order of nucleotides within a DNA or RNA molecule.
Nucleoside triphosphate	Nucleoside triphosphate is a molecule containing a nucleoside bound to three phosphates. Natural nucleoside triphosphates include adenosine triphosphate (ATP), guanosine triphosphate (GTP), cytidine triphosphate (CTP), 5-methyluridine triphosphate (m^5UTP), and uridine triphosphate (UTP). These terms refer to those nucleoside triphosphates that contain ribose.

3. The Importance of Weak and Strong Chemical Bonds,

CHAPTER HIGHLIGHTS & NOTES: KEY TERMS, PEOPLE, PLACES, CONCEPTS

Split	A split in phylogenetics is a bipartition of a set of taxa, and the smallest unit of information in unrooted phylogenetic trees: each edge of an unrooted phylogenetic tree represents one split, and the tree can be efficiently reconstructed from its set of splits. Moreover, when given several trees, the splits occurring in more than half of these trees give rise to a consensus tree, and the splits occurring in a smaller fraction of the trees generally give rise to a consensus Split Network.

CHAPTER QUIZ: KEY TERMS, PEOPLE, PLACES, CONCEPTS

1. A _________ is an enzyme whose central biological function is the synthesis of polymers of nucleic acids. DNA _________ and RNA _________ are used to assemble DNA and RNA molecules, respectively, generally by copying a DNA or RNA template strand using base-pairing interactions.

   It is an accident of history that the enzymes responsible for the generation of other biopolymers are not also referred to as _________s.

   a. 1L-myo-inositol 1-phosphate cytidylyltransferase
   b. 2-C-methyl-D-erythritol 4-phosphate cytidylyltransferase
   c. Polymerase
   d. 3-deoxy-manno-octulosonate cytidylyltransferase

2. _________ is the biomolecular structure of a protein molecule. Each protein is a polymer - specifically a polypeptide - that is a sequence formed from various L-a-amino acids (also referred to as residues). By convention, a chain under 40 residues is often identified as a peptide, rather than a protein.

   a. MF59
   b. Protein structure
   c. Best Friends Animal Society
   d. Black Pine Animal Sanctuary

3. . _________s are large biological molecules consisting of one or more chains of amino acids. _________s perform a vast array of functions within living organisms, including catalyzing metabolic reactions, replicating DNA, responding to stimuli, and transporting molecules from one location to another. _________s differ from one another primarily in their sequence of amino acids, which is dictated by the nucleotide sequence of their genes, and which usually results in folding of the _________ into a specific three-dimensional structure that determines its activity.

   a. Biomarker discovery
   b. Protein
   c. Cyanovirin-N

4. A _________ in phylogenetics is a bipartition of a set of taxa, and the smallest unit of information in unrooted phylogenetic trees: each edge of an unrooted phylogenetic tree represents one _________, and the tree can be efficiently reconstructed from its set of _________s. Moreover, when given several trees, the _________s occurring in more than half of these trees give rise to a consensus tree, and the _________s occurring in a smaller fraction of the trees generally give rise to a consensus _________ Network.

   a. Basal
   b. Catalogue of Life
   c. Split
   d. Cetruminantia

5. _________ describes a reaction that introduces an acetyl functional group into a chemical compound. (De_________ is the removal of the acetyl group).

   Specifically, _________ refers to the process of introducing an acetyl group (resulting in an acetoxy group) into a compound, namely, the substitution of an acetyl group for an active hydrogen atom.

   a. Acetylation
   b. Berberine
   c. Benzylisoquinoline
   d. 2-Methoxyethyl-18-methoxycoronaridinate

ANSWER KEY
3. The Importance of Weak and Strong Chemical Bonds,

---

1. c
2. b
3. b
4. c
5. a

---

4. The Structure of DNA,

CHAPTER OUTLINE: KEY TERMS, PEOPLE, PLACES, CONCEPTS

Dosage compensation

Complexity

Discovery

Double Helix

Basal

Deoxyribose

Glycosidic bond

Nucleoside

Sugar

Transcription

Bacteria

Kinase

Marker gene

Minor

Base pair

Conformation

Form

Antis

Denaturation

Hyperchromicity

Assay

4. The Structure of DNA,

CHAPTER OUTLINE: KEY TERMS, PEOPLE, PLACES, CONCEPTS

- Circular DNA
- Gel electrophoresis
- Nucleosome
- DNA gyrase
- Electrophoresis
- Deamination
- Ribose
- Insertion
- Transfer RNA
- Function
- Tetraloop
- Pseudoknot
- Listeria monocytogenes
- Ricin
- Virulence
- Gene
- Barbara
- Homeotic gene
- Synapsis
- Prediction
- Murine leukemia virus

4. The Structure of DNA,

CHAPTER OUTLINE: KEY TERMS, PEOPLE, PLACES, CONCEPTS

- Retinitis pigmentosa
- Victoria
- Strategy
- Aptamer
- Environment
- RNase P
- Ribozyme
- Directed evolution
- Green fluorescent protein
- Spinach
- Hammerhead ribozyme
- Peptidyl transferase
- RNA world hypothesis
- Ribosome
- Protein
- Protein structure
- RNA polymerase
- Amino acid
- Carbon
- Cysteine
- Cystine

4. The Structure of DNA,

CHAPTER OUTLINE: KEY TERMS, PEOPLE, PLACES, CONCEPTS

- Disulfide bond
- Glycine
- Proline
- Torsion
- Angle
- Polymerase
- Water
- Helix
- Oligomer
- Immunoglobulin G
- Chaperone
- Glycoprotein
- Glycosylase
- Conformational change
- Hexokinase
- Homology modeling
- Palindromic sequence
- Repressilator
- Bacteriophage
- Evolution
- Repressor

4. The Structure of DNA,

CHAPTER OUTLINE: KEY TERMS, PEOPLE, PLACES, CONCEPTS

________	Zinc finger
________	Active site
________	Enzyme
________	Ligand
________	Allosteric regulation
________	Inducer
________	Operator
________	Lac repressor

CHAPTER HIGHLIGHTS & NOTES: KEY TERMS, PEOPLE, PLACES, CONCEPTS

Dosage compensation

Dosage compensation is a hypothetical genetic regulatory mechanism which operates to equalize the phenotypic expression of characteristics determined by genes on the X chromosome so that they are equally expressed in the human XY male and the XX female.

Dosage compensation may occur in other organisms like the fruit fly Drosophila melanogaster, the roundworm Caenorhabditis elegans and the plant White campion .

Species can have different mechanisms of dosage compensation.

Complexity

In general usage, complexity tends to be used to characterize something with many parts in intricate arrangement. The study of these complex linkages is the main goal of complex systems theory.

In science, there are at this time a number of approaches to characterizing complexity, many of which are reflected in this article.

Discovery

Discovery is the act of detecting something new, or something 'old' that had been unknown.

With reference to science and academic disciplines, discovery is the observation of new phenomena, new actions, or new events and providing new reasoning to explain the knowledge gathered through such observations with previously acquired knowledge from abstract thought and everyday experiences. Visual discoveries are often called sightings.

Double Helix

Double Helix, a novel by Nancy Werlin, is about 18-year old Eli Samuels, who works for a famous molecular biologist named Dr. Quincy Wyatt. There is a mysterious connection between Dr. Wyatt and Eli's parents, and all Eli knows about the connection is that it has something to do with his mother, who has Huntington's disease. Because of the connection between Dr. Wyatt and the Samuels family, Eli's father is strongly against Eli working there.

Basal

In phylogenetics, a basal clade is the earliest clade to branch in a larger clade; it appears at the base of a cladogram.

A basal group forms an outgroup to the rest of the clade, such as in the following example:

The word 'basal' is preferred to the term 'primitive', which may carry false connotations of inferiority or a lack of complexity.

The term basal can only be correctly applied to clades of organisms, not to individual traits possessed by the organisms--although it can be misused in this manner in technical literature.

Deoxyribose

Deoxyribose, or more precisely 2-deoxyribose, is a monosaccharide with idealized formula H--(CH_2)-$(CHOH)_3$-H. Its name indicates that it is a deoxy sugar, meaning that it is derived from the sugar ribose by loss of an oxygen atom. Since the pentose sugars arabinose and ribose only differ by the stereochemistry at C2', 2-deoxyribose and 2-deoxyarabinose are equivalent, although the latter term is rarely used because ribose, not arabinose, is the precursor to deoxyribose.

Glycosidic bond

In chemistry, a glycosidic bond is a type of covalent bond that joins a carbohydrate molecule to another group, which may or may not be another carbohydrate.

A glycosidic bond is formed between the hemiacetal group of a saccharide (or a molecule derived from a saccharide) and the hydroxyl group of some organic compound such as an alcohol. If the group attached to the carbohydrate residue is not another saccharide it is referred to as an aglycone.

Nucleoside

Nucleosides are glycosylamines consisting of a nucleobase bound to a ribose or deoxyribose sugar via a beta-glycosidic linkage. Examples of nucleosides include cytidine, uridine, adenosine, guanosine, thymidine and inosine.

Sugar

Sugar is the generalized name for a class of chemically-related sweet-flavored substances, most of which are used as food. They are carbohydrates, composed of carbon, hydrogen and oxygen.

4. The Structure of DNA,

Transcription	Transcription is the first step of gene expression, in which a particular segment of DNA is copied into RNA by the enzyme, RNA polymerase. Both RNA and DNA are nucleic acids, which use base pairs of nucleotides as a complementary language that can be converted back and forth from DNA to RNA by the action of the correct enzymes. During transcription, a DNA sequence is read by an RNA polymerase, which produces a complementary, antiparallel RNA strand.
Bacteria	Bacteria constitute a large domain or kingdom of prokaryotic microorganisms. Typically a few micrometres in length, bacteria have a wide range of shapes, ranging from spheres to rods and spirals. Bacteria were among the first life forms to appear on Earth, and are present in most habitats on the planet.
Kinase	In enzymology, a [tyrosine 3-monooxygenase] kinase is an enzyme that catalyzes the chemical reactionATP + [tyrosine-3-monooxygenase] $\rightleftharpoons$ ADP + phospho-[tyrosine-3-monooxygenase] Thus, the two substrates of this enzyme are ATP and tyrosine-3-monooxygenase, whereas its two products are ADP and [[phospho-[tyrosine-3-monooxygenase]]]. This enzyme belongs to the family of transferases, specifically those transferring a phosphate group to the sidechain oxygen atom of serine or threonine residues in proteins (protein-serine/threonine kinases). The systematic name of this enzyme class is ATP:[tyrosine-3-monoxygenase] phosphotransferase.
Marker gene	A marker gene is a gene used in nuclear biology to determine if a nucleic acid sequence has been successfully inserted into an organism's DNA. There are two types of marker genes: a selectable marker and a marker for screening.
Minor	In law, a minor is a person under a certain age--usually the age of majority--which legally demarcates childhood from adulthood. The age depends upon jurisdiction and application, but is generally 18. Minor may also be used in contexts unconnected to the overall age of majority. For example, the drinking age in the United States is 21, and people below this age are sometimes called minors even if 18. The term underage often refers to those under the age of majority, but may also refer to persons under a certain age limit, such as the drinking age, smoking age, age of consent, marriageable age, driving age, voting age, etc.
Base pair	Base pairs are the building blocks of the DNA double helix, and contribute to the folded structure of both DNA and RNA. Dictated by specific hydrogen bonding patterns, Watson-Crick base pairs (guanine-cytosine and adenine-thymine) allow the DNA helix to maintain a regular helical structure that is independent of its nucleotide sequence. The complementary nature of this based-paired structure provides a backup copy of all genetic information encoded within double-stranded DNA.

The regular structure and data redundancy provided by the DNA double helix make DNA well suited to the storage of genetic information, while base-pairing between DNA and incoming nucleotides provides the mechanism through which DNA polymerase replicates DNA, and RNA polymerase transcribes DNA into RNA. Many DNA-binding proteins can recognize specific base pairing patterns that identify particular regulatory regions of genes.

Intramolecular base pairs can occur within single-stranded nucleic acids.

Conformation

Conformation in dogs refers solely to the externally visible details of a dog's structure and appearance, as defined in detail by each dog breed's written breed standard. A dog that conforms to most of the items of description in its individual breed standard is said to have good conformation. Unlike equine conformation, there are no fixed rules for dog conformation, as dogs are the most variable in appearance of any animals ('Phenotypic variation among dog breeds, whether it be in size, shape, or behavior, is greater than for any other animal').

Form

In botanical nomenclature, a form is one of the 'secondary' taxonomic ranks, below that of variety, which in turn is below that of species; it is an infraspecific taxon. If more than three ranks are listed in describing a taxon, the 'classification' is being specified, but only three parts make up the 'name' of the taxon: a genus name, a specific epithet, and an infraspecific epithet.

The abbreviation 'f.' or the full 'forma' should be put before the infraspecific epithet to indicate the rank.

Antis

Antis was a dog who received the Dickin Medal in 1949 from the People's Dispensary for Sick Animals for bravery in service during the Second World War.

Denaturation

Denaturation is a process in which proteins or nucleic acids lose the quaternary structure, tertiary structure and secondary structure which is present in their native state, by application of some external stress or compound such as a strong acid or base, a concentrated inorganic salt, an organic solvent, radiation or heat. If proteins in a living cell are denatured, this results in disruption of cell activity and possibly cell death. Denatured proteins can exhibit a wide range of characteristics, from loss of solubility to communal aggregation.

Hyperchromicity

Hyperchromicity is the increase of absorbance of a material. The most famous example is the hyperchromicity of DNA that occurs when the DNA duplex is denatured. The UV absorption is increased when the two single DNA strands are being separated, either by heat or by addition of denaturant or by increasing the pH level.

Assay

An assay is an investigative procedure in laboratory medicine, pharmacology, environmental biology, and molecular biology for qualitatively assessing or quantitatively measuring the presence or amount or the functional activity of a target entity (the analyte), which can be a drug or biochemical substance or a cell in an organism or organic sample.

The measured entity is generally called the analyte, or the measurand or the target of the assay. The assay usually aims to measure an intensive property of the analyte and express it in the relevant measurement unit (e.g. molarity, density, functional activity in enzyme international units, degree of some effect in comparison to a standard, etc)..

Circular DNA

Circular DNA is a form of DNA that is found in viruses, bacteria and archaea as well as in eukaryotic cells in the form of either mitochondrial DNA or plastid DNA.

While the individual strands of a linear double helix represent two distinct and separable molecules, this need not be true for circular DNA.

Gel electrophoresis

Gel electrophoresis is a method for separation and analysis of macromolecules and their fragments, based on their size and charge.

It is used in clinical chemistry to separate proteins by charge and/or size (IEF agarose, essentially size independent) and in biochemistry and molecular biology to separate a mixed population of DNA and RNA fragments by length, to estimate the size of DNA and RNA fragments or to separate proteins by charge. Nucleic acid molecules are separated by applying an electric field to move the negatively charged molecules through an agarose matrix.

Nucleosome

A nucleosome is the basic unit of DNA packaging in eukaryotes, consisting of a segment of DNA wound in sequence around eight histone protein cores. This structure is often compared to thread wrapped around a spool.

Nucleosomes form the fundamental repeating units of eukaryotic chromatin, which is used to pack the large eukaryotic genomes into the nucleus while still ensuring appropriate access to it (in mammalian cells approximately 2 m of linear DNA have to be packed into a nucleus of roughly 10 μm diameter).

DNA gyrase

DNA gyrase, often referred to simply as gyrase, is an enzyme that relieves strain while double-stranded DNA is being unwound by helicase. This causes negative supercoiling of the DNA. Bacterial DNA gyrase is the target of many antibiotics, including nalidixic acid, novobiocin, and ciprofloxacin.

DNA gyrase is a type II topoisomerase (EC 5.99.1.3) that introduces negative supercoils (or relaxes positive supercoils) into DNA by looping the template so as to form a crossing, then cutting one of the double helices and passing the other through it before releasing the break, changing the linking number by two in each enzymatic step.

Electrophoresis

Electrophoresis is the motion of dispersed particles relative to a fluid under the influence of a spatially uniform electric field.

This electrokinetic phenomenon was observed for the first time in 1807 by Ferdinand Frederic Reuss (Moscow State University), who noticed that the application of a constant electric field caused clay particles dispersed in water to migrate. It is ultimately caused by the presence of a charged interface between the particle surface and the surrounding fluid.

Deamination

Deamination is the removal of an amine group from a molecule. Enzymes which catalyse this reaction are called deaminases.

In the human body, deamination takes place primarily in the liver, however glutamate is also deaminated in the kidneys.

Ribose

Ribose is an organic compound with the formula $C_5H_{10}O_5$; specifically, a monosaccharide with linear form H-(C=O)-$(CHOH)_4$-H, which has all the hydroxyl groups on the same side in the Fischer projection.

The term may refer to either of two enantiomers. The term usually indicates -ribose, which occurs widely in nature and is discussed here.

Insertion

In genetics, an insertion is the addition of one or more nucleotide base pairs into a DNA sequence. This can often happen in microsatellite regions due to the DNA polymerase slipping. Insertions can be anywhere in size from one base pair incorrectly inserted into a DNA sequence to a section of one chromosome inserted into another.

Transfer RNA

A Transfer RNA is an adaptor molecule composed of RNA, typically 73 to 94 nucleotides in length, that serves as the physical link between the nucleotide sequence of nucleic acids (DNA and RNA) and the amino acid sequence of proteins. It does this by carrying an amino acid to the protein synthetic machinery of a cell (ribosome) as directed by a three-nucleotide sequence (codon) in a messenger RNA (mRNA). As such, tRNAs are a necessary component of protein translation, the biological synthesis of new proteins according to the genetic code.

Function

A function is the reason some object or process occurred in a system that evolved through a process of selection or Natural selection. Thus, function refers forward from the object or process, along some chain of causation, to the goal or success. Compare this to the mechanism of the object or process, which looks backward along some chain of causation, explaining how the feature occurred.

Tetraloop

Tetraloops are a type of four-base hairpin loop motifs in RNA secondary structure that cap many double helices. Three types of tetraloops are common in ribosomal RNA: GNRA, UNCG and CUUG. The GNRA tetraloop has a guanine-adenine base-pair where the guanine is 5' to the helix and the adenine is 3' to the helix.

4. The Structure of DNA,

CHAPTER HIGHLIGHTS & NOTES: KEY TERMS, PEOPLE, PLACES, CONCEPTS

Pseudoknot	A pseudoknot is a nucleic acid secondary structure containing at least two stem-loop structures in which half of one stem is intercalated between the two halves of another stem. The pseudoknot was first recognized in the turnip yellow mosaic virus in 1982. Pseudoknots fold into knot-shaped three-dimensional conformations but are not true topological knots.
Listeria monocytogenes	Listeria monocytogenes is the bacterium that causes the infection listeriosis. It is a facultative anaerobic bacterium, capable of surviving in the presence of oxygen. It can grow and reproduce inside the host's cells and is one of the most virulent food-borne pathogens, with 20 to 30 percent of clinical infections resulting in death.
Ricin	Ricin is a highly toxic, naturally occurring lectin produced in the seeds of the castor oil plant Ricinus communis. A dose the size of a few grains of table salt can kill an adult human. The median lethal dose (LD_{50}) of ricin is around 22 micrograms per kilogram (1.78 mg for an average adult, around $^{1}/_{228}$ of a standard aspirin tablet/0.4 g gross) in humans if exposure is from injection or inhalation.
Virulence	Virulence is, by MeSH definition, the degree of pathogenicity within a group or species of parasites as indicated by case fatality rates and/or the ability of the organism to invade the tissues of the host. The pathogenicity of an organism - its ability to cause disease - is determined by its virulence factors. The noun virulence derives from the adjective virulent.
Gene	A gene is a molecular unit of heredity of a living organism. It is widely accepted by the scientific community as a name given to some stretches of deoxyribonucleic acids (DNA) and ribonucleic acids (RNA) that code for a polypeptide or for an RNA chain that has a function in the organism, though there still are controversies about what plays the role of the genetic material. Living beings depend on genes, as they specify all proteins and functional RNA chains.
Barbara	Barbara, also referred to as Bilad al-Barbar, was an ancient region on the northern coast of the Somalia. The area was inhabited by the Eastern Baribah or Barbaroi (Berbers), as the ancestors of the Somalis were referred to by medieval Arab and ancient Greek geographers, respectively. Along with the neighboring Habash (Abyssinians) of al-Habash, the Barbaroi are recorded in the 1st century Greek document the Periplus of the Erythraean Sea as engaging in extensive commercial exchanges with Egypt and pre-Islamic Arabia.
Homeotic gene	Homeotic genes cause the development of specific structures in plants and animals. They include many of the Hox and ParaHox genes which are important for segmentation, They also include the MADS-box-containing genes involved the ABC model of flower development. It is important to note that not all homeotic genes are Hox genes; the MADS- box genes are homeotic but not Hox genes.
Synapsis	Synapsis is the pairing of two homologous chromosomes that occurs during meiosis. This is not to be confused with mitosis.

Prediction	A prediction or forecast is a statement about the way things will happen in the future, often but not always based on experience or knowledge. While there is much overlap between prediction and forecast, a prediction may be a statement that some outcome is expected, while a forecast is more specific, and may cover a range of possible outcomes. Although guaranteed information about the future is in many cases impossible, prediction is necessary to allow plans to be made about possible developments; Howard H. Stevenson writes that prediction in business '... is at least two things: Important and hard.'
Murine leukemia virus	The murine leukemia viruses are retroviruses named for their ability to cause cancer in murine (mouse) hosts. Some Murine leukemia viruss may infect other vertebrates. Murine leukemia viruss include both exogenous and endogenous viruses.
Retinitis pigmentosa	Retinitis pigmentosa is an inherited, degenerative eye disease that causes severe vision impairment and often blindness. The progress of RP is not consistent. Some people will exhibit symptoms from infancy, others may not notice symptoms until later in life.
Victoria	Victoria is a genus of water-lilies, in the plant family Nymphaeaceae, with very large green leaves that lie flat on the water's surface. Victoria amazonica has a leaf that is up to 3 m (9.8 ft) in diameter, on a stalk 7-8 m (22.9-26.2 ft) in length. The genus name was given in honour of Queen Victoria of the United Kingdom.
Strategy	A player's strategy, in game theory, refers to one of the options he can choose in a setting where the outcome depends not only on his own actions but on the action of others. A player's strategy will determine the action the player will take at any stage of the game. The strategy concept is sometimes (wrongly) confused with that of a move.
Aptamer	Aptamers are oligonucleic acid or peptide molecules that bind to a specific target molecule. Aptamers are usually created by selecting them from a large random sequence pool, but natural aptamers also exist in riboswitches. Aptamers can be used for both basic research and clinical purposes as macromolecular drugs.
Environment	The biophysical environment is the biotic and abiotic surrounding of an organism or population, and includes particularly the factors that have an influence in their survival, development and evolution. The naked term environment can make reference to different concepts, but it is often used as a short form for the biophysical environment. This practice is common, for instance, among governments, that usually name their departments and agencies dealing with the biophysical environment with denominations like Environment Agency.
RNase P	Ribonuclease P (EC 3.1.26.5, RNase P) is a type of ribonuclease which cleaves RNA.

RNase P is unique from other RNases in that it is a ribozyme - a ribonucleic acid that acts as a catalyst in the same way that a protein based enzyme would. Its function is to cleave off an extra, or precursor, sequence of RNA on tRNA molecules. Further RNase P is one of two known multiple turnover ribozymes in nature (the other being the ribosome), the discovery of which earned Sidney Altman and Thomas Cech the Nobel Prize in Chemistry in 1989: in the 1970s, Altman discovered the existence of precursor tRNA with flanking sequences and was the first to characterize RNase P and its activity in processing of the 5' leader sequence of precursor tRNA. Recent findings also reveal that RNase P has a new function.

Ribozyme

A ribozyme is an RNA molecule that is capable of performing specific biochemical reactions, similar to the action of protein enzymes. The 1981 discovery of ribozymes demonstrated that RNA can be both genetic material (like DNA) and a biological catalyst (like protein enzymes), and contributed to the RNA world hypothesis, which suggests that RNA may have been important in the evolution of prebiotic self-replicating systems. Also termed catalytic RNA, ribozymes function within the ribosome (as part of the large subunit ribosomal RNA) to link amino acids during protein synthesis, and in a variety of RNA processing reactions, including RNA splicing, viral replication, and transfer RNA biosynthesis.

Directed evolution

Directed evolution is a method used in protein engineering mimicks the process of natural selection to evolve proteins or nucleic acids towards a user defined goal.

Green fluorescent protein

The green fluorescent protein is a protein composed of 238 amino acid residues (26.9 kDa) that exhibits bright green fluorescence when exposed to light in the blue to ultraviolet range. Although many other marine organisms have similar green fluorescent proteins, Green fluorescent protein traditionally refers to the protein first isolated from the jellyfish Aequorea victoria. The Green fluorescent protein from A. victoria has a major excitation peak at a wavelength of 395 nm and a minor one at 475 nm.

Spinach

Spinach is an edible flowering plant in the family of Amaranthaceae. It is native to central and southwestern Asia. It is an annual plant (rarely biennial), which grows to a height of up to 30 cm.

Hammerhead ribozyme

The hammerhead ribozyme is a RNA module that catalyzes reversible cleavage and joining reactions at a specific site within an RNA molecule. It serves as a model system for research on the structure and properties of RNA, and is used for targeted RNA cleavage experiments, some with proposed therapeutic applications. Named for the resemblance of early secondary structure diagrams to a hammerhead shark hammerhead ribozymes RNAs were originally discovered in two classes of plant virus-like RNAs: satellite RNAs and viroids.

Peptidyl transferase

The Peptidyl transferase is an aminoacyltransferase as well as the primary enzymatic function of the ribosome, which forms peptide bonds between adjacent amino acids using tRNAs during the translation process of protein biosynthesis.

Peptidyl transferase activity is carried out by the ribosome. Peptidyl transferase activity is not mediated by any ribosomal proteins but by ribosomal RNA (rRNA), a ribozyme.

RNA world hypothesis

The RNA world hypothesis proposes that self-replicating ribonucleic acid molecules were precursors to current life, which is based on deoxyribonucleic acid (DNA), RNA and proteins.

RNA stores genetic information like DNA, and catalyzes chemical reactions like an enzyme protein. It may, therefore, have played a major step in the evolution of cellular life.

Ribosome

The ribosome is a large and complex molecular machine, found within all living cells, that serves as the primary site of biological protein synthesis (translation). Ribosomes link amino acids together in the order specified by messenger RNA (mRNA) molecules. Ribosomes consist of two major subunits--the small ribosomal subunit reads the mRNA, while the large subunit joins amino acids to form a polypeptide chain.

Protein

Proteins are large biological molecules consisting of one or more chains of amino acids. Proteins perform a vast array of functions within living organisms, including catalyzing metabolic reactions, replicating DNA, responding to stimuli, and transporting molecules from one location to another. Proteins differ from one another primarily in their sequence of amino acids, which is dictated by the nucleotide sequence of their genes, and which usually results in folding of the protein into a specific three-dimensional structure that determines its activity.

Protein structure

Protein structure is the biomolecular structure of a protein molecule. Each protein is a polymer - specifically a polypeptide - that is a sequence formed from various L-a-amino acids (also referred to as residues). By convention, a chain under 40 residues is often identified as a peptide, rather than a protein.

RNA polymerase

RNA polymerase, also known as DNA-dependent RNA polymerase, is an enzyme that produces RNA. In cells, RNAP is necessary for constructing RNA chains using DNA genes as templates, a process called transcription. RNA polymerase enzymes are essential to life and are found in all organisms and many viruses. In chemical terms, RNAP is a nucleotidyl transferase that polymerizes ribonucleotides at the 3' end of an RNA transcript.

Amino acid

Amino acids are biologically important organic compounds made from amine ($-NH_2$) and carboxylic acid (-COOH) functional groups, along with a side-chain specific to each amino acid. The key elements of an amino acid are carbon, hydrogen, oxygen, and nitrogen, though other elements are found in the side-chains of certain amino acids. About 500 amino acids are known and can be classified in many ways.

Carbon

Carbon is the chemical element with symbol C and atomic number 6.

As a member of group 14 on the periodic table, it is nonmetallic and tetravalent--making four electrons available to form covalent chemical bonds. There are three naturally occurring isotopes, with ^{12}C and ^{13}C being stable, while ^{14}C is radioactive, decaying with a half-life of about 5,730 years. Carbon is one of the few elements known since antiquity.

Cysteine

Cysteine is an a-amino acid with the chemical formula $HO_2CCH(NH_2)CH_2SH$. It is a semi-essential amino acid, which means that it can be biosynthesized in humans. The thiol side chain in cysteine often participates in enzymatic reactions, serving as a nucleophile. The thiol is susceptible to oxidization to give the disulfide derivative cystine, which serves an important structural role in many proteins.

Cystine

Cystine is the amino acid formed by the oxidation of two cysteine molecules that covalently link via a disulfide bond. This organosulfur compound has the formula $(SCH_2CH(NH_2)CO_2H)_2$. It is a white solid that is slightly soluble in water.

Disulfide bond

In chemistry, a disulfide bond is a covalent bond, usually derived by the coupling of two thiol groups. The linkage is also called an SS-bond or disulfide bridge. The overall connectivity is therefore R-S-S-R. The terminology is widely used in biochemistry.

Glycine

Glycine is an organic compound with the formula NH_2CH_2COOH. Having a hydrogen substituent as its side-chain, glycine is the smallest of the 20 amino acids commonly found in proteins. Its codons are GGU, GGC, GGA, GGG of the genetic code.

Glycine is a colourless, sweet-tasting crystalline solid.

Proline

Proline is an a-amino acid, one of the twenty DNA-encoded amino acids. Its codons are CCU, CCC, CCA, and CCG. It is not an essential amino acid, which means that the human body can synthesize it. It is unique among the 20 protein-forming amino acids in that the amine nitrogen is bound to not one but two alkyl groups, thus making it a secondary amine.

Torsion

Torsion is an anatomical event which takes place during the very early part of the life of snails and slugs of all kinds. In other words, torsion is a gastropod synapomorphy which occurs in all gastropods during larval development. Torsion is the rotation of the visceral mass, mantle, and shell 180° with respect to the head and foot of the gastropod.

Angle

The angle of a rib (costal angle) may both refer to the bending part of it, and a prominent line in this area, a little in front of the tubercle.

This line is directed downward and laterally; this gives attachment to a tendon of the iliocostalis muscle.

Polymerase	A polymerase is an enzyme whose central biological function is the synthesis of polymers of nucleic acids. DNA polymerase and RNA polymerase are used to assemble DNA and RNA molecules, respectively, generally by copying a DNA or RNA template strand using base-pairing interactions. It is an accident of history that the enzymes responsible for the generation of other biopolymers are not also referred to as polymerases.
Water	Water is a chemical compound with the chemical formula H2O. A water molecule contains one oxygen and two hydrogen atoms connected by covalent bonds. Water is a liquid at standard ambient temperature and pressure, but it often co-exists on Earth with its solid state, ice, and gaseous state, steam (water vapor).
Helix	The prominent rim of the auricula is called the helix. Where the helix turns downward behind, a small tubercle is frequently seen: the auricular tubercle of Darwin.
Oligomer	In chemistry, an oligomer is a molecular complex that consists of a few monomer units, in contrast to a polymer that, at least in principle, consists of a nearly unlimited number of monomers. Dimers, trimers, and tetramers are, for instance, oligomers respectively composed of two, three and four monomers. In the context of biochemistry, an oligomer is usually referred to a macromolecular complex formed by non-covalent bonding of few macromolecules like proteins or nucleic acids.
Immunoglobulin G	Immunoglobulin G is an antibody isotype. It is a protein complex composed of four peptide chains -- two identical heavy chains and two identical light chains arranged in a Y-shape typical of antibody monomers. Each IgG has two antigen binding sites.
Chaperone	In molecular biology, molecular chaperones are proteins that assist the non-covalent folding or unfolding and the assembly or disassembly of other macromolecular structures, but do not occur in these structures when the structures are performing their normal biological functions having completed the processes of folding and/or assembly. The common perception that chaperones are concerned primarily with protein folding is incorrect. The first protein to be called a chaperone assists the assembly of nucleosomes from folded histones and DNA and such assembly chaperones, especially in the nucleus, are concerned with the assembly of folded subunits into oligomeric structures.
Glycoprotein	Glycoproteins are proteins that contain oligosaccharide chains covalently attached to polypeptide side-chains. The carbohydrate is attached to the protein in a cotranslational or posttranslational modification. This process is known as glycosylation.
Glycosylase	Glycosylases are enzymes that hydrolyze glycosyl compounds.

They are a type of hydrolase (EC 3). In turn, glycosylases are divided into two groups: glycosidases -- enzymes that hydrolyze O- and S-glycosyl compounds (EC 3.2.1) -- and enzymes that hydrolyze N-glycosyl compounds (EC 3.2.2).

Conformational change

A macromolecule is usually flexible and dynamic. It can change its shape in response to changes in its environment or other factors; each possible shape is called a conformation, and a transition between them is called a conformational change. A macromolecular conformational change may be induced by many factors such as a change in temperature, pH, voltage, ion concentration, phosphorylation, or the binding of a ligand.

Hexokinase

A hexokinase is an enzyme that phosphorylates hexoses, forming hexose phosphate. In most organisms, glucose is the most important substrate of hexokinases, and glucose-6-phosphate the most important product.

Hexokinases should not be confused with glucokinase, which is a specific isoform of hexokinase.

Homology modeling

Homology modeling, also known as comparative modeling of protein, refers to constructing an atomic-resolution model of the 'target' protein from its amino acid sequence and an experimental three-dimensional structure of a related homologous protein . Homology modeling relies on the identification of one or more known protein structures likely to resemble the structure of the query sequence, and on the production of an alignment that maps residues in the query sequence to residues in the template sequence. It has been shown that protein structures are more conserved than protein sequences amongst homologues, but sequences falling below a 20% sequence identity can have very different structure.

Palindromic sequence

A palindromic sequence is a nucleic acid sequence that is the same whether read 5' (five-prime) to 3' (three prime) on one strand or 5' to 3' on the complementary strand with which it forms a double helix.

The meaning of palindrome in the context of genetics is slightly different from the definition used for words and sentences. Since a double helix is formed by two paired strands of nucleotides that run in opposite directions in the 5'-to-3' sense, and the nucleotides always pair in the same way (Adenine (A) with Thymine (T) for DNA, with Uracil (U) for RNA; Cytosine (C) with Guanine (G)), a (single-stranded) nucleotide sequence is said to be a palindrome if it is equal to its reverse complement.

Repressilator

The repressilator is a synthetic genetic regulatory network reported in a paper by Michael Elowitz and Stanislas Leibler. This network was designed from scratch to exhibit a stable oscillation which is reported via the expression of green fluorescent protein, and hence acts like an electrical oscillator system with fixed time periods.

Bacteriophage

A bacteriophage is a virus that infects and replicates within bacteria. The term is derived from 'bacteria' and the Greek fa?e?? phagein 'to devour'. Bacteriophages are composed of proteins that encapsulate a DNA or RNA genome, and may have relatively simple or elaborate structures.

Evolution

Evolution is a 2001 documentary series by the American broadcaster Public Broadcasting Service and WGBH on evolutionary biology.

The spokespeople for the series were Jane Goodall (overall spokesperson), Kenneth R. Miller and Stephen Jay Gould (science spokespeople), Eugenie C. Scott (education spokesperson), Arthur Peacocke and Arnold Thomas (religious spokespeople). The series was narrated by the Irish actor Liam Neeson.

Repressor

In molecular genetics, a repressor is a DNA- or RNA-binding protein that inhibits the expression of one or more genes by binding to the operator. A DNA-binding repressor blocks the attachment of RNA polymerase to the promoter, thus preventing transcription of the genes into messenger RNA. An RNA-binding repressor binds to the mRNA and prevents translation of the mRNA into protein. This blocking of expression is called repression.

Zinc finger

A zinc finger is a small protein structural motif that is characterized by the coordination of one or more zinc ions in order to stabilize the fold. Originally coined to describe the finger-like appearance of a hypothesized structure from Xenopus laevis transcription factor IIIA, the zinc finger name has now come to encompass a wide variety of differing protein structures.

Proteins that contain zinc fingers (zinc finger proteins) are classified into several different structural families.

Active site

In biology, the active site is the small portion of an enzyme where substrate molecules bind and undergo a chemical reaction. This chemical reaction occurs when a substrate collides with and slots into the active site of an enzyme. The active site is usually found in a 3-D groove or pocket of the enzyme, lined with amino acid residues (or nucleotides in RNA enzymes).

Enzyme

Enzymes are large biological molecules responsible for the thousands of metabolic processes that sustain life. They are highly selective catalysts, greatly accelerating both the rate and specificity of metabolic reactions, from the digestion of food to the synthesis of DNA. Most enzymes are proteins, although some catalytic RNA molecules have been identified. Enzymes adopt a specific three-dimensional structure, and may employ organic (e.g. biotin) and inorganic (e.g. magnesium ion) cofactors to assist in catalysis.

Ligand

In biochemistry and pharmacology, a ligand is a substance, that forms a complex with a biomolecule to serve a biological purpose. In a narrower sense, it is a signal triggering molecule, binding to a site on a target protein.

4. The Structure of DNA,

CHAPTER HIGHLIGHTS & NOTES: KEY TERMS, PEOPLE, PLACES, CONCEPTS

Allosteric regulation	In biochemistry, allosteric regulation is the regulation of an enzyme or other protein by binding an effector molecule at the protein's allosteric site . Effectors that enhance the protein's activity are referred to as allosteric activators, whereas those that decrease the protein's activity are called allosteric inhibitors. The term allostery comes from the Greek allos (?????), 'other', and stereos (ste?e??), 'solid (object)', in reference to the fact that the regulatory site of an allosteric protein is physically distinct from its active site.
Inducer	In molecular biology, an inducer is a molecule that starts gene expression. An inducer can bind to repressors or activators. Inducers function by disabling repressors.
Operator	In genetics, an operator is a segment of DNA to which a transcription factor protein binds. It is classically defined in the lac operon as a segment between the promoter and the genes of the operon. In the case of a repressor, the repressor protein physically obstructs the RNA polymerase from transcribing the genes.
Lac repressor	The lac repressor is a DNA-binding protein which inhibits the expression of genes coding for proteins involved in the metabolism of lactose in bacteria. These genes are repressed when lactose is not available to the cell, ensuring that the bacterium only invests energy in the production of machinery necessary for uptake and utilization of lactose when lactose is present. When lactose becomes available, it is converted into allolactose, which inhibits the lac repressor's DNA binding ability.

CHAPTER QUIZ: KEY TERMS, PEOPLE, PLACES, CONCEPTS

1. _________ is the first step of gene expression, in which a particular segment of DNA is copied into RNA by the enzyme, RNA polymerase. Both RNA and DNA are nucleic acids, which use base pairs of nucleotides as a complementary language that can be converted back and forth from DNA to RNA by the action of the correct enzymes. During _________, a DNA sequence is read by an RNA polymerase, which produces a complementary, antiparallel RNA strand.

   a. Transcription
   b. C1QL1
   c. CAG promoter
   d. Cap analysis gene expression

2. . A _________ is a gene used in nuclear biology to determine if a nucleic acid sequence has been successfully inserted into an organism's DNA. There are two types of _________s: a selectable marker and a marker for screening.

   a. 2q37 monosomy
   b. 5-HTTLPR

c. B chromosome
d. Marker gene

3. In phylogenetics, a _________ clade is the earliest clade to branch in a larger clade; it appears at the base of a cladogram.

   A _________ group forms an outgroup to the rest of the clade, such as in the following example:

   The word '_________' is preferred to the term 'primitive', which may carry false connotations of inferiority or a lack of complexity.

   The term _________ can only be correctly applied to clades of organisms, not to individual traits possessed by the organisms--although it can be misused in this manner in technical literature.

   a. Basal
   b. Neanderthal anatomy
   c. Vindija Cave
   d. 23andMe

4. _________s are a type of four-base hairpin loop motifs in RNA secondary structure that cap many double helices. Three types of _________s are common in ribosomal RNA: GNRA, UNCG and CUUG. The GNRA _________ has a guanine-adenine base-pair where the guanine is 5' to the helix and the adenine is 3' to the helix.

   a. Chimeric RNA
   b. Circular RNA
   c. Cis-acting replication element
   d. Tetraloop

5. _________ is the act of detecting something new, or something 'old' that had been unknown. With reference to science and academic disciplines, _________ is the observation of new phenomena, new actions, or new events and providing new reasoning to explain the knowledge gathered through such observations with previously acquired knowledge from abstract thought and everyday experiences. Visual _________(ies) are often called sightings.

   a. Bad habit
   b. Berliner Modell
   c. Blocking effect
   d. Discovery

ANSWER KEY
4. The Structure of DNA,

1. a
2. d
3. a
4. d
5. d

5. The Structure and Versatility of RNA, 107 6 The Structure of Proteins, ...

CHAPTER OUTLINE: KEY TERMS, PEOPLE, PLACES, CONCEPTS

- Molecular biology
- Agarose gel electrophoresis
- DNA sequencing
- Nucleic acid
- Polyacrylamide
- Agarose
- Electrophoresis
- Gel electrophoresis
- EcoRI
- Cleavage
- Restriction enzyme
- PstI
- Hybridization probe
- Northern blot
- Southern blot
- Dysgenesis
- Microarray
- DnaC
- Fusion protein
- Vector
- Plasmid

CHAPTER OUTLINE: KEY TERMS, PEOPLE, PLACES, CONCEPTS

- Expression vector
- Transformation
- Genomic library
- Reverse transcriptase
- CDNA library
- Colony
- Genomics
- Library
- Oligomer
- Site-directed mutagenesis
- Oligonucleotide synthesis
- Protein
- Response element
- Polymerase chain reaction
- Sequencing
- Nucleotide
- Haemophilus influenzae
- Shotgun sequencing
- Ferritin
- Human
- Human genome

Contig

Sequence

Forward genetics

Expressed sequence tag

Open reading frame

Transcriptome

Gene

Antisense RNA

BLAST

Enhancer

VISTA

Genome editing

Meganuclease

Chromatin immunoprecipitation

Column

Immunoprecipitation

Epitope

Coomassie Brilliant Blue

Sodium dodecyl sulfate

Edman degradation

Hfq protein

CHAPTER OUTLINE: KEY TERMS, PEOPLE, PLACES, CONCEPTS

____________	Chromatography
____________	Proteomics
____________	Interactome
____________	Assay
____________	DNA footprinting
____________	Chips
____________	Heredity
____________	Theory
____________	Hox gene

CHAPTER HIGHLIGHTS & NOTES: KEY TERMS, PEOPLE, PLACES, CONCEPTS

Molecular biology	Molecular biology is the branch of biology that deals with the molecular basis of biological activity. This field overlaps with other areas of biology and chemistry, particularly genetics and biochemistry. Molecular biology chiefly concerns itself with understanding the interactions between the various systems of a cell, including the interactions between the different types of DNA, RNA and protein biosynthesis as well as learning how these interactions are regulated.
Agarose gel electrophoresis	Agarose gel electrophoresis is a method of gel electrophoresis used in biochemistry, molecular biology, and clinical chemistry to separate a mixed population of DNA or proteins in a matrix of agarose. The proteins may be separated by charge and or size (IEF agarose, essentially size independent), and the DNA and RNA fragments by length. Biomolecules are separated by applying an electric field to move the negatively charged molecules through an agarose matrix, and the biomolecules are separated by size in the agarose gel matrix.
DNA sequencing	DNA sequencing is the process of determining the precise order of nucleotides within a DNA molecule. It includes any method or technology that is used to determine the order of the four bases--adenine, guanine, cytosine, and thymine--in a strand of DNA. The advent of rapid DNA sequencing methods has greatly accelerated biological and medical research and discovery.

CHAPTER HIGHLIGHTS & NOTES: KEY TERMS, PEOPLE, PLACES, CONCEPTS

Nucleic acid	The nucleic acids are polymeric macromolecules, or large biological molecules, essential for all known forms of life. Nucleic acids, which include DNA (deoxyribonucleic acid) and RNA (ribonucleic acid), are made from nucleotide monomers. Together with proteins, nucleic acids are the most important biological macromolecules; each is found in abundance in all living things, where they function in encoding, transmitting and expressing genetic information--in other words, information is conveyed through the nucleic acid sequence, or the order of nucleotides within a DNA or RNA molecule.
Polyacrylamide	Polyacrylamide (IUPAC poly or poly(1-carbamoylethylene)) is a polymer (-$CH_2CHCONH_2$-) formed from acrylamide subunits. It can be synthesized as a simple linear-chain structure or cross-linked, typically using N,N-methylenebisacrylamide. Polyacrylamide is not toxic.
Agarose	An agarose is a polysaccharide polymer material, generally extracted from seaweed. Agarose is a linear polymer made up of the repeating unit of agarobiose, which is a disaccharide made up of D-galactose and 3,6-anhydro-L-galactopyranose. Agarose is one of the two principal components of agar, and is purified from agar by removing agar's other component, agaropectin.
Electrophoresis	Electrophoresis is the motion of dispersed particles relative to a fluid under the influence of a spatially uniform electric field. This electrokinetic phenomenon was observed for the first time in 1807 by Ferdinand Frederic Reuss (Moscow State University), who noticed that the application of a constant electric field caused clay particles dispersed in water to migrate. It is ultimately caused by the presence of a charged interface between the particle surface and the surrounding fluid.
Gel electrophoresis	Gel electrophoresis is a method for separation and analysis of macromolecules and their fragments, based on their size and charge. It is used in clinical chemistry to separate proteins by charge and/or size (IEF agarose, essentially size independent) and in biochemistry and molecular biology to separate a mixed population of DNA and RNA fragments by length, to estimate the size of DNA and RNA fragments or to separate proteins by charge. Nucleic acid molecules are separated by applying an electric field to move the negatively charged molecules through an agarose matrix.
EcoRI	EcoRI is an endonuclease enzyme isolated from strains of E. coli, and is part of the restriction modification system. In molecular biology it is used as a restriction enzyme. It creates sticky ends with 5' end overhangs.
Cleavage	Cleavage, anatomically known as the intermammary cleft or the intermammary sulcus, is the space between a woman's breasts lying over the sternum. In popular culture, it is often defined by garments with low necklines, like ball gowns, evening gowns, lingerie and swimwear that expose or highlight cleavage.

Restriction enzyme

A restriction enzyme is an enzyme that cuts DNA at or near specific recognition nucleotide sequences known as restriction sites. Restriction enzymes are commonly classified into three types, which differ in their structure and whether they cut their DNA substrate at their recognition site, or if the recognition and cleavage sites are separate from one another. To cut DNA, all restriction enzymes make two incisions, once through each sugar-phosphate backbone (i.e. each strand) of the DNA double helix.

PstI

PstI, is a Type II restriction endonuclease from Providencia stuartii.

Hybridization probe

In molecular biology, a hybridization probe is a fragment of DNA or RNA of variable length which is used in DNA or RNA samples to detect the presence of nucleotide sequences (the DNA target) that are complementary to the sequence in the probe. The probe thereby hybridizes to single-stranded nucleic acid (DNA or RNA) whose base sequence allows probe-target base pairing due to complementarity between the probe and target. The labeled probe is first denatured (by heating or under alkaline conditions such as exposure to sodium hydroxide) into single stranded DNA (ssDNA) and then hybridized to the target ssDNA (Southern blotting) or RNA (Northern blotting) immobilized on a membrane or in situ.

Northern blot

The northern blot is a technique used in molecular biology research to study gene expression by detection of RNA in a sample.

With northern blotting it is possible to observe cellular control over structure and function by determining the particular gene expression levels during differentiation, morphogenesis, as well as abnormal or diseased conditions. Northern blotting involves the use of electrophoresis to separate RNA samples by size and detection with a hybridization probe complementary to part of or the entire target sequence.

Southern blot

A Southern blot is a method routinely used in molecular biology for detection of a specific DNA sequence in DNA samples. Southern blotting combines transfer of electrophoresis-separated DNA fragments to a filter membrane and subsequent fragment detection by probe hybridization. The method is named after its inventor, the British biologist Edwin Southern.

Dysgenesis

Dysgenesis

The term dysgenesis is used to describe abnormal organ development during embryonic growth and development. As opposed to agenesis, which refers to the complete failure of an organ to develop, dysgenesis usually implies disordered development or malformation and in some cases represents the milder end of a spectrum of abnormalities.

Examples:•Gonadal dysgenesis•Adrenal dysgenesis•Thyroid dysgenesis•Anterior segment dysgenesis.

Microarray	A microarray is a multiplex lab-on-a-chip. It is a 2D array on a solid substrate (usually a glass slide or silicon thin-film cell) that assays large amounts of biological material using high-throughput screening methods. The concept and methodology of microarrays was first introduced and illustrated in antibody microarrays (also referred to as antibody matrix) in 1983 in a scientific publication and a series of patents.
DnaC	DnaC is a loading factor for helicase dnaB. dnaB and dnaC associate with the dnaA bound origin. After loading dnaB at the origin, dnaC is released. This interaction of dnaC with dnaB requires the hydrolysis of ATP.
Fusion protein	Fusion proteins or chimeric proteins are proteins created through the joining of two or more genes which originally coded for separate proteins. Translation of this fusion gene results in a single polypeptide with functional properties derived from each of the original proteins. Recombinant fusion proteins are created artificially by recombinant DNA technology for use in biological research or therapeutics.
Vector	In molecular cloning, a vector is a DNA molecule used as a vehicle to artificially carry foreign genetic material into another cell, where it can be replicated and/or expressed. A vector containing foreign DNA is termed recombinant DNA. The four major types of vectors are plasmids, viral vectors, cosmids, and artificial chromosomes. Common to all engineered vectors are an origin of replication, a multicloning site, and a selectable marker.
Plasmid	A plasmid is a small DNA molecule that is physically separate from, and can replicate independently of, chromosomal DNA within a cell. Most commonly found as small circular, double-stranded DNA molecules in bacteria, plasmids are sometimes present in archaea and eukaryotic organisms. In nature, plasmids carry genes that may benefit survival of the organism (e.g. antibiotic resistance), and can frequently be transmitted from one bacterium to another (even of another species) via horizontal gene transfer.
Expression vector	An expression vector, otherwise known as an expression construct, is usually a plasmid or virus designed for protein expression in cells. The vector is used to introduce a specific gene into a target cell, and can commandeer the cell's mechanism for protein synthesis to produce the protein encoded by the gene. The plasmid is engineered to contain regulatory sequences that act as enhancer and promoter regions and lead to efficient transcription of the gene carried on the expression vector.
Transformation	In molecular biology, transformation is genetic alteration of a cell resulting from the direct uptake, incorporation and expression of exogenous genetic material from its surroundings and taken up through the cell membrane(s). Transformation occurs naturally in some species of bacteria, but it can also be effected by artificial means in other cells.

Genomic library	A genomic library is a collection of the total genomic DNA from a single organism. The DNA is stored in a population of identical vectors, each containing a different insert of DNA. In order to construct a genomic library, the organism's DNA is extracted from cells and then digested with a restriction enzyme to cut the DNA into fragments of a specific size. The fragments are then inserted into the vector using the enzyme, DNA ligase.
Reverse transcriptase	Reverse transcriptase is an enzyme used to generate complementary DNA (cDNA) from an RNA template, a process termed reverse transcription. RT is needed for the replication of retroviruses (e.g., HIV), and RT inhibitors are widely used as antiretroviral drugs. RT activity is also associated with the replication of chromosome ends (telomerase) and some mobile genetic elements (retrotransposons).
CDNA library	A cDNA library is a combination of cloned cDNA fragments inserted into a collection of host cells, which together constitute some portion of the transcriptome of the organism. cDNA is produced from fully transcribed mRNA found in the nucleus and therefore contains only the expressed genes of an organism. Similarly, tissue specific cDNA libraries can be produced.
Colony	In biology, a colony refers to individual organisms of the same species living closely together, usually for mutual benefit, such as stronger defense or the ability to attack bigger prey. Some insects (ants and honey bees, for example) live only in colonies. The Portuguese man o' war is an example of a colony of four different polyp forms.
Genomics	Genomics is a discipline in genetics that applies recombinant DNA, DNA sequencing methods, and bioinformatics to sequence, assemble, and analyze the function and structure of genomes . The field includes efforts to determine the entire DNA sequence of organisms and fine-scale genetic mapping. The field also includes studies of intragenomic phenomena such as heterosis, epistasis, pleiotropy and other interactions between loci and alleles within the genome.
Library	In molecular biology, a library is a collection of DNA fragments that is stored and propagated in a population of micro-organisms through the process of molecular cloning. There are different types of DNA libraries, including cDNA libraries (formed from reverse-transcribed RNA), genomic libraries (formed from genomic DNA) and randomized mutant libraries (formed by de novo gene synthesis where alternative nucleotides or codons are incorporated). DNA library technology is a mainstay of current molecular biology, and the applications of these libraries depends on the source of the original DNA fragments.
Oligomer	In chemistry, an oligomer is a molecular complex that consists of a few monomer units, in contrast to a polymer that, at least in principle, consists of a nearly unlimited number of monomers. Dimers, trimers, and tetramers are, for instance, oligomers respectively composed of two, three and four monomers.

CHAPTER HIGHLIGHTS & NOTES: KEY TERMS, PEOPLE, PLACES, CONCEPTS

Site-directed mutagenesis	Site-directed mutagenesis is a molecular biology method that is used to make specific and intentional changes to the DNA sequence of a gene and any gene products. Also called site-specific mutagenesis or oligonucleotide-directed mutagenesis, it is used for investigating the structure and biological activity of DNA, RNA, and protein molecules, and for protein engineering. With decreasing costs of oligonucleotide synthesis, artificial gene synthesis is now occasionally used as an alternative to site-directed mutagenesis.
Oligonucleotide synthesis	Oligonucleotide synthesis is the chemical synthesis of relatively short fragments of nucleic acids with defined chemical structure . The technique is extremely useful in current laboratory practice because it provides a rapid and inexpensive access to custom-made oligonucleotides of the desired sequence. Whereas enzymes synthesize DNA and RNA in a 5' to 3' direction, chemical oligonucleotide synthesis is carried out in the opposite, 3' to 5' direction.
Protein	Proteins are large biological molecules consisting of one or more chains of amino acids. Proteins perform a vast array of functions within living organisms, including catalyzing metabolic reactions, replicating DNA, responding to stimuli, and transporting molecules from one location to another. Proteins differ from one another primarily in their sequence of amino acids, which is dictated by the nucleotide sequence of their genes, and which usually results in folding of the protein into a specific three-dimensional structure that determines its activity.
Response element	Response elements are short sequences of DNA within a gene promoter region that are able to bind specific transcription factors and regulate transcription of genes. Under conditions of stress, a transcription activator protein binds to the response element and stimulates transcription. If the same response element sequence is located in the control regions of different genes, then these genes will be activated by the same stimuli, thus producing a coordinated response.
Polymerase chain reaction	The polymerase chain reaction is a biochemical technology in molecular biology to amplify a single or a few copies of a piece of DNA across several orders of magnitude, generating thousands to millions of copies of a particular DNA sequence. Developed in 1983 by Kary Mullis, Polymerase chain reaction is now a common and often indispensable technique used in medical and biological research labs for a variety of applications. These include DNA cloning for sequencing, DNA-based phylogeny, or functional analysis of genes; the diagnosis of hereditary diseases; the identification of genetic fingerprints (used in forensic sciences and paternity testing); and the detection and diagnosis of infectious diseases.
Sequencing	In genetics and biochemistry, sequencing means to determine the primary structure of an unbranched biopolymer. Sequencing results in a symbolic linear depiction known as a sequence which succinctly summarizes much of the atomic-level structure of the sequenced molecule.

Nucleotide	Nucleotides are organic molecules that form the basic building blocks of nucleic acids, such as DNA and RNA. A nucleotide is composed of a nucleobase, a pentose (ribose or deoxyribose) and at least one phosphate group. Nucleotides serve to carry packets of energy within the cell (ATP). In the form of the nucleoside triphosphates (ATP, GTP, CTP and UTP), nucleotides play central roles in metabolism.
Haemophilus influenzae	Haemophilus influenzae, formerly called Pfeiffer's bacillus or Bacillus influenzae, is a Gram-negative, coccobacilli bacterium first described in 1892 by Richard Pfeiffer during an influenza pandemic. A member of the Pasteurellaceae family, it is generally aerobic, but can grow as a facultative anaerobe. H. influenzae was mistakenly considered to be the cause of influenza until 1933, when the viral etiology of influenza became apparent.
Shotgun sequencing	In genetics, shotgun sequencing, also known as shotgun cloning, is a method used for sequencing long DNA strands. It is named by analogy with the rapidly expanding, quasi-random firing pattern of a shotgun. Since the chain termination method of DNA sequencing can only be used for fairly short strands (100 to 1000 basepairs), longer sequences must be subdivided into smaller fragments, and subsequently re-assembled to give the overall sequence.
Ferritin	Ferritin is a ubiquitous intracellular protein that stores iron and releases it in a controlled fashion. The amount of ferritin stored reflects the amount of iron stored. The protein is produced by almost all living organisms, including algae, bacteria, higher plants, and animals.
Human	Humans are primates of the family Hominidae, and the only extant species of the genus Homo. Humans are distinguished from other primates by their bipedal locomotion, and especially by their relatively larger brain with its particularly well developed neocortex, prefrontal cortex and temporal lobes, which enable high levels of abstract reasoning, language, problem solving, and culture through social learning. Humans use tools to a much higher degree than any other animal, and are the only extant species known to build fires and cook their food, as well as the only known species to clothe themselves and create and use numerous other technologies and arts.
Human genome	The human genome is the complete set of genetic information for humans . This information is located as DNA sequences within the 23 chromosome pairs in cell nuclei and in a small DNA molecule found within individual mitochondria. Human genomes include both protein-coding DNA genes and noncoding DNA. Haploid human genomes (contained in egg and sperm cells) consist of three billion DNA base pairs, while diploid genomes (found in somatic cells) have twice the DNA content.

Contig	A contig is a set of overlapping DNA segments that together represent a consensus region of DNA. In bottom-up sequencing projects, a contig refers to overlapping sequence data (reads); in top-down sequencing projects, contig refers to the overlapping clones that form a physical map of the genome that is used to guide sequencing and assembly. Contigs can thus refer both to overlapping DNA sequence and to overlapping physical segments (fragments) contained in clones depending on the context.
Sequence	In medicine, a sequence is a series of ordered consequences due to a single cause. It differs from a syndrome in that seriality is more predictable: if A causes B, and B causes C, and C causes D, then D would not be seen if C is not seen. However, in less formal contexts, the term 'syndrome' is sometimes used instead of sequence.
Forward genetics	Forward genetics encompasses several means of identifying the genotype that is responsible for a phenotype. Initially, this was done by generating random mutations in an organism, often with radiation or insertional mutagenesis (ex. Sleeping Beauty), and after subsequent breeding, isolating individuals with an aberrant phenotype.
Expressed sequence tag	An expressed sequence tag is a short sub-sequence of a cDNA sequence. They may be used to identify gene transcripts, and are instrumental in gene discovery and gene sequence determination. The identification of Expressed sequence tags has proceeded rapidly, with approximately 74.2 million Expressed sequence tags now available in public databases (e.g. GenBank 1 January 2013, all species).
Open reading frame	In molecular genetics, an open reading frame is the part of a reading frame that contains no stop codons. The transcription termination pause site is located after the Open reading frame, beyond the translation stop codon, because if transcription were to cease before the stop codon, an incomplete protein would be made during translation. Normally, inserts which interrupt the reading frame of a subsequent region after the start codon cause frameshift mutation of the sequence and dislocate the sequences for stop codons.
Transcriptome	The transcriptome is the set of all RNA molecules, including mRNA, rRNA, tRNA, and other non-coding RNA produced in one or a population of cells. It differs from the exome in that it includes only those RNA molecules found in a specified cell population, and usually includes the amount or concentration of each RNA molecule in addition to the molecular identities.
Gene	A gene is a molecular unit of heredity of a living organism. It is widely accepted by the scientific community as a name given to some stretches of deoxyribonucleic acids (DNA) and ribonucleic acids (RNA) that code for a polypeptide or for an RNA chain that has a function in the organism, though there still are controversies about what plays the role of the genetic material.

Antisense RNA	Antisense RNA is a single-stranded RNA that is complementary to a messenger RNA (mRNA) strand transcribed within a cell. Some authors have used the term micRNA (mRNA-interfering complementary RNA) to refer to these RNAs but it is not widely used. Antisense RNA may be introduced into a cell to inhibit translation of a complementary mRNA by base pairing to it and physically obstructing the translation machinery.
BLAST	In bioinformatics, BLAST, or BLAST, is an algorithm for comparing primary biological sequence information, such as the amino-acid sequences of different proteins or the nucleotides of DNA sequences. A BLAST search enables a researcher to compare a query sequence with a library or database of sequences, and identify library sequences that resemble the query sequence above a certain threshold. Different types of BLASTs are available according to the query sequences.
Enhancer	In genetics, an enhancer is a short region of DNA that can be bound with proteins to enhance transcription levels of genes (hence the name) in a gene cluster. While enhancers are usually cis-acting, an enhancer does not need to be particularly close to the genes it acts on, and sometimes need not be located on the same chromosome.
VISTA	VISTA is a collection of databases, tools, and servers that permit extensive comparative genomics analyses.
Genome editing	Genome editing, or genome editing with engineered nucleases is a type of genetic engineering in which DNA is inserted, replaced, or removed from a genome using artificially engineered nucleases, or 'molecular scissors.' The nucleases create specific double-stranded break (DSBs) at desired locations in the genome, and harness the cell's endogenous mechanisms to repair the induced break by natural processes of homologous recombination (HR) and nonhomologous end-joining (NHEJ). There are currently four families of engineered nucleases being used: Zinc finger nucleases (ZFNs), Transcription Activator-Like Effector Nucleases (TALENs), CRISPR, and engineered meganuclease re-engineered homing endonucleases. It is commonly practiced in genetic analysis that in order to understand the function of a gene or a protein function one interferes with it in a sequence-specific way and monitors its effects on the organism.
Meganuclease	Meganucleases are endodeoxyribonucleases characterized by a large recognition site ; as a result this site generally occurs only once in any given genome. For example, the 18-base pair sequence recognized by the I-SceI meganuclease would on average require a genome twenty times the size of the human genome to be found once by chance (although sequences with a single mismatch occur about three times per human-sized genome). Meganucleases are therefore considered to be the most specific naturally occurring restriction enzymes.

CHAPTER HIGHLIGHTS & NOTES: KEY TERMS, PEOPLE, PLACES, CONCEPTS

Chromatin immunoprecipitation	Chromatin Immunoprecipitation is a type of immunoprecipitation experimental technique used to investigate the interaction between proteins and DNA in the cell. It aims to determine whether specific proteins are associated with specific genomic regions, such as transcription factors on promoters or other DNA binding sites, and possibly defining cistromes. ChIP also aims to determine the specific location in the genome that various histone modifications are associated with, indicating the target of the histone modifiers.
Column	The column, or technically the gynostemium, is a reproductive structure that can be found in several plant families: Aristolochiaceae, Orchidaceae, and Stylidiaceae. It is derived from the fusion of both male and female parts into a single organ. This means that the style and stigma of the pistil, with the filaments and one or more anthers, are all united.
Immunoprecipitation	Immunoprecipitation is the technique of precipitating a protein antigen out of solution using an antibody that specifically binds to that particular protein. This process can be used to isolate and concentrate a particular protein from a sample containing many thousands of different proteins. Immunoprecipitation requires that the antibody be coupled to a solid substrate at some point in the procedure.
Epitope	An epitope, also known as antigenic determinant, is the part of an antigen that is recognized by the immune system, specifically by antibodies, B cells, or T cells. The part of an antibody that recognizes the epitope is called a paratope. Although epitopes are usually non-self proteins, sequences derived from the host that can be recognized are also epitopes.
Coomassie Brilliant Blue	Coomassie Brilliant Blue is the name of two similar triphenylmethane dyes that were developed for use in the textile industry but are now commonly used for staining proteins in analytical biochemistry. Coomassie Brilliant Blue G-250 differs from Coomassie Brilliant Blue R-250 by the addition of two methyl groups. The name 'Coomassie' is a registered trademark of Imperial Chemical Industries.
Sodium dodecyl sulfate	Sodium dodecyl sulfate, sodium laurilsulfate or sodium lauryl sulfate (SLS) is an organic compound with the formula $CH_3(CH_2)_{11}OSO_3Na$. It is an anionic surfactant used in many cleaning and hygiene products. The salt is of an organosulfate consisting of a 12-carbon tail attached to a sulfate group, giving the material the amphiphilic properties required of a detergent.
Edman degradation	Edman degradation, developed by Pehr Edman, is a method of sequencing amino acids in a peptide. In this method, the amino-terminal residue is labeled and cleaved from the peptide without disrupting the peptide bonds between other amino acid residues.
Hfq protein	The Hfq protein encoded by the hfq gene was discovered in 1968 as an Escherichia. coli host factor that was essential for replication of the bacteriophage Qß.

Chromatography	Chromatography [?kr??m??t?gr?fi] is the collective term for a set of laboratory techniques for the separation of mixtures. The mixture is dissolved in a fluid called the mobile phase, which carries it through a structure holding another material called the stationary phase. The various constituents of the mixture travel at different speeds, causing them to separate.
Proteomics	Proteomics is the large-scale study of proteins, particularly their structures and functions. Proteins are vital parts of living organisms, as they are the main components of the physiological metabolic pathways of cells. The term proteomics was first coined in 1997 to make an analogy with genomics, the study of the genome.
Interactome	In molecular biology, an interactome is the whole set of molecular interactions in a particular cell. The term specifically refers to physical interactions among molecules but can also mean indirect interactions among genes, i.e. genetic interactions. It is generally displayed as an undirected graph.
Assay	An assay is an investigative procedure in laboratory medicine, pharmacology, environmental biology, and molecular biology for qualitatively assessing or quantitatively measuring the presence or amount or the functional activity of a target entity (the analyte), which can be a drug or biochemical substance or a cell in an organism or organic sample. The measured entity is generally called the analyte, or the measurand or the target of the assay. The assay usually aims to measure an intensive property of the analyte and express it in the relevant measurement unit (e.g. molarity, density, functional activity in enzyme international units, degree of some effect in comparison to a standard, etc)..
DNA footprinting	DNA footprinting is a method of investigating the sequence specificity of DNA-binding proteins in vitro. This technique can be used to study protein-DNA interactions both outside and within cells. The regulation of transcription has been studied extensively, and yet there is still much that is not known.
Chips	Chips the dog was the most decorated war dog from World War II. Chips was a German Shepherd-Collie-Siberian Husky mix owned by Edward J. Wren of Pleasantville, NY. During the war, private citizens like Wren donated their dogs for duty. Chips shipped out to the War Dog Training Center, Front Royal, Virginia, in 1942 for training as a sentry dog. He served with the 3rd Infantry Division in North Africa, Sicily, Italy, France and Germany.
Heredity	Heredity is the passing of traits to offspring from its parents or ancestor. This is the process by which an offspring cell or organism acquires or becomes predisposed to the characteristics of its parent cell or organism. Through heredity, variations exhibited by individuals can accumulate and cause some species to evolve.

CHAPTER HIGHLIGHTS & NOTES: KEY TERMS, PEOPLE, PLACES, CONCEPTS

Theory

Theory is a contemplative and rational type of abstract or generalizing thinking, or the results of such thinking. Depending on the context, the results might for example include generalized explanations of how nature works. The word has its roots in ancient Greek, but in modern use it has taken on several different related meanings.

Hox gene

Hox genes are a group of related genes that control the body plan of the embryo along the anterior-posterior (head-tail) axis. After the embryonic segments have formed, the Hox proteins determine the type of segment structures (e.g. legs, antennae, and wings in fruit flies or the different vertebrate ribs in humans) that will form on a given segment. Hox proteins thus confer segmental identity, but do not form the actual segments themselves

Hox genes are defined as having the following properties:•their protein product is a transcription factor•they contain a DNA sequence known as the homeobox•in many animals, the organization of the Hox genes on the chromosome is the same as the order of their expression along the anterior-posterior axis of the developing animal, and are thus said to display colinearity..

CHAPTER QUIZ: KEY TERMS, PEOPLE, PLACES, CONCEPTS

1. __________, formerly called Pfeiffer's bacillus or Bacillus influenzae, is a Gram-negative, coccobacilli bacterium first described in 1892 by Richard Pfeiffer during an influenza pandemic. A member of the Pasteurellaceae family, it is generally aerobic, but can grow as a facultative anaerobe.

   H. influenzae was mistakenly considered to be the cause of influenza until 1933, when the viral etiology of influenza became apparent.

   a. Haemophilus influenzae
   b. Horizontal gene transfer
   c. R-factor
   d. Carbapenem resistant enterobacteriaceae

2. . In genetics, __________, also known as shotgun cloning, is a method used for sequencing long DNA strands. It is named by analogy with the rapidly expanding, quasi-random firing pattern of a shotgun.

   Since the chain termination method of DNA sequencing can only be used for fairly short strands (100 to 1000 basepairs), longer sequences must be subdivided into smaller fragments, and subsequently re-assembled to give the overall sequence.

   a. Shotgun sequencing
   b. BFAST

c. Carlson Curve
d. ChIP-exo

3. A _________ is a multiplex lab-on-a-chip. It is a 2D array on a solid substrate (usually a glass slide or silicon thin-film cell) that assays large amounts of biological material using high-throughput screening methods. The concept and methodology of microarrays was first introduced and illustrated in antibody microarrays (also referred to as antibody matrix) in 1983 in a scientific publication and a series of patents.

a. Biochip
b. CaSNP
c. Microarray
d. Chemical compound microarray

4. _________, sodium laurilsulfate or sodium lauryl sulfate (SLS) is an organic compound with the formula $CH_3(CH_2)_{11}OSO_3Na$. It is an anionic surfactant used in many cleaning and hygiene products. The salt is of an organosulfate consisting of a 12-carbon tail attached to a sulfate group, giving the material the amphiphilic properties required of a detergent.

a. Dioctyl sodium sulfosuccinate
b. MBAS assay
c. Sodium dodecyl sulfate
d. Perfluorononanoic acid

5. _________ is the branch of biology that deals with the molecular basis of biological activity. This field overlaps with other areas of biology and chemistry, particularly genetics and biochemistry. _________ chiefly concerns itself with understanding the interactions between the various systems of a cell, including the interactions between the different types of DNA, RNA and protein biosynthesis as well as learning how these interactions are regulated.

a. Bacteremia
b. Fungemia
c. Hypercalcaemia
d. Molecular biology

1. a

2. a

3. c

4. c

5. d

6. Genome Structure, Chromatin, and the Nucleosome,

CHAPTER OUTLINE: KEY TERMS, PEOPLE, PLACES, CONCEPTS

- Chromatid
- Histone methyltransferase
- Function
- Protein
- Nucleoid
- Polyploid
- Ploidy
- Genome
- Genome size
- Megakaryocyte
- Nucleus
- Chromosome
- Complexity
- DNA gyrase
- DNA polymerase
- Escherichia coli
- Gene density
- Virulence
- Gene
- Origin
- Origin of replication

6. Genome Structure, Chromatin, and the Nucleosome,

CHAPTER OUTLINE: KEY TERMS, PEOPLE, PLACES, CONCEPTS

- Ferritin
- Intron
- MicroRNA
- Reverse transcriptase
- Microsatellite
- Centromere
- Escherichia
- Kinetochore
- Microtubule
- Telomerase
- Cell
- Cell division
- Centrosome
- Chromosome segregation
- Cohesin
- Mitosis
- S phase
- Sister chromatids
- Cell cycle
- Division
- Interphase

6. Genome Structure, Chromatin, and the Nucleosome,

CHAPTER OUTLINE: KEY TERMS, PEOPLE, PLACES, CONCEPTS

Condensin

Prophase

Anaphase

Cell cycle checkpoint

Cytokinesis

Fusion protein

Metaphase

Telophase

Microscopy

Linker DNA

DNA replication

Core

Nucleosome

Axis

Modifications

Minor

Gel electrophoresis

Euchromatin

Heterochromatin

Solenoid

Acetylation

6. Genome Structure, Chromatin, and the Nucleosome,

CHAPTER OUTLINE: KEY TERMS, PEOPLE, PLACES, CONCEPTS

______	Histone
______	Bromodomain
______	Histone acetyltransferase
______	DNA synthesis
______	Inheritance
______	Chaperone

CHAPTER HIGHLIGHTS & NOTES: KEY TERMS, PEOPLE, PLACES, CONCEPTS

Chromatid	A chromatid is one copy of a duplicated chromosome, which generally is joined to the other copy by a centromere, for the process of nuclear division . They are normally identical ('homozygous') but may have slight differences in the case of mutations, in which case they are heterozygous. They are called sister chromatids so long as they are joined by the centromeres.
Histone methyltransferase	Histone methyltransferases are histone-modifying enzymes, (including histone-lysine N-methyltransferase and histone-arginine N-methyltransferase), that catalyze the transfer of one, two, or three methyl groups to lysine and arginine residues of histone proteins. The attachment of methyl groups occurs predominantly at specific lysine or arginine residues on histones H3 and H4. Two major types of histone methyltranferases exist, lysine-specific (which can be SET (Su(var)3-9, Enhancer of Zeste, Trithorax) domain containing or non-SET domain containing) and arginine-specific. In both types of histone methyltransferases, cofactor S-Adenosyl methionine (SAM) serves as a cofactor and methyl donor group.
Function	A function is the reason some object or process occurred in a system that evolved through a process of selection or Natural selection. Thus, function refers forward from the object or process, along some chain of causation, to the goal or success. Compare this to the mechanism of the object or process, which looks backward along some chain of causation, explaining how the feature occurred.
Protein	Proteins are large biological molecules consisting of one or more chains of amino acids. Proteins perform a vast array of functions within living organisms, including catalyzing metabolic reactions, replicating DNA, responding to stimuli, and transporting molecules from one location to another.

6. Genome Structure, Chromatin, and the Nucleosome,

CHAPTER HIGHLIGHTS & NOTES: KEY TERMS, PEOPLE, PLACES, CONCEPTS

Nucleoid

The nucleoid is an irregularly-shaped region within the cell of a prokaryote that contains all or most of the genetic material. In contrast to the nucleus of a eukaryotic cell, it is not surrounded by a nuclear membrane. The genome of prokaryotic organisms generally is a circular, double-stranded piece of DNA, of which multiple copies may exist at any time.

Polyploid

Polyploid cells and organisms are those containing more than two paired sets of chromosomes. Most eukaryotic species are diploid, meaning they have two sets of chromosomes -- one set inherited from each parent. However polyploidy is found in some organisms and is especially common in plants.

Ploidy

Ploidy is the number of sets of chromosomes in the nucleus of a biological cell. Normally a gamete (sperm or egg) carries a full set of chromosomes that includes a single copy of each chromosome, as aneuploidy generally leads to severe genetic disease in the offspring. The haploid number (n) is the number of chromosomes in a gamete.

Genome

In modern molecular biology and genetics, the genome is the entirety of an organism's hereditary information. It is encoded either in DNA or, for many types of viruses, in RNA. The genome includes both the genes and the non-coding sequences of the DNA/RNA.

Genome size

Genome size is the total amount of DNA contained within one copy of a single genome. It is typically measured in terms of mass in picograms (trillionths (10^{-12}) of a gram, abbreviated pg) or less frequently in Daltons or as the total number of nucleotide base pairs typically in megabases (millions of base pairs, abbreviated Mb or Mbp). One picogram equals 978 megabases.

Megakaryocyte

A megakaryocyte is a bone marrow cell responsible for the production of blood thrombocytes (platelets), which are necessary for normal blood clotting. Megakaryocytes normally account for 1 out of 10,000 bone marrow cells but can increase in number nearly 10-fold during the course of certain diseases. Owing to variations in word roots and spelling, synonyms include megalokaryocyte and megacaryocyte.

Nucleus

In neuroanatomy, a nucleus is a brain structure consisting of a relatively compact cluster of neurons. It is one of the two most common forms of nerve cell organization, the other being layered structures such as the cerebral cortex or cerebellar cortex. In anatomical sections, a nucleus shows up as a region of gray matter, often bordered by white matter.

Chromosome

A chromosome is an organized structure of DNA, protein, and RNA found in cells. It is a single piece of coiled DNA containing many genes, regulatory elements and other nucleotide sequences. Chromosomes also contain DNA-bound proteins, which serve to package the DNA and control its functions.

Complexity

In general usage, complexity tends to be used to characterize something with many parts in intricate arrangement.

The study of these complex linkages is the main goal of complex systems theory.

In science, there are at this time a number of approaches to characterizing complexity, many of which are reflected in this article.

DNA gyrase

DNA gyrase, often referred to simply as gyrase, is an enzyme that relieves strain while double-stranded DNA is being unwound by helicase. This causes negative supercoiling of the DNA. Bacterial DNA gyrase is the target of many antibiotics, including nalidixic acid, novobiocin, and ciprofloxacin.

DNA gyrase is a type II topoisomerase (EC 5.99.1.3) that introduces negative supercoils (or relaxes positive supercoils) into DNA by looping the template so as to form a crossing, then cutting one of the double helices and passing the other through it before releasing the break, changing the linking number by two in each enzymatic step.

DNA polymerase

A DNA polymerase is a cellular or viral polymerase enzyme that synthesizes DNA molecules from their nucleotide building blocks. DNA polymerases are essential for DNA replication, and usually function in pairs while copying one double-stranded DNA molecule into two double-stranded DNAs in a process termed semiconservative DNA replication. DNA polymerases also play key roles in other processes within cells, including DNA repair, genetic recombination, reverse transcription, and the generation of antibody diversity via the specialized DNA polymerase, terminal deoxynucleotidyl transferase.

Escherichia coli

Escherichia coli is a Gram-negative, facultative anaerobic, rod-shaped bacterium that is commonly found in the lower intestine of warm-blooded organisms (endotherms). Most E. coli strains are harmless, but some serotypes can cause serious food poisoning in humans, and are occasionally responsible for product recalls due to food contamination. The harmless strains are part of the normal flora of the gut, and can benefit their hosts by producing vitamin K_2, and by preventing the establishment of pathogenic bacteria within the intestine.

Gene density

In genetics, the gene density of an organism's genome is the ratio of the number of genes per number of base pairs, usually written in terms of a million base pairs, or megabase . The human genome has a gene density of 12-15 genes/Mb, while the genome of the C. elegans roundworm is estimated to have only 1 gene per 5000 base pairs.

Curiously, seemingly simple organisms such as bacteria and amoebas have a much higher gene density than humans.

Virulence

Virulence is, by MeSH definition, the degree of pathogenicity within a group or species of parasites as indicated by case fatality rates and/or the ability of the organism to invade the tissues of the host. The pathogenicity of an organism - its ability to cause disease - is determined by its virulence factors.

6. Genome Structure, Chromatin, and the Nucleosome,

CHAPTER HIGHLIGHTS & NOTES: KEY TERMS, PEOPLE, PLACES, CONCEPTS

Gene	A gene is a molecular unit of heredity of a living organism. It is widely accepted by the scientific community as a name given to some stretches of deoxyribonucleic acids (DNA) and ribonucleic acids (RNA) that code for a polypeptide or for an RNA chain that has a function in the organism, though there still are controversies about what plays the role of the genetic material. Living beings depend on genes, as they specify all proteins and functional RNA chains.
Origin	The anatomical origin is a concept used when describing muscles, tendons, ligaments, nerves, and blood and lymph vessels. While it often has a slightly different meaning depending on which kind of origin is referred to, it is generally used to explain the relative location of the anatomical structure in question. It is not to be understood in a temporal/ontogenetical sense.
Origin of replication	The origin of replication is a particular sequence in a genome at which replication is initiated. This can either involve the replication of DNA in living organisms such as prokaryotes and eukaryotes, or that of DNA or RNA in viruses, such as double-stranded RNA viruses. DNA replication may proceed from this point bidirectionally or unidirectionally.
Ferritin	Ferritin is a ubiquitous intracellular protein that stores iron and releases it in a controlled fashion. The amount of ferritin stored reflects the amount of iron stored. The protein is produced by almost all living organisms, including algae, bacteria, higher plants, and animals.
Intron	An intron is any nucleotide sequence within a gene that is removed by RNA splicing while the final mature RNA product of a gene is being generated. The term intron refers to both the DNA sequence within a gene and the corresponding sequence in RNA transcripts. Sequences that are joined together in the final mature RNA after RNA splicing are exons.
MicroRNA	A microRNA is a small non-coding RNA molecule (ca. 22 nucleotides) found in plants and animals, which functions in transcriptional and post-transcriptional regulation of gene expression. Encoded by eukaryotic nuclear DNA, miRNAs function via base-pairing with complementary sequences within mRNA molecules, usually resulting in gene silencing via translational repression or target degradation. The human genome may encode over 1000 miRNAs, which may target about 60% of mammalian genes and are abundant in many human cell types.
Reverse transcriptase	Reverse transcriptase is an enzyme used to generate complementary DNA (cDNA) from an RNA template, a process termed reverse transcription. RT is needed for the replication of retroviruses (e.g., HIV), and RT inhibitors are widely used as antiretroviral drugs. RT activity is also associated with the replication of chromosome ends (telomerase) and some mobile genetic elements (retrotransposons).
Microsatellite	Microsatellites, also known as Simple Sequence Repeats or Short Tandem Repeats (STRs), are repeating sequences of 2-6 base pairs of DNA. It is a type of Variable Number Tandem Repeat (VNTR). Microsatellites are typically co-dominant.

Centromere — The centromere is the part of a chromosome that links sister chromatids. During mitosis, spindle fibers attach to the centromere via the kinetochore. Centromeres were first defined as genetic loci that direct the behavior of chromosomes.

Escherichia — Escherichia is a genus of Gram-negative, non-spore forming, facultatively anaerobic, rod-shaped bacteria from the family Enterobacteriaceae. In those species which are inhabitants of the gastrointestinal tracts of warm-blooded animals, Escherichia species provide a portion of the microbially derived vitamin K for their host. A number of the species of Escherichia are pathogenic.

Kinetochore — The kinetochore is the protein structure on chromatids where the spindle fibers attach during cell division to pull sister chromatids apart.

The kinetochore forms in eukaryotes, assembles on the centromere and links the chromosome to microtubule polymers from the mitotic spindle during mitosis and meiosis.

'Monocentric' organisms, including vertebrates, fungi, and most plants, have a single centromeric region on each chromosome which assembles one kinetochore.

Microtubule — Microtubules are a component of the cytoskeleton, found throughout the cytoplasm. These tubular polymers of tubulin can grow as long as 50 micrometres, with an average length of 25 μm and are highly dynamic. The outer diameter of a microtubule is about 25 nm while the inner diameter is about 12 nm.

Telomerase — Telomerase is a ribonucleoprotein that is an enzyme that adds DNA sequence repeats to the 3' end of DNA strands in the telomere regions, which are found at the ends of eukaryotic chromosomes. This region of repeated nucleotide called telomeres contains noncoding DNA and hinders the loss of important DNA from chromosome ends. As a result, every time the chromosome is copied, only 100-200 nucleotides are lost, which causes no damage to the organism's DNA. Telomerase is a reverse transcriptase that carries its own RNA molecule, which is used as a template when it elongates telomeres, which are shortened after each replication cycle.

Cell — The cell is the basic structural, functional and biological unit of all known living organisms. Cells are the smallest unit of life that is classified as a living thing, and are often called the 'building blocks of life'.

Cells consist of a protoplasm enclosed within a membrane, which contains many biomolecules such as proteins and nucleic acids.

Cell division — Cell division is the process by which a parent cell divides into two or more daughter cells. Cell division usually occurs as part of a larger cell cycle.

6. Genome Structure, Chromatin, and the Nucleosome,

CHAPTER HIGHLIGHTS & NOTES: KEY TERMS, PEOPLE, PLACES, CONCEPTS

Centrosome	In cell biology, the centrosome is an organelle that serves as the main microtubule organizing center of the animal cell as well as a regulator of cell-cycle progression. It was discovered by Edouard Van Beneden in 1883. and was described and named in 1888 by Theodor Boveri. The centrosome is thought to have evolved only in the metazoan lineage of eukaryotic cells.
Chromosome segregation	Chromosome segregation is a step in cell reproduction or division, where chromosomes pair off with their similar homologous chromosome. In mitosis, a complete copy of each one is made. In meiosis, one chromosome from each pair migrates to opposite ends of the cell and the genes are split to make a gamete.
Cohesin	Cohesin is a protein complex that regulates the separation of sister chromatids during cell division, either mitosis or meiosis.
Mitosis	Mitosis is the process by which a cell, which has previously replicated each of its chromosomes, separates the chromosomes in its cell nucleus into two identical sets of chromosomes, each set in its own new nucleus. It is a form of nuclear division. It is generally followed immediately by cytokinesis, which divides the nuclei, cytoplasm, organelles, and cell membrane into two cells containing roughly equal shares of these cellular components.
S phase	S-phase (synthesis phase) is the part of the cell cycle in which DNA is replicated, occurring between G_1 phase and G_2 phase. Precise and accurate DNA replication is necessary to prevent genetic abnormalities which often lead to cell death or disease. Due to the importance, the regulatory pathways that govern this event in eukaryotes are highly conserved.
Sister chromatids	Sister chromatids are generated when a single chromosome is replicated into two copies of itself, these copies being called sister chromatids. Compare sister chromatids to homologous chromosomes, which are the two different copies of a chromosome that diploid organisms (like humans) inherit, one from each parent. In other words, while sister chromatids are by and large identical (since they carry the same alleles, also called variants or versions, of genes) because they derive from one original chromosome, homologous chromosomes might or might not be the same as each other because they derive from different parents.
Cell cycle	The cell cycle, or cell-division cycle, is the series of events that take place in a cell leading to its division and duplication . In cells without a nucleus (prokaryotic), the cell cycle occurs via a process termed binary fission. In cells with a nucleus (eukaryotes), the cell cycle can be divided in three periods: interphase--during which the cell grows, accumulating nutrients needed for mitosis and duplicating its DNA--and the mitotic (M) phase, during which the cell splits itself into two distinct cells, often called 'daughter cells' and the final phase, cytokinesis, where the new cell is completely divided.
Division	In biology, a phylum is a taxonomic rank below kingdom and above class.

Traditionally, in botany the term division is used instead of 'phylum', although in 1993 the International Botanical Congress accepted the designation 'phylum'. The kingdom Animalia contains approximately 35 phyla; the kingdom Plantae contains 12 phyla.

Interphase

Interphase is the phase of the cell cycle in which the cell spends the majority of its time and performs the majority of its purposes including preparation for cell division. In preparation for cell division, it increases its size and makes a copy of its DNA, which is made during the S phase. Interphase is also considered to be the 'living' phase of the cell, in which the cell obtains nutrients, grows, reads its DNA, and conducts other 'normal' cell functions.

Condensin

Condensins are large protein complexes that play a central role in chromosome assembly and segregation during mitosis and meiosis.

Prophase

Prophase, from the ancient Greek p?? and f?s?? (stage), is a stage of mitosis in which the chromatin condenses into double rod-shaped structures called chromosomes in which the chromatin becomes visible. This process, called chromatin condensation, is involved with the condensin complex. Since the genetic material has been replicated in the prior interphase of the cell cycle, there are two identical copies of each chromosome in the cell.

Anaphase

Anaphase, from the ancient Greek ??? and f?s?? (stage), is the stage of mitosis or meiosis when chromosomes are split and the sister chromatids move to opposite poles of the cell.

Anaphase accounts for approximately 1% of the cell cycle's duration. It begins with the regulated triggering of the metaphase-to-anaphase transition.

Cell cycle checkpoint

Cell cycle checkpoints are control mechanisms that ensure the fidelity of cell division in eukaryotic cells. These checkpoints verify whether the processes at each phase of the cell cycle have been accurately completed before progression into the next phase. Multiple checkpoints have been identified, though some of them are less understood than others.

Cytokinesis

Cytokinesis (from the greek cyto- and kinesis (motion, movement)) is the process in which the cytoplasm of a single eukaryotic cell is divided to form two daughter cells. It usually initiates during the late stages of mitosis, and sometimes meiosis, splitting a mitotic cell in two, to ensure that chromosome number is maintained from one generation to the next. In animal cells, one notable exception to the normal process of cytokinesis is oogenesis (the creation of an ovum in the ovarian follicle of the ovary), where the ovum takes almost all the cytoplasm and organelles, leaving very little for the resulting polar bodies, which then die.

Fusion protein

Fusion proteins or chimeric proteins are proteins created through the joining of two or more genes which originally coded for separate proteins. Translation of this fusion gene results in a single polypeptide with functional properties derived from each of the original proteins.

6. Genome Structure, Chromatin, and the Nucleosome,

CHAPTER HIGHLIGHTS & NOTES: KEY TERMS, PEOPLE, PLACES, CONCEPTS

Metaphase

Metaphase, from the ancient Greek μet? and f?s?? (stage)is a stage of mitosis in the eukaryotic cell cycle in which condensed and highly coiled chromosomes, carrying genetic information, align in the middle of the cell before being separated into each of the two daughter cells. Metaphase accounts for approximately 4% of the cell cycle's duration. Preceded by events in prometaphase and followed by anaphase, microtubules formed in prophase have already found and attached themselves to kinetochores in metaphase.

Telophase

Telophase, from the ancient Greek 'te???' and 'fas??' (stage), is the final stage in both meiosis and mitosis in a eukaryotic cell.

During telophase, the effects of prophase and prometaphase (the nuclear membrane and nucleolus disintegrating) are reversed. Two daughter nuclei form in each daughter cell, and phosphatases de-phosphorylate the nuclear lamins at the ends of the cell, forming nuclear envelopes around each nucleus.

Microscopy

Microscopy is the technical field of using microscopes to view samples and objects that cannot be seen with the unaided eye . There are three well-known branches of microscopy: optical, electron, and scanning probe microscopy.

Optical and electron microscopy involve the diffraction, reflection, or refraction of electromagnetic radiation/electron beams interacting with the specimen, and the subsequent collection of this scattered radiation or another signal in order to create an image.

Linker DNA

Linker DNA is double-stranded DNA in between two nucleosome cores that, in association with histone H1, holds the cores together. Linker DNA is seen as the string in the 'beads and string model', which is made by using an ionic solution on the chromatin. Linker DNA connects to histone H1 and histone H1 sits on the nucleosome core.

DNA replication

DNA replication is the process of producing two identical copies from one original DNA molecule. This biological process occurs in all living organisms and is the basis for biological inheritance. DNA is composed of two strands and each strand of the original DNA molecule serves as template for the production of the complementary strand, a process referred to as semiconservative replication.

Core

In anatomy, the core refers, in its most general of definitions, to the body minus the legs and arms. Functional movements are highly dependent on the core, and lack of core development can result in a predisposition to injury. The major muscles of the core reside in the area of the belly and the mid and lower back (not the shoulders), and peripherally include the hips, the shoulders and the neck.

Nucleosome

A nucleosome is the basic unit of DNA packaging in eukaryotes, consisting of a segment of DNA wound in sequence around eight histone protein cores.

This structure is often compared to thread wrapped around a spool.

Nucleosomes form the fundamental repeating units of eukaryotic chromatin, which is used to pack the large eukaryotic genomes into the nucleus while still ensuring appropriate access to it (in mammalian cells approximately 2 m of linear DNA have to be packed into a nucleus of roughly 10 μm diameter).

Axis

In anatomy, the second cervical vertebra of the spine is named the axis or epistropheus.

It forms the pivot upon which the first cervical vertebra (the atlas), which carries the head, rotates.

The most distinctive characteristic of this bone is the strong odontoid process ('dens') which rises perpendicularly from the upper surface of the body.

Modifications

In opposition to mutations, modifications are included in the band width of the genome of an individual creature. Modifications are dependent on the plentifulness of the substrate, light, warmths, stress, training, and so on.

A modification is a change in the physical appearance of an organism (phenotype) caused by environmental factors.

Minor

In law, a minor is a person under a certain age--usually the age of majority--which legally demarcates childhood from adulthood. The age depends upon jurisdiction and application, but is generally 18. Minor may also be used in contexts unconnected to the overall age of majority. For example, the drinking age in the United States is 21, and people below this age are sometimes called minors even if 18. The term underage often refers to those under the age of majority, but may also refer to persons under a certain age limit, such as the drinking age, smoking age, age of consent, marriageable age, driving age, voting age, etc.

Gel electrophoresis

Gel electrophoresis is a method for separation and analysis of macromolecules and their fragments, based on their size and charge.

It is used in clinical chemistry to separate proteins by charge and/or size (IEF agarose, essentially size independent) and in biochemistry and molecular biology to separate a mixed population of DNA and RNA fragments by length, to estimate the size of DNA and RNA fragments or to separate proteins by charge. Nucleic acid molecules are separated by applying an electric field to move the negatively charged molecules through an agarose matrix.

Euchromatin

Euchromatin is a lightly packed form of chromatin that is rich in gene concentration, and is often (but not always) under active transcription. Euchromatin comprises the most active portion of the genome within the cell nucleus. 92% of the human genome is euchromatic.

6. Genome Structure, Chromatin, and the Nucleosome,

CHAPTER HIGHLIGHTS & NOTES: KEY TERMS, PEOPLE, PLACES, CONCEPTS

Heterochromatin	Heterochromatin is a tightly packed form of DNA, which comes in different varieties. These varieties lie on a continuum between the two extremes of constitutive and facultative heterochromatin. Both play a role in the expression of genes, where constitutive heterochromatin can affect the genes near them (position-effect variegation) and where facultative heterochromatin is the result of genes that are silenced through a mechanism such as histone methylation or siRNA through RNAi.
Solenoid	The solenoid defines the packing of DNA as a 30 nm fiber of chromatin and results from the helical winding of at least five nucleosome strands. In eukaryotic cells, 146 bp of DNA are wrapped approximately 1.65 times around a histone octamer which together are called a nucleosome. Histone H1, which is not part of the binding histones, tightens the DNA bound to the eight protein complex.
Acetylation	Acetylation describes a reaction that introduces an acetyl functional group into a chemical compound. (Deacetylation is the removal of the acetyl group). Specifically, acetylation refers to the process of introducing an acetyl group (resulting in an acetoxy group) into a compound, namely, the substitution of an acetyl group for an active hydrogen atom.
Histone	In biology, histones are highly alkaline proteins found in eukaryotic cell nuclei that package and order the DNA into structural units called nucleosomes. They are the chief protein components of chromatin, acting as spools around which DNA winds, and play a role in gene regulation. Without histones, the unwound DNA in chromosomes would be very long (a length to width ratio of more than 10 million to 1 in human DNA).
Bromodomain	A bromodomain is a protein domain that recognizes acetylated lysine residues such as those on the N-terminal tails of histones. This recognition is often a prerequisite for protein-histone association and chromatin remodeling. The domain itself adopts an all-a protein fold, a bundle of four alpha helices.
Histone acetyltransferase	Histone acetyltransferases are enzymes that acetylate conserved lysine amino acids on histone proteins by transferring an acetyl group from acetyl CoA to form e-N-acetyllysine. DNA is wrapped around histones, and by transferring an acetyl group to the histones, genes can be turned on and off. Histone acetylation increases gene expression.
DNA synthesis	DNA synthesis is the natural or artificial creation of deoxyribonucleic acid molecules. In nature, such molecules are created by all living cells through the process of DNA replication, with replication initiator proteins splitting the existing DNA of the cell and making a copy of each split strand, with the copied strands then being joined together with their template strand into a new DNA molecule.

CHAPTER HIGHLIGHTS & NOTES: KEY TERMS, PEOPLE, PLACES, CONCEPTS

Inheritance	In genetic algorithms, inheritance is the ability of modelled objects to mate, mutate and propagate their problem solving genes to the next generation, in order to produce an evolved solution to a particular problem.
Chaperone	In molecular biology, molecular chaperones are proteins that assist the non-covalent folding or unfolding and the assembly or disassembly of other macromolecular structures, but do not occur in these structures when the structures are performing their normal biological functions having completed the processes of folding and/or assembly. The common perception that chaperones are concerned primarily with protein folding is incorrect. The first protein to be called a chaperone assists the assembly of nucleosomes from folded histones and DNA and such assembly chaperones, especially in the nucleus, are concerned with the assembly of folded subunits into oligomeric structures.

CHAPTER QUIZ: KEY TERMS, PEOPLE, PLACES, CONCEPTS

1. In law, a _________ is a person under a certain age--usually the age of majority--which legally demarcates childhood from adulthood. The age depends upon jurisdiction and application, but is generally 18. _________ may also be used in contexts unconnected to the overall age of majority. For example, the drinking age in the United States is 21, and people below this age are sometimes called _________s even if 18. The term underage often refers to those under the age of majority, but may also refer to persons under a certain age limit, such as the drinking age, smoking age, age of consent, marriageable age, driving age, voting age, etc.

   a. Bairn
   b. Birth in Sri Lanka
   c. Chartier v. Chartier
   d. Minor

2. The _________ is an irregularly-shaped region within the cell of a prokaryote that contains all or most of the genetic material. In contrast to the nucleus of a eukaryotic cell, it is not surrounded by a nuclear membrane. The genome of prokaryotic organisms generally is a circular, double-stranded piece of DNA, of which multiple copies may exist at any time.

   a. Nucleoid
   b. Bacterial growth
   c. Bacterial morphological plasticity
   d. Bacterial phyla

3. . The _________ is the part of a chromosome that links sister chromatids. During mitosis, spindle fibers attach to the _________ via the kinetochore. _________s were first defined as genetic loci that direct the behavior of chromosomes.

a. Bivalent
b. Chromosome
c. Microchromosome
d. Centromere

4. _________ is the natural or artificial creation of deoxyribonucleic acid molecules. In nature, such molecules are created by all living cells through the process of DNA replication, with replication initiator proteins splitting the existing DNA of the cell and making a copy of each split strand, with the copied strands then being joined together with their template strand into a new DNA molecule. Various means also exist to artificially stimulate the replication of naturally occurring DNA, or to create artificial gene sequences.

a. Cdc6
b. DNA clamp
c. DNA ligase
d. DNA synthesis

5. _________ (from the greek cyto- and kinesis (motion, movement)) is the process in which the cytoplasm of a single eukaryotic cell is divided to form two daughter cells. It usually initiates during the late stages of mitosis, and sometimes meiosis, splitting a mitotic cell in two, to ensure that chromosome number is maintained from one generation to the next. In animal cells, one notable exception to the normal process of _________ is oogenesis (the creation of an ovum in the ovarian follicle of the ovary), where the ovum takes almost all the cytoplasm and organelles, leaving very little for the resulting polar bodies, which then die.

a. Bivalent
b. Cdc25
c. Cytokinesis
d. CDKN1B

ANSWER KEY
6. Genome Structure, Chromatin, and the Nucleosome,

1. d
2. a
3. d
4. d
5. c

7. The Replication of DNA,

CHAPTER OUTLINE: KEY TERMS, PEOPLE, PLACES, CONCEPTS

	DNA replication
	DNA synthesis
	Nucleoside triphosphate
	Extension
	DNA damage
	DNA photolyase
	DNA polymerase
	Proofreading
	Active site
	Kinetic proofreading
	Pyrophosphate
	Metal
	Polymerase
	Environment
	Plant
	Processivity
	Exon skipping
	Methylation
	Okazaki fragments
	Primer
	Primase

7. The Replication of DNA,

CHAPTER OUTLINE: KEY TERMS, PEOPLE, PLACES, CONCEPTS

- RNA polymerase
- Ligase ribozyme
- Helicase
- DNA-binding protein
- Electrophoresis
- Enzyme
- Gel electrophoresis
- Topoisomerase
- Response element
- Experiment
- Replisome
- Escherichia coli
- Jacob
- Origin
- Origin of replication
- ATP-binding motif
- DnaA
- DnaC
- Edman degradation
- Escherichia
- Origin recognition complex

7. The Replication of DNA,

CHAPTER OUTLINE: KEY TERMS, PEOPLE, PLACES, CONCEPTS

	Cooperative binding
	Degradation
	S phase
	Eukaryote
	Telomerase
	Telomerase reverse transcriptase
	Ferritin
	Marker gene

CHAPTER HIGHLIGHTS & NOTES: KEY TERMS, PEOPLE, PLACES, CONCEPTS

DNA replication	DNA replication is the process of producing two identical copies from one original DNA molecule. This biological process occurs in all living organisms and is the basis for biological inheritance. DNA is composed of two strands and each strand of the original DNA molecule serves as template for the production of the complementary strand, a process referred to as semiconservative replication.
DNA synthesis	DNA synthesis is the natural or artificial creation of deoxyribonucleic acid molecules. In nature, such molecules are created by all living cells through the process of DNA replication, with replication initiator proteins splitting the existing DNA of the cell and making a copy of each split strand, with the copied strands then being joined together with their template strand into a new DNA molecule. Various means also exist to artificially stimulate the replication of naturally occurring DNA, or to create artificial gene sequences.
Nucleoside triphosphate	Nucleoside triphosphate is a molecule containing a nucleoside bound to three phosphates. Natural nucleoside triphosphates include adenosine triphosphate (ATP), guanosine triphosphate (GTP), cytidine triphosphate (CTP), 5-methyluridine triphosphate (m^5UTP), and uridine triphosphate (UTP). These terms refer to those nucleoside triphosphates that contain ribose.

7. The Replication of DNA,

CHAPTER HIGHLIGHTS & NOTES: KEY TERMS, PEOPLE, PLACES, CONCEPTS

Extension	In kinesiology, extension is a movement of a joint that results in increased angle between two bones or body surfaces at a joint. Extension usually results in straightening of the bones or body surfaces involved. For example, extension is produced by extending the flexed (bent) elbow.
DNA damage	DNA damage is an alteration in the chemical structure of DNA, such as a break in a strand of DNA, a base missing from the backbone of DNA, or a chemically changed base such as 8-OHdG. Damage to DNA that occurs naturally can result from metabolic or hydrolytic processes. Metabolism releases compounds that damage DNA including reactive oxygen species, reactive nitrogen species, reactive carbonyl species, lipid peroxidation products and alkylating agents, among others, while hydrolysis cleaves chemical bonds in DNA. Naturally occurring DNA damages arise about 10,000 to 100,000 times per day per mammalian cell. DNA damage is distinctly different from mutation, although both are types of error in DNA. DNA damage is an abnormal chemical structure in DNA, while a mutation is a change in the sequence of standard base pairs.
DNA photolyase	DNA photolyase is an evolutionary conserved protein domain. This domain binds a light harvesting cofactor. Deoxyribodipyrimidine photolyase (DNA photolyase) is a DNA repair enzyme.
DNA polymerase	A DNA polymerase is a cellular or viral polymerase enzyme that synthesizes DNA molecules from their nucleotide building blocks. DNA polymerases are essential for DNA replication, and usually function in pairs while copying one double-stranded DNA molecule into two double-stranded DNAs in a process termed semiconservative DNA replication. DNA polymerases also play key roles in other processes within cells, including DNA repair, genetic recombination, reverse transcription, and the generation of antibody diversity via the specialized DNA polymerase, terminal deoxynucleotidyl transferase.
Proofreading	The term proofreading is used in genetics to refer to the error-correcting processes, first proposed by John Hopfield and Jacques Ninio, involved in DNA replication, immune system specificity, enzyme-substrate recognition among many other processes that require enhanced specificity. The proofreading mechanisms of Hopfield and Ninio are non-equilibrium active processes that consume ATP to enhance specificity of various biochemical reactions. In bacteria, all three DNA polymerases (I, II, and III) have the ability to proofread, using 3'->5' exonuclease activity.
Active site	In biology, the active site is the small portion of an enzyme where substrate molecules bind and undergo a chemical reaction. This chemical reaction occurs when a substrate collides with and slots into the active site of an enzyme.

Kinetic proofreading

Kinetic proofreading is a mechanism for error correction in biochemical reactions, proposed independently by John Hopfield (1974) and Jacques Ninio (1975). Kinetic proofreading allows enzymes to discriminate between two possible reaction pathways leading to correct or incorrect products with an accuracy higher than what one would predict based on the difference in the activation energy between these two pathways.

Increased specificity is obtained by introducing an irreversible step exiting the pathway, with reaction intermediates leading to incorrect products more likely to prematurely exit the pathway than reaction intermediates leading to the correct product.

Pyrophosphate

In chemistry, the anion, the salts, and the esters of pyrophosphoric acid are called pyrophosphates. Any salt or ester containing two phosphate groups is called a diphosphate. As a food additive, diphosphates are known as E450. As well as the normal pyrophosphates, a number of hydrogen pyrophosphates also exist, such as $Na_2H_2P_2O_7$.

Metal

A metal is a solid material that is typically hard, opaque, shiny, and features good electrical and thermal conductivity. Metals are generally malleable--that is, they can be hammered or pressed permanently out of shape without breaking or cracking--as well as fusible (able to be fused or melted) and ductile (able to be drawn out into a thin wire). 91 of the 118 elements in the periodic table are metals.

Polymerase

A polymerase is an enzyme whose central biological function is the synthesis of polymers of nucleic acids. DNA polymerase and RNA polymerase are used to assemble DNA and RNA molecules, respectively, generally by copying a DNA or RNA template strand using base-pairing interactions.

It is an accident of history that the enzymes responsible for the generation of other biopolymers are not also referred to as polymerases.

Environment

The biophysical environment is the biotic and abiotic surrounding of an organism or population, and includes particularly the factors that have an influence in their survival, development and evolution. The naked term environment can make reference to different concepts, but it is often used as a short form for the biophysical environment. This practice is common, for instance, among governments, that usually name their departments and agencies dealing with the biophysical environment with denominations like Environment Agency.

Plant

Plants, also called green plants (Viridiplantae in Latin), are living multicellular organisms of the kingdom Plantae. They form a clade that includes the flowering plants, conifers and other gymnosperms, ferns, clubmosses, hornworts, liverworts and mosses, as well as, depending on definition, the green algae. Plants exclude the red and brown seaweeds such as kelp, the fungi, Archaea and bacteria.

7. The Replication of DNA,

CHAPTER HIGHLIGHTS & NOTES: KEY TERMS, PEOPLE, PLACES, CONCEPTS

Processivity

In molecular biology and biochemistry, processivity is an enzyme's ability to catalyze 'consecutive reactions without releasing its substrate'.

For example, processivity is the average number of nucleotides added by a polymerase enzyme, such as DNA polymerase, per association/disassociation with the template. DNA polymerases associated with DNA replication tend to be highly processive, while those associated with DNA repair tend to have low processivity.

Exon skipping

Exon skipping is a method used to cause cells to “skip” over faulty or misaligned sections of genetic code, leading to a truncated but still functional protein despite the genetic mutation.

Methylation

In the chemical sciences, methylation denotes the addition of a methyl group to a substrate or the substitution of an atom or group by a methyl group. Methylation is a form of alkylation with a methyl group, rather than a larger carbon chain, replacing a hydrogen atom. These terms are commonly used in chemistry, biochemistry, soil science, and the biological sciences.

Okazaki fragments

Okazaki fragments are short, newly synthesized DNA fragments that are formed on the lagging template strand during DNA replication. They are complementary to the lagging template strand, together forming short double-stranded DNA sections. Okazaki fragments are between 1,000 and 2,000 nucleotides long in Escherichia coli and are between 100 and 200 nucleotides long in eukaryotes.

Primer

A primer is a strand of nucleic acid that serves as a starting point for DNA synthesis. It is required for DNA replication because the enzymes that catalyze this process, DNA polymerases, can only add new nucleotides to an existing strand of DNA. The polymerase starts replication at the 3'-end of the primer, and copies the opposite strand.

In most cases of natural DNA replication, the primer for DNA synthesis and replication is a short strand of RNA (which can be made de novo).

Primase

DNA primase is an enzyme involved in the replication of DNA. DNA primase is, in fact, a type of RNA polymerase which creates an RNA primer (later this RNA piece is removed by a 5' to 3' exonuclease); next, DNA polymerase uses the RNA primer to replicate ssDNA.

Primase catalyzes the synthesis of a short RNA (or DNA in some organisms) segment called a primer complementary to a ssDNA template. Primase is of key importance in DNA replication because no known DNA polymerases can initiate the synthesis of a DNA strand without an initial RNA or DNA primer (for temporary DNA elongation).

RNA polymerase

RNA polymerase, also known as DNA-dependent RNA polymerase, is an enzyme that produces RNA. In cells, RNAP is necessary for constructing RNA chains using DNA genes as templates, a process called transcription.

RNA polymerase enzymes are essential to life and are found in all organisms and many viruses. In chemical terms, RNAP is a nucleotidyl transferase that polymerizes ribonucleotides at the 3' end of an RNA transcript.

Ligase ribozyme

The RNA Ligase ribozyme was the first of several types of synthetic ribozymes produced by in vitro evolution and selection techniques. They are an important class of ribozymes because they catalyze the assembly of RNA fragments into phosphodiester RNA polymers, a reaction required of all extant nucleic acid polymerases and thought to be required for any self-replicating molecule. Ideas that the origin of life may have involved the first self-replicating molecules being ribozymes are called RNA World hypotheses.

Helicase

Helicases are a class of enzymes vital to all living organisms. Their main function is to unpackage an organism's genes. They are motor proteins that move directionally along a nucleic acid phosphodiester backbone, separating two annealed nucleic acid strands (i.e., DNA, RNA, or RNA-DNA hybrid) using energy derived from ATP hydrolysis.

DNA-binding protein

DNA-binding proteins are proteins that are composed of DNA-binding domains and thus have a specific or general affinity for either single or double stranded DNA. Sequence-specific DNA-binding proteins generally interact with the major groove of B-DNA, because it exposes more functional groups that identify a base pair. However there are some known minor groove DNA-binding ligands such as Netropsin, Distamycin, Hoechst 33258, Pentamidine, DAPI and others.

Electrophoresis

Electrophoresis is the motion of dispersed particles relative to a fluid under the influence of a spatially uniform electric field. This electrokinetic phenomenon was observed for the first time in 1807 by Ferdinand Frederic Reuss (Moscow State University), who noticed that the application of a constant electric field caused clay particles dispersed in water to migrate. It is ultimately caused by the presence of a charged interface between the particle surface and the surrounding fluid.

Enzyme

Enzymes are large biological molecules responsible for the thousands of metabolic processes that sustain life. They are highly selective catalysts, greatly accelerating both the rate and specificity of metabolic reactions, from the digestion of food to the synthesis of DNA. Most enzymes are proteins, although some catalytic RNA molecules have been identified. Enzymes adopt a specific three-dimensional structure, and may employ organic (e.g. biotin) and inorganic (e.g. magnesium ion) cofactors to assist in catalysis.

Gel electrophoresis

Gel electrophoresis is a method for separation and analysis of macromolecules and their fragments, based on their size and charge.

It is used in clinical chemistry to separate proteins by charge and/or size (IEF agarose, essentially size independent) and in biochemistry and molecular biology to separate a mixed population of DNA and RNA fragments by length, to estimate the size of DNA and RNA fragments or to separate proteins by charge.

7. The Replication of DNA,

CHAPTER HIGHLIGHTS & NOTES: KEY TERMS, PEOPLE, PLACES, CONCEPTS

Topoisomerase	Topoisomerases are enzymes that regulate the overwinding or underwinding of DNA. The winding problem of DNA arises due to the intertwined nature of its double helical structure. For example, during DNA replication, DNA becomes overwound ahead of a replication fork. If left unabated, this tension would eventually halt DNA replication.
Response element	Response elements are short sequences of DNA within a gene promoter region that are able to bind specific transcription factors and regulate transcription of genes. Under conditions of stress, a transcription activator protein binds to the response element and stimulates transcription. If the same response element sequence is located in the control regions of different genes, then these genes will be activated by the same stimuli, thus producing a coordinated response.
Experiment	The Experiment was an early nineteenth century boat powered by horses and incorporated the then novel idea of a screw propeller.
Replisome	The replisome is a complex molecular machine that carries out replication of DNA. The replisome first unwinds double stranded DNA into two single strands. For each of the resulting single strands, a new complementary sequence of DNA is synthesized. The net result is formation of two new double stranded DNA sequences that are exact copies of the original double stranded DNA sequence.
Escherichia coli	Escherichia coli is a Gram-negative, facultative anaerobic, rod-shaped bacterium that is commonly found in the lower intestine of warm-blooded organisms (endotherms). Most E. coli strains are harmless, but some serotypes can cause serious food poisoning in humans, and are occasionally responsible for product recalls due to food contamination. The harmless strains are part of the normal flora of the gut, and can benefit their hosts by producing vitamin K_2, and by preventing the establishment of pathogenic bacteria within the intestine.
Jacob	The Jacob sheep is a rare breed of small, piebald, polycerate (multi-horned) sheep. Jacobs may have from two to six horns, but most commonly have four. The most common color is black and white.
Origin	The anatomical origin is a concept used when describing muscles, tendons, ligaments, nerves, and blood and lymph vessels. While it often has a slightly different meaning depending on which kind of origin is referred to, it is generally used to explain the relative location of the anatomical structure in question. It is not to be understood in a temporal/ontogenetical sense.
Origin of replication	The origin of replication is a particular sequence in a genome at which replication is initiated. This can either involve the replication of DNA in living organisms such as prokaryotes and eukaryotes, or that of DNA or RNA in viruses, such as double-stranded RNA viruses.

ATP-binding motif	An ATP-Binding Motif is a specific sequence of protein subunits that promotes the attachment of ATP to a target protein. An ATP binding site is a protein micro-environment where ATP is captured and hydrolyzed to ADP, releasing energy that is utilized by the protein to 'do work' by changing the protein shape and/or making the enzyme catalytically active. The same ATP binding motif is used in many proteins: hence a 'motif' that is similar across a range of proteins.
DnaA	DnaA is a protein that activates initiation of DNA replication in prokaryotes. It is a replication initiation factor which promotes the unwinding of DNA at oriC. The onset of the initiation phase of DNA replication is determined by the concentration of DnaA. DnaA accumulates during growth and then triggers the initiation of replication. Replication begins with active DnaA binding to 9-mer (9-bp) repeats upstream of oriC. Binding of DnaA leads to strand separation at the 13-mer repeats.
DnaC	DnaC is a loading factor for helicase dnaB. dnaB and dnaC associate with the dnaA bound origin. After loading dnaB at the origin, dnaC is released. This interaction of dnaC with dnaB requires the hydrolysis of ATP.
Edman degradation	Edman degradation, developed by Pehr Edman, is a method of sequencing amino acids in a peptide. In this method, the amino-terminal residue is labeled and cleaved from the peptide without disrupting the peptide bonds between other amino acid residues.
Escherichia	Escherichia is a genus of Gram-negative, non-spore forming, facultatively anaerobic, rod-shaped bacteria from the family Enterobacteriaceae. In those species which are inhabitants of the gastrointestinal tracts of warm-blooded animals, Escherichia species provide a portion of the microbially derived vitamin K for their host. A number of the species of Escherichia are pathogenic.
Origin recognition complex	In molecular biology, Origin recognition complex is a multi-subunit DNA binding complex that binds in all eukaryotes in an ATP-dependent manner to origins of replication. The subunits of this complex are encoded by the Origin recognition complex1, Origin recognition complex2, Origin recognition complex3, Origin recognition complex4, Origin recognition complex5 and Origin recognition complex6 genes. Origin recognition complex is a central component for eukaryotic DNA replication, and binds chromatin at replication origins throughout the cell cycle.
Cooperative binding	Molecular binding is an interaction between molecules that results in a stable association between those molecules. Cooperative binding occurs if the number of binding sites of a macromolecule that are occupied by a specific type of ligand is a non-linear function of this ligand's concentration. This can be due, for instance, to an affinity for the ligand that depends on the amount of ligand bound.
Degradation	In geology, degradation refers to the lowering of a fluvial surface, such as a stream bed or floodplain, through erosional processes. It is the opposite of aggradation. Degradation is characteristic of channel networks in which either bedrock erosion is taking place, or in systems that are sediment-starved and are therefore entraining more material than is being deposited.

7. The Replication of DNA,

CHAPTER HIGHLIGHTS & NOTES: KEY TERMS, PEOPLE, PLACES, CONCEPTS

S phase	S-phase (synthesis phase) is the part of the cell cycle in which DNA is replicated, occurring between G_1 phase and G_2 phase. Precise and accurate DNA replication is necessary to prevent genetic abnormalities which often lead to cell death or disease. Due to the importance, the regulatory pathways that govern this event in eukaryotes are highly conserved.
Eukaryote	A eukaryote is an organism whose cells contain a nucleus and other structures (organelles) enclosed within membranes. Eukaryotes are formally the taxon Eukarya or Eukaryota. The defining membrane-bound structure that sets eukaryotic cells apart from prokaryotic cells is the nucleus, or nuclear envelope, within which the genetic material is carried.
Telomerase	Telomerase is a ribonucleoprotein that is an enzyme that adds DNA sequence repeats to the 3' end of DNA strands in the telomere regions, which are found at the ends of eukaryotic chromosomes. This region of repeated nucleotide called telomeres contains noncoding DNA and hinders the loss of important DNA from chromosome ends. As a result, every time the chromosome is copied, only 100-200 nucleotides are lost, which causes no damage to the organism's DNA. Telomerase is a reverse transcriptase that carries its own RNA molecule, which is used as a template when it elongates telomeres, which are shortened after each replication cycle.
Telomerase reverse transcriptase	Telomerase reverse transcriptase is a catalytic subunit of the enzyme telomerase, which, together with the telomerase RNA component (TERC), comprises the most important unit of the telomerase complex. Telomerases are part of a distinct subgroup of RNA-dependent polymerases. Telomerase lengthens telomeres in DNA strands, thereby allowing senescent cells that would otherwise become postmitotic and undergo apoptosis to exceed the Hayflick limit and become potentially immortal, as is often the case with cancerous cells.
Ferritin	Ferritin is a ubiquitous intracellular protein that stores iron and releases it in a controlled fashion. The amount of ferritin stored reflects the amount of iron stored. The protein is produced by almost all living organisms, including algae, bacteria, higher plants, and animals.
Marker gene	A marker gene is a gene used in nuclear biology to determine if a nucleic acid sequence has been successfully inserted into an organism's DNA. There are two types of marker genes: a selectable marker and a marker for screening.

1. _________ is a ubiquitous intracellular protein that stores iron and releases it in a controlled fashion. The amount of _________ stored reflects the amount of iron stored. The protein is produced by almost all living organisms, including algae, bacteria, higher plants, and animals.

   a. Ferritin
   b. Biochemical sensor
   c. Biocrystallization
   d. Biomarker

2. _________ is a ribonucleoprotein that is an enzyme that adds DNA sequence repeats to the 3' end of DNA strands in the telomere regions, which are found at the ends of eukaryotic chromosomes. This region of repeated nucleotide called telomeres contains noncoding DNA and hinders the loss of important DNA from chromosome ends. As a result, every time the chromosome is copied, only 100-200 nucleotides are lost, which causes no damage to the organism's DNA. _________ is a reverse transcriptase that carries its own RNA molecule, which is used as a template when it elongates telomeres, which are shortened after each replication cycle.

   a. Cell division
   b. Chromatid
   c. Chromatin bridge
   d. Telomerase

3. In the chemical sciences, _________ denotes the addition of a methyl group to a substrate or the substitution of an atom or group by a methyl group. _________ is a form of alkylation with a methyl group, rather than a larger carbon chain, replacing a hydrogen atom. These terms are commonly used in chemistry, biochemistry, soil science, and the biological sciences.

   a. Bisulfite sequencing
   b. Methylation
   c. DAnCER
   d. Genomic imprinting

4. _________ is the natural or artificial creation of deoxyribonucleic acid molecules. In nature, such molecules are created by all living cells through the process of DNA replication, with replication initiator proteins splitting the existing DNA of the cell and making a copy of each split strand, with the copied strands then being joined together with their template strand into a new DNA molecule. Various means also exist to artificially stimulate the replication of naturally occurring DNA, or to create artificial gene sequences.

   a. Cdc6
   b. DNA synthesis
   c. DNA ligase
   d. DNA polymerase eta

5. . _________s, also called green _________s (Viridiplantae in Latin), are living multicellular organisms of the kingdom Plantae.

They form a clade that includes the flowering _________s, conifers and other gymnosperms, ferns, clubmosses, hornworts, liverworts and mosses, as well as, depending on definition, the green algae. _________s exclude the red and brown seaweeds such as kelp, the fungi, Archaea and bacteria.

a. Plant
b. Breviata
c. Ceratiomyxa
d. Cochliopodium

ANSWER KEY
7. The Replication of DNA,

1. a
2. d
3. b
4. b
5. a

---

8. The Mutability and Repair of DNA,

CHAPTER OUTLINE: KEY TERMS, PEOPLE, PLACES, CONCEPTS

Chromosome

Hot spot

DNA synthesis

Lesion

Prediction

DNA replication

Exon skipping

Polymorphism

Proofreading

Cooperative binding

Microsatellite

Mutation

SpoT

DNA polymerase

Minor spliceosome

Exonuclease VII

Methionine

Okazaki fragments

Basal

DNA damage

Deamination

8. The Mutability and Repair of DNA,

CHAPTER OUTLINE: KEY TERMS, PEOPLE, PLACES, CONCEPTS

- Mutagen
- Modifications
- Transcription
- Adenosine
- Depurination
- Xanthine
- 5-Methylcytosine
- Nitrosamine
- 5-Bromouracil
- Base analog
- Bleomycin
- Mutagenesis
- Kinase
- Marker gene
- Protein
- DNA photolyase
- DNA repair
- Response element
- Base excision repair
- Glycosylase
- Excision repair

8. The Mutability and Repair of DNA,

CHAPTER OUTLINE: KEY TERMS, PEOPLE, PLACES, CONCEPTS

______	Nucleotide
______	Nucleotide excision repair
______	RNA polymerase
______	Xeroderma pigmentosum
______	Homologous recombination
______	Family
______	RecA
______	SOS response
______	Ubiquitin
______	Clamp

CHAPTER HIGHLIGHTS & NOTES: KEY TERMS, PEOPLE, PLACES, CONCEPTS

Chromosome	A chromosome is an organized structure of DNA, protein, and RNA found in cells. It is a single piece of coiled DNA containing many genes, regulatory elements and other nucleotide sequences. Chromosomes also contain DNA-bound proteins, which serve to package the DNA and control its functions.
Hot spot	In veterinary medicine, a 'hot spot' (or acute pyoderma, acute moist pyotraumatic dermatitis) is one of the many names for a raw, painful, irritated skin lesion that results in and worsens from a pet (such as a dog or a cat) constantly biting, scratching, chewing, and licking an area of its skin that is irritated or itchy. If it is covered by the dog's hair, the hair holds in the moisture and further irritates it. It is a patch that appears suddenly and is often bright red, hairless, and scaly looking.
DNA synthesis	DNA synthesis is the natural or artificial creation of deoxyribonucleic acid molecules.

In nature, such molecules are created by all living cells through the process of DNA replication, with replication initiator proteins splitting the existing DNA of the cell and making a copy of each split strand, with the copied strands then being joined together with their template strand into a new DNA molecule. Various means also exist to artificially stimulate the replication of naturally occurring DNA, or to create artificial gene sequences.

Lesion

A lesion is any abnormality in the tissue of an organism, usually caused by disease or trauma. Lesion is derived from the Latin word laesio meaning injury.

Prediction

A prediction or forecast is a statement about the way things will happen in the future, often but not always based on experience or knowledge. While there is much overlap between prediction and forecast, a prediction may be a statement that some outcome is expected, while a forecast is more specific, and may cover a range of possible outcomes.

Although guaranteed information about the future is in many cases impossible, prediction is necessary to allow plans to be made about possible developments; Howard H. Stevenson writes that prediction in business '... is at least two things: Important and hard.'

DNA replication

DNA replication is the process of producing two identical copies from one original DNA molecule. This biological process occurs in all living organisms and is the basis for biological inheritance. DNA is composed of two strands and each strand of the original DNA molecule serves as template for the production of the complementary strand, a process referred to as semiconservative replication.

Exon skipping

Exon skipping is a method used to cause cells to “skip” over faulty or misaligned sections of genetic code, leading to a truncated but still functional protein despite the genetic mutation.

Polymorphism

Polymorphism in biology occurs when two or more clearly different phenotypes exist in the same population of a species -- in other words, the occurrence of more than one form or morph. In order to be classified as such, morphs must occupy the same habitat at the same time and belong to a panmictic population (one with random mating).

Polymorphism as described here involves morphs of the phenotype.

Proofreading

The term proofreading is used in genetics to refer to the error-correcting processes, first proposed by John Hopfield and Jacques Ninio, involved in DNA replication, immune system specificity, enzyme-substrate recognition among many other processes that require enhanced specificity. The proofreading mechanisms of Hopfield and Ninio are non-equilibrium active processes that consume ATP to enhance specificity of various biochemical reactions.

Cooperative binding	Molecular binding is an interaction between molecules that results in a stable association between those molecules. Cooperative binding occurs if the number of binding sites of a macromolecule that are occupied by a specific type of ligand is a non-linear function of this ligand's concentration. This can be due, for instance, to an affinity for the ligand that depends on the amount of ligand bound.
Microsatellite	Microsatellites, also known as Simple Sequence Repeats or Short Tandem Repeats (STRs), are repeating sequences of 2-6 base pairs of DNA. It is a type of Variable Number Tandem Repeat (VNTR). Microsatellites are typically co-dominant. They are used as molecular markers in genetics, for kinship, population and other studies.
Mutation	In genetics, a mutation is a change of the nucleotide sequence of the genome of an organism, virus, or extrachromosomal genetic element. Mutations result from unrepaired damage to DNA or to RNA genomes (typically caused by radiation or chemical mutagens), errors in the process of replication, or from the insertion or deletion of segments of DNA by mobile genetic elements. Mutations may or may not produce discernible changes in the observable characteristics (phenotype) of an organism.
SpoT	SpoT is a bacterial protein that hydrolizes alarmones, ppGpp, in the bacterial stringent response. Its hydrolase activity is Mn2+-dependent with a conserved His-Asp (HD) motif. In E. coli, SpoT protein consists of 693 amino acids.
DNA polymerase	A DNA polymerase is a cellular or viral polymerase enzyme that synthesizes DNA molecules from their nucleotide building blocks. DNA polymerases are essential for DNA replication, and usually function in pairs while copying one double-stranded DNA molecule into two double-stranded DNAs in a process termed semiconservative DNA replication. DNA polymerases also play key roles in other processes within cells, including DNA repair, genetic recombination, reverse transcription, and the generation of antibody diversity via the specialized DNA polymerase, terminal deoxynucleotidyl transferase.
Minor spliceosome	The minor spliceosome is a ribonucleoprotein complex that catalyses the removal of an atypical class of spliceosomal introns (U12-type) from eukaryotic messenger RNAs in plant, insects, vertebrates and some fungi (Rhizopus oryzae). This process is called noncanonical splicing, as opposed to U2-dependent canonical splicing. U12-type introns represent less than 1% of all introns in human cells.
Exonuclease VII	In molecular biology, exonuclease VII is a bacterial exonuclease enzyme. It is composed of two nonidentical subunits; one large subunit and 4 small ones. Exonuclease VII catalyses exonucleolytic cleavage in either 5'-3' or 3'-5' direction to yield 5'-phosphomononucleotides.
Methionine	Methionine is an a-amino acid with the chemical formula $HO_2CCH(NH_2)CH_2CH_2SCH_3$. This essential amino acid is classified as nonpolar.

8. The Mutability and Repair of DNA,

CHAPTER HIGHLIGHTS & NOTES: KEY TERMS, PEOPLE, PLACES, CONCEPTS

Okazaki fragments

Okazaki fragments are short, newly synthesized DNA fragments that are formed on the lagging template strand during DNA replication. They are complementary to the lagging template strand, together forming short double-stranded DNA sections. Okazaki fragments are between 1,000 and 2,000 nucleotides long in Escherichia coli and are between 100 and 200 nucleotides long in eukaryotes.

Basal

In phylogenetics, a basal clade is the earliest clade to branch in a larger clade; it appears at the base of a cladogram.

A basal group forms an outgroup to the rest of the clade, such as in the following example:

The word 'basal' is preferred to the term 'primitive', which may carry false connotations of inferiority or a lack of complexity.

The term basal can only be correctly applied to clades of organisms, not to individual traits possessed by the organisms--although it can be misused in this manner in technical literature.

DNA damage

DNA damage is an alteration in the chemical structure of DNA, such as a break in a strand of DNA, a base missing from the backbone of DNA, or a chemically changed base such as 8-OHdG. Damage to DNA that occurs naturally can result from metabolic or hydrolytic processes. Metabolism releases compounds that damage DNA including reactive oxygen species, reactive nitrogen species, reactive carbonyl species, lipid peroxidation products and alkylating agents, among others, while hydrolysis cleaves chemical bonds in DNA. Naturally occurring DNA damages arise about 10,000 to 100,000 times per day per mammalian cell.

DNA damage is distinctly different from mutation, although both are types of error in DNA. DNA damage is an abnormal chemical structure in DNA, while a mutation is a change in the sequence of standard base pairs.

Deamination

Deamination is the removal of an amine group from a molecule. Enzymes which catalyse this reaction are called deaminases.

In the human body, deamination takes place primarily in the liver, however glutamate is also deaminated in the kidneys.

Mutagen

In genetics, a mutagen is a physical or chemical agent that changes the genetic material, usually DNA, of an organism and thus increases the frequency of mutations above the natural background level. As many mutations cause cancer, mutagens are therefore also likely to be carcinogens. Not all mutations are caused by mutagens: so-called 'spontaneous mutations' occur due to spontaneous hydrolysis, errors in DNA replication, repair and recombination.

Modifications

In opposition to mutations, modifications are included in the band width of the genome of an individual creature. Modifications are dependent on the plentifulness of the substrate, light, warmths, stress, training, and so on.

A modification is a change in the physical appearance of an organism (phenotype) caused by environmental factors.

Transcription

Transcription is the first step of gene expression, in which a particular segment of DNA is copied into RNA by the enzyme, RNA polymerase. Both RNA and DNA are nucleic acids, which use base pairs of nucleotides as a complementary language that can be converted back and forth from DNA to RNA by the action of the correct enzymes. During transcription, a DNA sequence is read by an RNA polymerase, which produces a complementary, antiparallel RNA strand.

Adenosine

Adenosine is a purine nucleoside comprising a molecule of adenine attached to a ribose sugar molecule (ribofuranose) moiety via a ß-N_9-glycosidic bond.

Adenosine plays an important role in biochemical processes, such as energy transfer--as adenosine triphosphate (ATP) and adenosine diphosphate (ADP)--as well as in signal transduction as cyclic adenosine monophosphate, cAMP. It is also an inhibitory neurotransmitter, believed to play a role in promoting sleep and suppressing arousal.

Depurination

Depurination is a chemical reaction of purine deoxyribonucleosides, deoxyadenosine and deoxyguanosine, and ribonucleosides, adenosine or guanosine, in which the ß-N-glycosidic bond is hydrolytically cleaved releasing a nucleic base, adenine or guanine, respectively. The second product of depurination of deoxyribonucleosides and ribonucleosides is sugar, 2'-deoxyribose and ribose, respectively. More complex compounds containing nucleoside residues, nucleotides and nucleic acids, also suffer from depurination.

Xanthine

Xanthine is a purine base found in most human body tissues and fluids and in other organisms. A number of stimulants are derived from xanthine, including caffeine and theobromine.

Xanthine is a product on the pathway of purine degradation.

5-Methylcytosine

5-Methylcytosine is a methylated form of the DNA base cytosine that may be involved in the regulation of gene transcription. When cytosine is methylated, the DNA maintains the same sequence, but the expression of methylated genes can be altered (the study of this is part of the field of epigenetics). 5-Methylcytosine is incorporated in the nucleoside 5-methylcytidine.

Nitrosamine

Nitrosamines are chemical compounds of the chemical structure $R^1N\text{-}N{=}O$, most of which are carcinogenic.

8. The Mutability and Repair of DNA,

CHAPTER HIGHLIGHTS & NOTES: KEY TERMS, PEOPLE, PLACES, CONCEPTS

5-Bromouracil	5-Bromouracil is a brominated derivative of uracil that acts as an antimetabolite or base analog, substituting for thymine in DNA, and can induce DNA mutation in the same way as 2-aminopurine. It is used mainly as an experimental mutagen, but its deoxyriboside derivative (5-bromo-2-deoxy-uridine) is used to treat neoplasms. 5-BrU exists in three tautomeric forms that have different base pairing properties.
Base analog	A base analog is a chemical that can substitute for a normal nucleobase in nucleic acids. One of the more common base analogs is 5-bromouracil, the abnormal base found in the mutagenic nucleotide analog BrdU. When a nucleotide containing 5-bromouracil is incorporated into the DNA, it is most likely to pair with adenine; however, it can spontaneously shift into another isomer which pairs with a different nucleobase, guanine. If this happens during DNA replication, a guanine will be inserted opposite the base analog, and in the next DNA replication, that guanine will pair with a cytosine.
Bleomycin	Bleomycin is a glycopeptide antibiotic produced by the bacterium Streptomyces verticillus. Bleomycin refers to a family of structurally related compounds. When used as an anticancer agent, the chemotherapeutical forms are primarily bleomycin A_2 and B_2.
Mutagenesis	Mutagenesis in the laboratory is an important technique whereby DNA mutations are deliberately engineered to produce mutant genes, proteins, strains of bacteria, or other genetically-modified organisms. Various constituents of a gene, such as its control elements and its gene product, may be mutated so that the functioning of a gene or protein can be examined in detail. The mutation may also produce mutant proteins with interesting properties, or enhanced or novel functions that may be of commercial use.
Kinase	In enzymology, a [tyrosine 3-monooxygenase] kinase is an enzyme that catalyzes the chemical reactionATP + [tyrosine-3-monooxygenase] $\rightleftharpoons$ ADP + phospho-[tyrosine-3-monooxygenase] Thus, the two substrates of this enzyme are ATP and tyrosine-3-monooxygenase, whereas its two products are ADP and [[phospho-[tyrosine-3-monooxygenase]]]. This enzyme belongs to the family of transferases, specifically those transferring a phosphate group to the sidechain oxygen atom of serine or threonine residues in proteins (protein-serine/threonine kinases). The systematic name of this enzyme class is ATP:[tyrosine-3-monoxygenase] phosphotransferase.
Marker gene	A marker gene is a gene used in nuclear biology to determine if a nucleic acid sequence has been successfully inserted into an organism's DNA. There are two types of marker genes: a selectable marker and a marker for screening.

Protein	Proteins are large biological molecules consisting of one or more chains of amino acids. Proteins perform a vast array of functions within living organisms, including catalyzing metabolic reactions, replicating DNA, responding to stimuli, and transporting molecules from one location to another. Proteins differ from one another primarily in their sequence of amino acids, which is dictated by the nucleotide sequence of their genes, and which usually results in folding of the protein into a specific three-dimensional structure that determines its activity.
DNA photolyase	DNA photolyase is an evolutionary conserved protein domain. This domain binds a light harvesting cofactor. Deoxyribodipyrimidine photolyase (DNA photolyase) is a DNA repair enzyme.
DNA repair	DNA repair is a collection of processes by which a cell identifies and corrects damage to the DNA molecules that encode its genome. In human cells, both normal metabolic activities and environmental factors such as UV light and radiation can cause DNA damage, resulting in as many as 1 million individual molecular lesions per cell per day. Many of these lesions cause structural damage to the DNA molecule and can alter or eliminate the cell's ability to transcribe the gene that the affected DNA encodes.
Response element	Response elements are short sequences of DNA within a gene promoter region that are able to bind specific transcription factors and regulate transcription of genes. Under conditions of stress, a transcription activator protein binds to the response element and stimulates transcription. If the same response element sequence is located in the control regions of different genes, then these genes will be activated by the same stimuli, thus producing a coordinated response.
Base excision repair	In biochemistry and genetics, base excision repair is a cellular mechanism that repairs damaged DNA throughout the cell cycle. It is responsible primarily for removing small, non-helix-distorting base lesions from the genome. The related nucleotide excision repair pathway repairs bulky helix-distorting lesions.
Glycosylase	Glycosylases are enzymes that hydrolyze glycosyl compounds. They are a type of hydrolase (EC 3). In turn, glycosylases are divided into two groups: glycosidases -- enzymes that hydrolyze O- and S-glycosyl compounds (EC 3.2.1) -- and enzymes that hydrolyze N-glycosyl compounds (EC 3.2.2).
Excision repair	Excision repair is a term applied to several DNA repair mechanisms. They remove the damaged nucleotides and are able to determine the correct sequence from the complementary strand of DNA.

	Specific mechanisms include:•Base excision repair which repairs damage due to a single nucleotide caused by oxidation, alkylation, hydrolysis, or deamination;•Nucleotide excision repair which repairs damage affecting 2-30 nucleotide-length strands. These include bulky, helix distorting damage, such as thymine dimerization and other types of cyclobutyl dimerization caused by UV light as well as single-strand breaks.
Nucleotide	Nucleotides are organic molecules that form the basic building blocks of nucleic acids, such as DNA and RNA. A nucleotide is composed of a nucleobase, a pentose (ribose or deoxyribose) and at least one phosphate group. Nucleotides serve to carry packets of energy within the cell (ATP). In the form of the nucleoside triphosphates (ATP, GTP, CTP and UTP), nucleotides play central roles in metabolism.
Nucleotide excision repair	Nucleotide excision repair is a DNA repair mechanism. DNA damage occurs constantly because of chemicals (ie intercalating agents), radiation and other mutagens. Three excision repair pathways exist to repair single stranded DNA damage: Nucleotide excision repair base excision repair (BER), and DNA mismatch repair (MMR).
RNA polymerase	RNA polymerase, also known as DNA-dependent RNA polymerase, is an enzyme that produces RNA. In cells, RNAP is necessary for constructing RNA chains using DNA genes as templates, a process called transcription. RNA polymerase enzymes are essential to life and are found in all organisms and many viruses. In chemical terms, RNAP is a nucleotidyl transferase that polymerizes ribonucleotides at the 3' end of an RNA transcript.
Xeroderma pigmentosum	Xeroderma pigmentosum, or XP, is an autosomal recessive genetic disorder of DNA repair in which the ability to repair damage caused by ultraviolet light is deficient. In extreme cases, all exposure to sunlight must be forbidden, no matter how small; as such, individuals with the disease are often colloquially referred to as Children of the Night. Multiple basal cell carcinomas (basaliomas) and other skin malignancies frequently occur at a young age in those with XP. In fact, metastatic malignant melanoma and squamous cell carcinoma are the two most common causes of death in XP victims.
Homologous recombination	Homologous recombination is a type of genetic recombination in which nucleotide sequences are exchanged between two similar or identical molecules of DNA. It is most widely used by cells to accurately repair harmful breaks that occur on both strands of DNA, known as double-strand breaks. Homologous recombination also produces new combinations of DNA sequences during meiosis, the process by which eukaryotes make gamete cells, like sperm and egg cells in animals. These new combinations of DNA represent genetic variation in offspring, which in turn enables populations to adapt during the course of evolution.

Family

In biological classification, family isExample: Walnuts and hickories belong to Juglandaceae, the walnut family

What does and does not belong to each family is determined by a taxonomist. Similarly for the question if a particular family should be recognized at all. Often there is no exact agreement, with different taxonomists each taking a different position.

RecA

RecA is a 38 kilodalton protein essential for the repair and maintenance of DNA. A RecA structural and functional homolog has been found in every species in which one has been seriously sought and serves as an archetype for this class of homologous DNA repair proteins. The homologous protein in Homo sapiens is called RAD51.

RecA has multiple activities, all related to DNA repair.

SOS response

The SOS response is a global response to DNA damage in which the cell cycle is arrested and DNA repair and mutagenesis are induced. The system involves the RecA protein (Rad51 in eukaryotes). The RecA protein, stimulated by single-stranded DNA, is involved in the inactivation of the LexA repressor thereby inducing the response.

Ubiquitin

Ubiquitin is a small regulatory protein that has been found in almost all tissues (ubiquitously) of eukaryotic organisms. It was discovered in 1975 by Goldstein and further characterized throughout the 1970s and 80s. There are four genes in the human genome that produce ubiquitin; UBB, UBC, UBA52 and RPS27A.

Ubiquitination is a post translational modification (an addition to a protein after it has been made) where ubiquitin is attached to a substrate protein.

Clamp

Clamps are the main attachment structure of the Polyopisthocotylean monogeneans.These ectoparasitic worms have a variable number of clamps on their haptor ; each clamp is attached to the host fish, generally to its gill. Clamps include sclerotised elements, called the sclerites, and muscles. The structure of clamps varies according to the groups within the Polyopisthocotylean monogeneans; microcotylids have relatively simple clamps, whereas gastrocotylids have more complex clamps.

8. The Mutability and Repair of DNA,

CHAPTER QUIZ: KEY TERMS, PEOPLE, PLACES, CONCEPTS

1. The _________ is a global response to DNA damage in which the cell cycle is arrested and DNA repair and mutagenesis are induced. The system involves the RecA protein (Rad51 in eukaryotes). The RecA protein, stimulated by single-stranded DNA, is involved in the inactivation of the LexA repressor thereby inducing the response.

   a. 8-Oxoguanine
   b. Base excision repair
   c. DNA glycosylase
   d. SOS response

2. _________ in the laboratory is an important technique whereby DNA mutations are deliberately engineered to produce mutant genes, proteins, strains of bacteria, or other genetically-modified organisms. Various constituents of a gene, such as its control elements and its gene product, may be mutated so that the functioning of a gene or protein can be examined in detail. The mutation may also produce mutant proteins with interesting properties, or enhanced or novel functions that may be of commercial use.

   a. Biosafety Clearing-House
   b. BioSteel
   c. Mutagenesis
   d. Diamond v. Chakrabarty

3. _________ is a small regulatory protein that has been found in almost all tissues (ubiquitously) of eukaryotic organisms. It was discovered in 1975 by Goldstein and further characterized throughout the 1970s and 80s. There are four genes in the human genome that produce _________; UBB, UBC, UBA52 and RPS27A.

   Ubiquitination is a post translational modification (an addition to a protein after it has been made) where _________ is attached to a substrate protein.

   a. Ubiquitin
   b. Carboxylation
   c. Citrullination
   d. Clostripain

4. _________ is the process of producing two identical copies from one original DNA molecule. This biological process occurs in all living organisms and is the basis for biological inheritance. DNA is composed of two strands and each strand of the original DNA molecule serves as template for the production of the complementary strand, a process referred to as semiconservative replication.

   a. Cationic liposome
   b. DNA replication
   c. BacMam
   d. Biodistribution

5. . _________s are chemical compounds of the chemical structure $R^1N\text{-}N\text{=}O$, most of which are carcinogenic.

a. Nitrosamine
b. Cyanamide
c. Denitrification
d. Denitrifying bacteria

ANSWER KEY

8. The Mutability and Repair of DNA,

1. d
2. c
3. a
4. b
5. a

9. Homologous Recombination at the Molecular Level,

CHAPTER OUTLINE: KEY TERMS, PEOPLE, PLACES, CONCEPTS

- Homologous recombination
- Discovery
- Gene
- Gene orders
- DNA polymerase
- Holliday junction
- Bacteria
- Eukaryote
- Branch migration
- Heteroduplex
- Resolution
- Cleavage
- RecBCD
- Chi site
- RecA
- Rada
- Chromosome segregation
- Sister chromatids
- Meiosis
- Genetics
- Cooperative binding

9. Homologous Recombination at the Molecular Level,

CHAPTER OUTLINE: KEY TERMS, PEOPLE, PLACES, CONCEPTS

____________ Gene conversion

____________ Minor spliceosome

CHAPTER HIGHLIGHTS & NOTES: KEY TERMS, PEOPLE, PLACES, CONCEPTS

Homologous recombination	Homologous recombination is a type of genetic recombination in which nucleotide sequences are exchanged between two similar or identical molecules of DNA. It is most widely used by cells to accurately repair harmful breaks that occur on both strands of DNA, known as double-strand breaks. Homologous recombination also produces new combinations of DNA sequences during meiosis, the process by which eukaryotes make gamete cells, like sperm and egg cells in animals. These new combinations of DNA represent genetic variation in offspring, which in turn enables populations to adapt during the course of evolution.
Discovery	Discovery is the act of detecting something new, or something 'old' that had been unknown. With reference to science and academic disciplines, discovery is the observation of new phenomena, new actions, or new events and providing new reasoning to explain the knowledge gathered through such observations with previously acquired knowledge from abstract thought and everyday experiences. Visual discoveries are often called sightings.
Gene	A gene is a molecular unit of heredity of a living organism. It is widely accepted by the scientific community as a name given to some stretches of deoxyribonucleic acids (DNA) and ribonucleic acids (RNA) that code for a polypeptide or for an RNA chain that has a function in the organism, though there still are controversies about what plays the role of the genetic material. Living beings depend on genes, as they specify all proteins and functional RNA chains.
Gene orders	Gene orders is the permutation of genome arrangement. So far a fair amount of work trying to describe whether gene orders evolve according to a molecular clock (molecular clock hypothesis) or in jumps (punctuated equilibrium). Some research on Gene orders in animals' mitochondrial gemone reveal that the mutation rate of gene orders is not a constant in some degrees.
DNA polymerase	A DNA polymerase is a cellular or viral polymerase enzyme that synthesizes DNA molecules from their nucleotide building blocks. DNA polymerases are essential for DNA replication, and usually function in pairs while copying one double-stranded DNA molecule into two double-stranded DNAs in a process termed semiconservative DNA replication.

Holliday junction

A Holliday junction is a mobile junction between four strands of DNA. The structure is named after Robin Holliday, who proposed it in 1964 to account for a particular type of exchange of genetic information he observed in Ustilago maydis known as homologous recombination. Holliday junctions are highly conserved structures, from prokaryotes to mammals.

Because these junctions are between homologous sequences, they can slide up and down the DNA. In bacteria, this sliding (or branch migration) is facilitated by the RuvABC complex or RecG protein, molecular motors that use the energy of ATP hydrolysis to push the junction around.

Bacteria

Bacteria constitute a large domain or kingdom of prokaryotic microorganisms. Typically a few micrometres in length, bacteria have a wide range of shapes, ranging from spheres to rods and spirals. Bacteria were among the first life forms to appear on Earth, and are present in most habitats on the planet.

Eukaryote

A eukaryote is an organism whose cells contain a nucleus and other structures (organelles) enclosed within membranes. Eukaryotes are formally the taxon Eukarya or Eukaryota. The defining membrane-bound structure that sets eukaryotic cells apart from prokaryotic cells is the nucleus, or nuclear envelope, within which the genetic material is carried.

Branch migration

Branch migration describes the ability of a DNA strand partially paired with its complement in a duplex to extend its pairing by displacing the resident strand with which it is homologous. This usually happens when two homologous double strands form a Holliday junction and the whole structure slides into one direction; the 'branch migrates'. This procedure can influence the amount of information that is transferred between two recombining partners.

Heteroduplex

A heteroduplex is a double-stranded molecule of nucleic acid originated through the genetic recombination of single complementary strands derived from different sources, such as from different homologous chromosomes or even from different organisms. One such example is the heteroduplex DNA strand formed in hybridization processes, usually for biochemistry-based phylogenetical analyses. Another example is the heteroduplexes formed when non-natural analogs of nucleic acids are used to bind with nucleic acids; these heteroduplexes result from performing antisense techniques using single-stranded peptide nucleic acid, 2'-O-methyl phosphorothioate or Morpholino oligos to bind with RNA.

In meiosis, the process of crossing-over occurs between non-sister chromatids, which results in new allelic combinations of a population.

Resolution

Resolution in terms of electron density is a measure of the resolvability in the electron density map of a molecule. In X-ray crystallography, resolution is the highest resolvable peak in the diffraction pattern. While cryo-electron microscopy is a frequency space comparison of two halves of the data, which strives to correlate with the X-ray definition.

9. Homologous Recombination at the Molecular Level,

CHAPTER HIGHLIGHTS & NOTES: KEY TERMS, PEOPLE, PLACES, CONCEPTS

Cleavage

Cleavage, anatomically known as the intermammary cleft or the intermammary sulcus, is the space between a woman's breasts lying over the sternum. In popular culture, it is often defined by garments with low necklines, like ball gowns, evening gowns, lingerie and swimwear that expose or highlight cleavage.

Most people in Western culture, both male and female, consider breasts an important aspect of femininity and many women use cleavage to enhance their physical and sexual attractiveness and to improve their sense of femininity.

RecBCD

RecBCD is an enzyme of the E. coli bacterium that initiates recombinational repair from potentially lethal double strand breaks in DNA which may result from ionizing radiation, replication errors, endonucleases, oxidative damage, and a host of other factors. The RecBCD enzyme is both a helicase that unwinds, or separates the strands of DNA, and a nuclease that makes single-stranded nicks in DNA.

Chi site

A Chi site or Chi sequence is a short stretch of DNA in the genome of a bacterium near which homologous recombination is more likely than expected to occur. Chi sites serve as stimulators of DNA double-strand break repair in bacteria, which can arise from radiation or chemical treatments, or result from replication fork breakage during DNA replication. The sequence of the Chi site is unique to each group of closely related organisms; in E. coli and other enteric bacteria, such as Salmonella, the sequence is 5'-GCTGGTGG-3'.

RecA

RecA is a 38 kilodalton protein essential for the repair and maintenance of DNA. A RecA structural and functional homolog has been found in every species in which one has been seriously sought and serves as an archetype for this class of homologous DNA repair proteins. The homologous protein in Homo sapiens is called RAD51.

RecA has multiple activities, all related to DNA repair.

Rada

Ra?a? or ri?a?a is a technical term from Sunni Islamic jurisprudence meaning 'the suckling which produces the legal impediment to marriage of foster-kinship'. The term derives from the infinitive noun of the Arabic word radi?a or rada?a ('he sucked the breast of his mother'). Often it is translated as 'fosterage' or 'milk-kinship'.

Chromosome segregation

Chromosome segregation is a step in cell reproduction or division, where chromosomes pair off with their similar homologous chromosome. In mitosis, a complete copy of each one is made. In meiosis, one chromosome from each pair migrates to opposite ends of the cell and the genes are split to make a gamete.

Sister chromatids

Sister chromatids are generated when a single chromosome is replicated into two copies of itself, these copies being called sister chromatids.

Compare sister chromatids to homologous chromosomes, which are the two different copies of a chromosome that diploid organisms (like humans) inherit, one from each parent. In other words, while sister chromatids are by and large identical (since they carry the same alleles, also called variants or versions, of genes) because they derive from one original chromosome, homologous chromosomes might or might not be the same as each other because they derive from different parents.

Meiosis

Meiosis is a special type of cell division necessary for sexual reproduction in eukaryotes, such as animals, plants and fungi. The number of sets of chromosomes in the cell undergoing meiosis is reduced to half the original number, typically from two sets (diploid) to one set (haploid). The cells produced by meiosis are either gametes (the usual case in animals) or otherwise usually spores from which gametes are ultimately produced (the case in land plants).

Genetics

Genetics, a discipline of biology, is the science of genes, heredity, and variation in living organisms.

Genetics concerns the process of trait inheritance from parents to offspring, including the molecular structure and function of genes, gene behavior in the context of a cell or organism (e.g. dominance and epigenetics), gene distribution, and variation and change in populations (such as through Genome-Wide Association Studies). Given that genes are universal to living organisms, genetics can be applied to the study of all living systems; including bacteria, plants, animals, and humans.

Cooperative binding

Molecular binding is an interaction between molecules that results in a stable association between those molecules. Cooperative binding occurs if the number of binding sites of a macromolecule that are occupied by a specific type of ligand is a non-linear function of this ligand's concentration. This can be due, for instance, to an affinity for the ligand that depends on the amount of ligand bound.

Gene conversion

Gene conversion is a form of genetic recombination, in which one version of a gene is observed to replace a different version. At the level of DNA, gene conversion differs from typical homologous recombination in that a duplicate copy of the donor allele appears in the recipient DNA, while the recipient allele is lost. That is, DNA sequence information is transferred from one DNA helix (which remains unchanged) to another DNA helix, whose sequence is altered.

Minor spliceosome

The minor spliceosome is a ribonucleoprotein complex that catalyses the removal of an atypical class of spliceosomal introns (U12-type) from eukaryotic messenger RNAs in plant, insects, vertebrates and some fungi (Rhizopus oryzae). This process is called noncanonical splicing, as opposed to U2-dependent canonical splicing. U12-type introns represent less than 1% of all introns in human cells.

9. Homologous Recombination at the Molecular Level,

CHAPTER QUIZ: KEY TERMS, PEOPLE, PLACES, CONCEPTS

1. A _________ is a mobile junction between four strands of DNA. The structure is named after Robin Holliday, who proposed it in 1964 to account for a particular type of exchange of genetic information he observed in Ustilago maydis known as homologous recombination. _________s are highly conserved structures, from prokaryotes to mammals.

   Because these junctions are between homologous sequences, they can slide up and down the DNA. In bacteria, this sliding (or branch migration) is facilitated by the RuvABC complex or RecG protein, molecular motors that use the energy of ATP hydrolysis to push the junction around.

   a. Binding site
   b. Boom method
   c. Holliday junction
   d. CccDNA

2. _________ is a 38 kilodalton protein essential for the repair and maintenance of DNA. A _________ structural and functional homolog has been found in every species in which one has been seriously sought and serves as an archetype for this class of homologous DNA repair proteins. The homologous protein in Homo sapiens is called RAD51.

   _________ has multiple activities, all related to DNA repair.

   a. 8-Oxoguanine
   b. Base excision repair
   c. RecA
   d. DNA mismatch repair

3. _________, a discipline of biology, is the science of genes, heredity, and variation in living organisms.

   _________ concerns the process of trait inheritance from parents to offspring, including the molecular structure and function of genes, gene behavior in the context of a cell or organism (e.g. dominance and epi_________), gene distribution, and variation and change in populations (such as through Genome-Wide Association Studies). Given that genes are universal to living organisms, _________ can be applied to the study of all living systems; including bacteria, plants, animals, and humans.

   a. Gordo
   b. Ham
   c. Laika
   d. Genetics

4. . _________ describes the ability of a DNA strand partially paired with its complement in a duplex to extend its pairing by displacing the resident strand with which it is homologous. This usually happens when two homologous double strands form a Holliday junction and the whole structure slides into one direction; the 'branch migrates'. This procedure can influence the amount of information that is transferred between two recombining partners.

   a. Bacterial one-hybrid system

b. Baek Sung-hee
c. Biopolymer
d. Branch migration

5. _________ is a type of genetic recombination in which nucleotide sequences are exchanged between two similar or identical molecules of DNA. It is most widely used by cells to accurately repair harmful breaks that occur on both strands of DNA, known as double-strand breaks. _________ also produces new combinations of DNA sequences during meiosis, the process by which eukaryotes make gamete cells, like sperm and egg cells in animals. These new combinations of DNA represent genetic variation in offspring, which in turn enables populations to adapt during the course of evolution.

a. 2q37 monosomy
b. 5-HTTLPR
c. B chromosome
d. Homologous recombination

ANSWER KEY

9. Homologous Recombination at the Molecular Level,

1. c

2. c

3. d

4. d

5. d

---

10. Site-Specific Recombination and Transposition of DNA,

CHAPTER OUTLINE: KEY TERMS, PEOPLE, PLACES, CONCEPTS

- Conformation
- Ribosome
- Bacteriophage
- Growth factor
- Insect
- Intron
- Deletion
- Insertion
- Inversion
- Limb
- Site-specific recombination
- Serine
- Tyrosine
- Cre recombinase
- Evolution
- Integrase
- DNA replication
- Flagellin
- Hin recombinase
- Saga
- Salmonella

10. Site-Specific Recombination and Transposition of DNA,

CHAPTER OUTLINE: KEY TERMS, PEOPLE, PLACES, CONCEPTS

- Enhancer
- Circular DNA
- Saccharomyces
- Saccharomyces cerevisiae
- Chromosome
- Discovery
- Ferritin
- Hot spot
- Mutagen
- Retinitis pigmentosa
- Reverse transcriptase
- Cleavage
- Hermes
- Replicative transposition
- Translocase
- Retrotransposon
- Composite transposon
- SAFE
- Haven
- Immunity
- Antisense RNA

10. Site-Specific Recombination and Transposition of DNA,

CHAPTER OUTLINE: KEY TERMS, PEOPLE, PLACES, CONCEPTS

	Insertion sequence
	RNA polymerase
	Footprint
	Antibody
	Immune system
	Recombination signal sequences

CHAPTER HIGHLIGHTS & NOTES: KEY TERMS, PEOPLE, PLACES, CONCEPTS

Conformation	Conformation in dogs refers solely to the externally visible details of a dog's structure and appearance, as defined in detail by each dog breed's written breed standard. A dog that conforms to most of the items of description in its individual breed standard is said to have good conformation. Unlike equine conformation, there are no fixed rules for dog conformation, as dogs are the most variable in appearance of any animals ('Phenotypic variation among dog breeds, whether it be in size, shape, or behavior, is greater than for any other animal').
Ribosome	The ribosome is a large and complex molecular machine, found within all living cells, that serves as the primary site of biological protein synthesis (translation). Ribosomes link amino acids together in the order specified by messenger RNA (mRNA) molecules. Ribosomes consist of two major subunits--the small ribosomal subunit reads the mRNA, while the large subunit joins amino acids to form a polypeptide chain.
Bacteriophage	A bacteriophage is a virus that infects and replicates within bacteria. The term is derived from 'bacteria' and the Greek fa?e?? phagein 'to devour'. Bacteriophages are composed of proteins that encapsulate a DNA or RNA genome, and may have relatively simple or elaborate structures.
Growth factor	A growth factor is a naturally occurring substance capable of stimulating cellular growth, proliferation and cellular differentiation. Usually it is a protein or a steroid hormone. Growth factors are important for regulating a variety of cellular processes.
Insect	Insects (from Latin insectum, a calque of Greek ??t?μ?? [

éntomon], 'cut into sections') are a class of invertebrates within the arthropod phylum that have a chitinous exoskeleton, a three-part body, three pairs of jointed legs, compound eyes and one pair of antennae. They are among the most diverse groups of animals on the planet, including more than a million described species and representing more than half of all known living organisms. The number of extant species is estimated at between six and ten million, and potentially represent over 90% of the differing animal life forms on Earth.

Intron

An intron is any nucleotide sequence within a gene that is removed by RNA splicing while the final mature RNA product of a gene is being generated. The term intron refers to both the DNA sequence within a gene and the corresponding sequence in RNA transcripts. Sequences that are joined together in the final mature RNA after RNA splicing are exons.

Deletion

In genetics, a deletion is a mutation (a genetic aberration) in which a part of a chromosome or a sequence of DNA is missing. Deletion is the loss of genetic material. Any number of nucleotides can be deleted, from a single base to an entire piece of chromosome.

Insertion

In genetics, an insertion is the addition of one or more nucleotide base pairs into a DNA sequence. This can often happen in microsatellite regions due to the DNA polymerase slipping. Insertions can be anywhere in size from one base pair incorrectly inserted into a DNA sequence to a section of one chromosome inserted into another.

Inversion

In evolutionary developmental biology, inversion refers to the hypothesis that during the course of animal evolution, the structures along the dorsoventral axis have taken on an orientation opposite that of the ancestral form. In the early 19th century, the French naturalist Étienne Geoffroy Saint-Hilaire noted that the organization of dorsal and ventral structures in arthropods is opposite that of mammals. Decades later, in light of Darwin's theory of "descent with modification," Anton Dohrn proposed that these groups arose from a common ancestor which possessed a body plan similar to that of modern annelids with a ventral nerve cord and dorsal heart.

Limb

A limb, or extremity, is a jointed, or prehensile (as octopus tentacles or new world monkey tails), appendage of the human or other animal body. In the human body, the upper and lower limbs are commonly called the arms and the legs.

Most animals use limbs for locomotion, such as walking, running, or climbing.

Site-specific recombination

Site-specific recombination, also known as conservative site-specific recombination, is a type of genetic recombination in which DNA strand exchange takes place between segments possessing only a limited degree of sequence homology. Site-specific recombinases perform rearrangements of DNA segments by recognizing and binding to short DNA sequences (sites), at which they cleave the DNA backbone, exchange the two DNA helices involved and rejoin the DNA strands.

10. Site-Specific Recombination and Transposition of DNA,

CHAPTER HIGHLIGHTS & NOTES: KEY TERMS, PEOPLE, PLACES, CONCEPTS

Serine	Serine is an amino acid with the formula $HO_2CCH(NH_2)CH_2OH$. It is one of the proteinogenic amino acids. Its codons in the genetic code are UCU, UCC, UCA, UCG, AGU and AGC. By virtue of the hydroxyl group, serine is classified as a polar amino acid.
Tyrosine	Tyrosine or 4-hydroxyphenylalanine, is one of the 20 amino acids that are used by cells to synthesize proteins. Its codons are UAC and UAU. It is a non-essential amino acid with a polar side group. The word 'tyrosine' is from the Greek tyri, meaning cheese, as it was first discovered in 1846 by German chemist Justus von Liebig in the protein casein from cheese.
Cre recombinase	Cre Recombinase is a tyrosine recombinase enzyme derived from the P1 Bacteriophage. The enzyme uses a topoisomerase I like mechanism to carry out site specific recombination events. The enzyme (38kDa) is a member of the Integrase family of site specific recombinase and it is known to catalyse the site specific recombination event between two DNA recognition sites (loxP sites).
Evolution	Evolution is a 2001 documentary series by the American broadcaster Public Broadcasting Service and WGBH on evolutionary biology. The spokespeople for the series were Jane Goodall (overall spokesperson), Kenneth R. Miller and Stephen Jay Gould (science spokespeople), Eugenie C. Scott (education spokesperson), Arthur Peacocke and Arnold Thomas (religious spokespeople). The series was narrated by the Irish actor Liam Neeson.
Integrase	Retroviral integrase is an enzyme produced by a retrovirus (such as HIV) that enables its genetic material to be integrated into the DNA of the infected cell. Retroviral INs are not to be confused with phage integrases, such as ? phage integrase . IN is a key component in the retroviral pre-integration complex (PIC).
DNA replication	DNA replication is the process of producing two identical copies from one original DNA molecule. This biological process occurs in all living organisms and is the basis for biological inheritance. DNA is composed of two strands and each strand of the original DNA molecule serves as template for the production of the complementary strand, a process referred to as semiconservative replication.
Flagellin	Flagellin is a globular protein that arranges itself in a hollow cylinder to form the filament in bacterial flagellum. It has a mass of about 30,000 to 60,000 daltons. Flagellin is the principal substituent of bacterial flagellum, and is present in large amounts on nearly all flagellated bacteria.
Hin recombinase	Hin recombinase is a 21kD protein composed of 198 amino acids that is found in the bacteria Salmonella. Hin belongs to the serine recombinase family of DNA invertases in which it relies on the active site serine to initiate DNA cleavage and recombination.

Saga	Saga cheese is a mix of blue cheese and brie, originated in Denmark, a creamy, blue-veined cheese with a white-mould rind. Saga is a very mild blue-veined cheese. It comes with a delicate blue mold, that may not appear in other varieties of blue cheeses.
Salmonella	Salmonella is a genus of rod-shaped, Gram-negative, non-spore-forming, predominantly motile enterobacteria with diameters around 0.7 to 1.5 µm, lengths from 2 to 5 µm, and flagella that grade in all directions . They are chemoorganotrophs, obtaining their energy from oxidation and reduction reactions using organic sources, and are facultative anaerobes. Most species produce hydrogen sulfide, which can readily be detected by growing them on media containing ferrous sulfate, such as TSI. Most isolates exist in two phases: a motile phase I and a nonmotile phase II. Cultures that are nonmotile upon primary culture may be switched to the motile phase using a Cragie tube.
Enhancer	In genetics, an enhancer is a short region of DNA that can be bound with proteins to enhance transcription levels of genes (hence the name) in a gene cluster. While enhancers are usually cis-acting, an enhancer does not need to be particularly close to the genes it acts on, and sometimes need not be located on the same chromosome.
Circular DNA	Circular DNA is a form of DNA that is found in viruses, bacteria and archaea as well as in eukaryotic cells in the form of either mitochondrial DNA or plastid DNA. While the individual strands of a linear double helix represent two distinct and separable molecules, this need not be true for circular DNA.
Saccharomyces	Saccharomyces is a genus in the kingdom of fungi that includes many species of yeast. Saccharomyces is from Greek s???a? (sugar) and µ???? (mushroom) and means sugar fungus. Many members of this genus are considered very important in food production.
Saccharomyces cerevisiae	Saccharomyces cerevisiae is a species of yeast. It is perhaps the most useful yeast, having been instrumental to winemaking, baking and brewing since ancient times. It is believed that it was originally isolated from the skin of grapes .
Chromosome	A chromosome is an organized structure of DNA, protein, and RNA found in cells. It is a single piece of coiled DNA containing many genes, regulatory elements and other nucleotide sequences. Chromosomes also contain DNA-bound proteins, which serve to package the DNA and control its functions.
Discovery	Discovery is the act of detecting something new, or something 'old' that had been unknown. With reference to science and academic disciplines, discovery is the observation of new phenomena, new actions, or new events and providing new reasoning to explain the knowledge gathered through such observations with previously acquired knowledge from abstract thought and everyday experiences. Visual discoveries are often called sightings.
Ferritin	Ferritin is a ubiquitous intracellular protein that stores iron and releases it in a controlled fashion.

	The amount of ferritin stored reflects the amount of iron stored. The protein is produced by almost all living organisms, including algae, bacteria, higher plants, and animals.
Hot spot	In veterinary medicine, a 'hot spot' (or acute pyoderma, acute moist pyotraumatic dermatitis) is one of the many names for a raw, painful, irritated skin lesion that results in and worsens from a pet (such as a dog or a cat) constantly biting, scratching, chewing, and licking an area of its skin that is irritated or itchy. If it is covered by the dog's hair, the hair holds in the moisture and further irritates it. It is a patch that appears suddenly and is often bright red, hairless, and scaly looking.
Mutagen	In genetics, a mutagen is a physical or chemical agent that changes the genetic material, usually DNA, of an organism and thus increases the frequency of mutations above the natural background level. As many mutations cause cancer, mutagens are therefore also likely to be carcinogens. Not all mutations are caused by mutagens: so-called 'spontaneous mutations' occur due to spontaneous hydrolysis, errors in DNA replication, repair and recombination.
Retinitis pigmentosa	Retinitis pigmentosa is an inherited, degenerative eye disease that causes severe vision impairment and often blindness. The progress of RP is not consistent. Some people will exhibit symptoms from infancy, others may not notice symptoms until later in life.
Reverse transcriptase	Reverse transcriptase is an enzyme used to generate complementary DNA (cDNA) from an RNA template, a process termed reverse transcription. RT is needed for the replication of retroviruses (e.g., HIV), and RT inhibitors are widely used as antiretroviral drugs. RT activity is also associated with the replication of chromosome ends (telomerase) and some mobile genetic elements (retrotransposons).
Cleavage	Cleavage, anatomically known as the intermammary cleft or the intermammary sulcus, is the space between a woman's breasts lying over the sternum. In popular culture, it is often defined by garments with low necklines, like ball gowns, evening gowns, lingerie and swimwear that expose or highlight cleavage. Most people in Western culture, both male and female, consider breasts an important aspect of femininity and many women use cleavage to enhance their physical and sexual attractiveness and to improve their sense of femininity.
Hermes	Hermes is a proposed genus of sea snails, marine gastropod mollusks in the family Conidae, the cone snails and their allies. This genus currently (November 2011) is still treated by some experts as an 'alternative representation' of this group of species.

Replicative transposition	Replicative transposition is a mechanism of transposition in molecular biology, proposed by James A. Shapiro in 1979, in which the transposable element is duplicated during the reaction, so that the transposing entity is a copy of the original element. In this mechanism, the donor and receptor DNA sequences form a characteristic intermediate 'theta' configuration, sometimes called a 'Shapiro intermediate'. Replicative transposition is characteristic to retrotransposons and occurs from time to time in class II transposons.Chaconas, George; Harshey, Rasika M. (2002), 'Transposition of phage Mu DNA', in Craig, N. L.; Craigie, R.; Gellert, M. et al., Mobile DNA II, American Society for Microbiology, pp. 384-402 suggested (help).</ref>
Translocase	Translocase is a general term for a protein that assists in moving another molecule, usually across a membrane. Translocases are most common secretion system in Gram positive bacteria. Examples include:•ornithine translocase associated with ornithine translocase deficiency.•carnitine-acylcarnitine translocase associated with carnitine-acylcarnitine translocase deficiency.•Translocase of outer mitochondrial membrane 40 (TOMM40), a protein encoded by the TOMM40 gene, whose alleles differentially impact the risk for Alzheimer's disease.
Retrotransposon	Retrotransposons are genetic elements that can amplify themselves in a genome and are ubiquitous components of the DNA of many eukaryotic organisms. They are a subclass of transposon. They are particularly abundant in plants, where they are often a principal component of nuclear DNA. In maize, 49-78% of the genome is made up of retrotransposons.
Composite transposon	A composite transposon is similar in function to simple transposons and Insertion Sequence elements in that it has protein coding DNA segments flanked by inverted, repeated sequences that can be recognized by transposase enzymes. A composite transposon, however, is flanked by two separate IS elements which may or may not be exact replicas. Instead of each IS element moving separately, the entire length of DNA spanning from one IS element to the other is transposed as one complete unit.
SAFE	SAFE is a New Zealand animal rights advocacy group. The group's purpose is to oppose practices of perceived unnecessary animal exploitation and experimentation. SAFE actively campaigns against current intensive pig and chicken farming practices.
Haven	In graph theory, a haven is a way of describing a strategy for an evader to win a certain type of pursuit-evasion game on an undirected graph. Havens were first introduced by Seymour & Thomas (1993); they may be used to characterize the treewidth of graphs, to prove the existence of small separators on minor-closed families of graphs, and to characterize the ends and clique minors of infinite graphs.
Immunity	In biology, immunity is the state of having sufficient biological defences to avoid infection, disease, or other unwanted biological invasion. It is the capability of the body to resist harmful microbes from entering it.

10. Site-Specific Recombination and Transposition of DNA,

CHAPTER HIGHLIGHTS & NOTES: KEY TERMS, PEOPLE, PLACES, CONCEPTS

Antisense RNA	Antisense RNA is a single-stranded RNA that is complementary to a messenger RNA (mRNA) strand transcribed within a cell. Some authors have used the term micRNA (mRNA-interfering complementary RNA) to refer to these RNAs but it is not widely used. Antisense RNA may be introduced into a cell to inhibit translation of a complementary mRNA by base pairing to it and physically obstructing the translation machinery.
Insertion sequence	An insertion sequence is a short DNA sequence that acts as a simple transposable element. Insertion sequences have two major characteristics: they are small relative to other transposable elements (generally around 700 to 2500 bp in length) and only code for proteins implicated in the transposition activity (they are thus different from other transposons, which also carry accessory genes such as antibiotic resistance genes). These proteins are usually the transposase which catalyses the enzymatic reaction allowing the IS to move, and also one regulatory protein which either stimulates or inhibits the transposition activity.
RNA polymerase	RNA polymerase, also known as DNA-dependent RNA polymerase, is an enzyme that produces RNA. In cells, RNAP is necessary for constructing RNA chains using DNA genes as templates, a process called transcription. RNA polymerase enzymes are essential to life and are found in all organisms and many viruses. In chemical terms, RNAP is a nucleotidyl transferase that polymerizes ribonucleotides at the 3' end of an RNA transcript.
Footprint	Footprints are the impressions or images left behind by a person walking or running. Hoofprints and pawprints are those left by animals with hooves or paws rather than feet, while 'shoeprints' is the specific term for prints made by shoes. They may either be indentations in the ground or something placed onto the surface that was stuck to the bottom of the foot.
Antibody	An antibody, also known as an immunoglobulin (Ig), is a large Y-shaped protein produced by B cells that is used by the immune system to identify and neutralize foreign objects such as bacteria and viruses. The antibody recognizes a unique part of the foreign target, called an antigen. Each tip of the 'Y' of an antibody contains a paratope (a structure analogous to a lock) that is specific for one particular epitope (similarly analogous to a key) on an antigen, allowing these two structures to bind together with precision.
Immune system	The immune system is a system of biological structures and processes within an organism that protects against disease. To function properly, an immune system must detect a wide variety of agents, from viruses to parasitic worms, and distinguish them from the organism's own healthy tissue. Pathogens can rapidly evolve and adapt, and thereby avoid detection and neutralization by the immune system, however, multiple defense mechanisms have also evolved to recognize and neutralize pathogens.

CHAPTER HIGHLIGHTS & NOTES: KEY TERMS, PEOPLE, PLACES, CONCEPTS

Recombination signal sequences	The regional genes, used to generate T-cell receptors and Immunoglobulin molecules, are flanked by recombination signal sequences that are recognized by a group of enzymes known collectively as the VDJ recombinase. Recombination signal sequencess are composed of seven conserved nucleotides (a heptamer) that reside next to the gene encoding sequence followed by a spacer (containing either 12 or 23 unconserved nucleotides) followed by a conserved nonamer (9 base pairs). The Recombination signal sequencess are present on the 3' side (downstream) of a V region and the 5' side (upstream) of the J region.

CHAPTER QUIZ: KEY TERMS, PEOPLE, PLACES, CONCEPTS

1. An _________, also known as an immunoglobulin (Ig), is a large Y-shaped protein produced by B cells that is used by the immune system to identify and neutralize foreign objects such as bacteria and viruses. The _________ recognizes a unique part of the foreign target, called an antigen. Each tip of the 'Y' of an _________ contains a paratope (a structure analogous to a lock) that is specific for one particular epitope (similarly analogous to a key) on an antigen, allowing these two structures to bind together with precision.

    a. Bacteremia
    b. Fungemia
    c. Antibody
    d. Hyperglycemia

2. In graph theory, a _________ is a way of describing a strategy for an evader to win a certain type of pursuit-evasion game on an undirected graph. _________s were first introduced by Seymour & Thomas (1993); they may be used to characterize the treewidth of graphs, to prove the existence of small separators on minor-closed families of graphs, and to characterize the ends and clique minors of infinite graphs.

    a. Backgammon opening theory
    b. Haven
    c. Bandwidth-sharing game
    d. Bankruptcy problem

3. . The _________ is a large and complex molecular machine, found within all living cells, that serves as the primary site of biological protein synthesis (translation). _________s link amino acids together in the order specified by messenger RNA (mRNA) molecules. _________s consist of two major subunits--the small ribosomal subunit reads the mRNA, while the large subunit joins amino acids to form a polypeptide chain.

    a. GIR1 branching ribozyme
    b. Ribosome

c. Leadzyme
d. Kleine Feldhofer Grotte

4. In genetics, an _________ is a short region of DNA that can be bound with proteins to enhance transcription levels of genes (hence the name) in a gene cluster. While _________s are usually cis-acting, an _________ does not need to be particularly close to the genes it acts on, and sometimes need not be located on the same chromosome.

a. Bacterial transcription
b. C1QL1
c. Enhancer
d. Cap analysis gene expression

5. _________ is a 2001 documentary series by the American broadcaster Public Broadcasting Service and WGBH on evolutionary biology.

The spokespeople for the series were Jane Goodall (overall spokesperson), Kenneth R. Miller and Stephen Jay Gould (science spokespeople), Eugenie C. Scott (education spokesperson), Arthur Peacocke and Arnold Thomas (religious spokespeople). The series was narrated by the Irish actor Liam Neeson.

a. Biological dispersal
b. Evolution
c. Decellularization
d. Gordo

ANSWER KEY
10. Site-Specific Recombination and Transposition of DNA,

1. c
2. b
3. b
4. c
5. b

You can take the complete Chapter Practice Test

for 10. Site-Specific Recombination and Transposition of DNA,
on all key terms, persons, places, and concepts.

Online 99 Cents

http://www.JustTheFacts101.com

11. Mechanisms of Transcription,

CHAPTER OUTLINE: KEY TERMS, PEOPLE, PLACES, CONCEPTS

- DNA replication
- Transcription
- Ligase ribozyme
- RNA polymerase
- Core
- Core enzyme
- RNA polymerase I
- RNA polymerase II
- RNA polymerase III
- RNA polymerase IV
- Enzyme
- Polymerase
- Transcription bubble
- Bacteria
- Conformation
- Consensus sequence
- Promoter
- Amino acid
- Carbon
- Helix
- Molecular mimicry

11. Mechanisms of Transcription,

CHAPTER OUTLINE: KEY TERMS, PEOPLE, PLACES, CONCEPTS

	Processivity
	Proofreading
	Rho factor
	Hairless
	General transcription factor
	Eukaryote
	Insulator
	Minor
	Saga
	Forward genetics
	Ferritin
	Genetics
	Mediator
	Elongation factor
	FACT
	Polyadenylation
	Nucleosome

DNA replication	DNA replication is the process of producing two identical copies from one original DNA molecule. This biological process occurs in all living organisms and is the basis for biological inheritance. DNA is composed of two strands and each strand of the original DNA molecule serves as template for the production of the complementary strand, a process referred to as semiconservative replication.
Transcription	Transcription is the first step of gene expression, in which a particular segment of DNA is copied into RNA by the enzyme, RNA polymerase. Both RNA and DNA are nucleic acids, which use base pairs of nucleotides as a complementary language that can be converted back and forth from DNA to RNA by the action of the correct enzymes. During transcription, a DNA sequence is read by an RNA polymerase, which produces a complementary, antiparallel RNA strand.
Ligase ribozyme	The RNA Ligase ribozyme was the first of several types of synthetic ribozymes produced by in vitro evolution and selection techniques. They are an important class of ribozymes because they catalyze the assembly of RNA fragments into phosphodiester RNA polymers, a reaction required of all extant nucleic acid polymerases and thought to be required for any self-replicating molecule. Ideas that the origin of life may have involved the first self-replicating molecules being ribozymes are called RNA World hypotheses.
RNA polymerase	RNA polymerase, also known as DNA-dependent RNA polymerase, is an enzyme that produces RNA. In cells, RNAP is necessary for constructing RNA chains using DNA genes as templates, a process called transcription. RNA polymerase enzymes are essential to life and are found in all organisms and many viruses. In chemical terms, RNAP is a nucleotidyl transferase that polymerizes ribonucleotides at the 3' end of an RNA transcript.
Core	In anatomy, the core refers, in its most general of definitions, to the body minus the legs and arms. Functional movements are highly dependent on the core, and lack of core development can result in a predisposition to injury. The major muscles of the core reside in the area of the belly and the mid and lower back (not the shoulders), and peripherally include the hips, the shoulders and the neck.
Core enzyme	A core enzyme consists of the subunits of an enzyme that are needed for catalytic activity, as in the core enzyme RNA polymerase. An example of a core enzyme is a RNA polymerase enzyme without the sigma factor . This enzyme consists of only two alpha (2a), one beta (ß) and one beta prime (ß').
RNA polymerase I	RNA polymerase I is, in higher eukaryotes, the enzyme that only transcribes ribosomal RNA (but not 5S rRNA, which is synthesized by RNA Polymerase III), a type of RNA that accounts for over 50% of the total RNA synthesized in a cell. Pol I consists of 8-14 protein subunits (polypeptides).

All 12 subunits have identical or related counterparts in Pol II and Pol III. rDNA transcription is confined to the nucleolus where several hundreds of copies of rRNA genes are present, arranged as tandem head-to-tail repeats.

RNA polymerase II

RNA polymerase II is an enzyme found in eukaryotic cells. It catalyzes the transcription of DNA to synthesize precursors of mRNA and most snRNA and microRNA. A 550 kDa complex of 12 subunits, RNAP II is the most studied type of RNA polymerase. A wide range of transcription factors are required for it to bind to upstream gene promoters and begin transcription.

RNA polymerase III

In eukaryote cells, RNA polymerase III transcribes DNA to synthesize ribosomal 5S rRNA, tRNA and other small RNAs. This enzyme complex has a more limited role than the Pol III in prokaryote cells.

The genes transcribed by RNA Pol III fall in the category of 'housekeeping' genes whose expression is required in all cell types and most environmental conditions.

RNA polymerase IV

RNA polymerase IV is an enzyme which synthesizes small interfering RNA in plants. Polymerase IV is specific to plants genomes and is required for the synthesis of over 90% of 24-nt heterochromatic siRNA.

Enzyme

Enzymes are large biological molecules responsible for the thousands of metabolic processes that sustain life. They are highly selective catalysts, greatly accelerating both the rate and specificity of metabolic reactions, from the digestion of food to the synthesis of DNA. Most enzymes are proteins, although some catalytic RNA molecules have been identified. Enzymes adopt a specific three-dimensional structure, and may employ organic (e.g. biotin) and inorganic (e.g. magnesium ion) cofactors to assist in catalysis.

Polymerase

A polymerase is an enzyme whose central biological function is the synthesis of polymers of nucleic acids. DNA polymerase and RNA polymerase are used to assemble DNA and RNA molecules, respectively, generally by copying a DNA or RNA template strand using base-pairing interactions.

It is an accident of history that the enzymes responsible for the generation of other biopolymers are not also referred to as polymerases.

Transcription bubble

A transcription bubble is a molecular structure that occurs during the transcription of DNA when a limited portion of the DNA double strand is unwound. RNA polymerase (Main Article: transcription) may then bind to the exposed DNA and begin synthesizing a new strand of RNA. As RNA polymerase progresses down the DNA strand in the 3' to 5' direction, more of the DNA double strand is unwound upstream of the polymerase while DNA downstream of the polymerase re-anneals, moving a transcription bubble in the process that may be seen with specialized staining techniques, spectroscopy or microscopy.

Bacteria	Bacteria constitute a large domain or kingdom of prokaryotic microorganisms. Typically a few micrometres in length, bacteria have a wide range of shapes, ranging from spheres to rods and spirals. Bacteria were among the first life forms to appear on Earth, and are present in most habitats on the planet.
Conformation	Conformation in dogs refers solely to the externally visible details of a dog's structure and appearance, as defined in detail by each dog breed's written breed standard. A dog that conforms to most of the items of description in its individual breed standard is said to have good conformation. Unlike equine conformation, there are no fixed rules for dog conformation, as dogs are the most variable in appearance of any animals ('Phenotypic variation among dog breeds, whether it be in size, shape, or behavior, is greater than for any other animal').
Consensus sequence	In molecular biology and bioinformatics, the consensus sequence is the calculated order of most frequent residues, either nucleotide or amino acid, found at each position in a sequence alignment. It represents the results of a multiple sequence alignments in which related sequences are compared to each other and similar sequence motifs are calculated. Such information is important when considering sequence dependent enzymes such as RNA polymerase.
Promoter	In genetics, a promoter is a region of DNA that initiates transcription of a particular gene. Promoters are located near the genes they transcribe, on the same strand and upstream on the DNA (towards the 3' region of the anti-sense strand, also called template strand and non-coding strand). Promoters can be about 100-1000 base pairs long.
Amino acid	Amino acids are biologically important organic compounds made from amine ($-NH_2$) and carboxylic acid ($-COOH$) functional groups, along with a side-chain specific to each amino acid. The key elements of an amino acid are carbon, hydrogen, oxygen, and nitrogen, though other elements are found in the side-chains of certain amino acids. About 500 amino acids are known and can be classified in many ways.
Carbon	Carbon is the chemical element with symbol C and atomic number 6. As a member of group 14 on the periodic table, it is nonmetallic and tetravalent--making four electrons available to form covalent chemical bonds. There are three naturally occurring isotopes, with ^{12}C and ^{13}C being stable, while ^{14}C is radioactive, decaying with a half-life of about 5,730 years. Carbon is one of the few elements known since antiquity.
Helix	The prominent rim of the auricula is called the helix. Where the helix turns downward behind, a small tubercle is frequently seen: the auricular tubercle of Darwin.
Molecular mimicry	Molecular mimicry is defined as the theoretical possibility that sequence similarities between foreign and self-peptides are sufficient to result in the cross-activation of autoreactive T or B cells by pathogen-derived peptides.

Despite the promiscuity of several peptide sequences which can be both foreign and self in nature, a single antibody or TCR (T cell receptor) can be activated by even a few crucial residues which stresses the importance of structural homology in the theory of molecular mimicry. Upon the activation of B or T cells, it is believed that these 'peptide mimic' specific T or B cells can cross-react with self-epitopes, thus leading to tissue pathology (autoimmunity).

Processivity

In molecular biology and biochemistry, processivity is an enzyme's ability to catalyze 'consecutive reactions without releasing its substrate'.

For example, processivity is the average number of nucleotides added by a polymerase enzyme, such as DNA polymerase, per association/disassociation with the template. DNA polymerases associated with DNA replication tend to be highly processive, while those associated with DNA repair tend to have low processivity.

Proofreading

The term proofreading is used in genetics to refer to the error-correcting processes, first proposed by John Hopfield and Jacques Ninio, involved in DNA replication, immune system specificity, enzyme-substrate recognition among many other processes that require enhanced specificity. The proofreading mechanisms of Hopfield and Ninio are non-equilibrium active processes that consume ATP to enhance specificity of various biochemical reactions.

In bacteria, all three DNA polymerases (I, II, and III) have the ability to proofread, using 3'->5' exonuclease activity.

Rho factor

A ? factor (Rho factor) is a prokaryotic protein involved in the termination of transcription. Rho factor binds to the transcription terminator pause site, an exposed region of single stranded RNA (a stretch of 72 nucleotides) after the open reading frame at GC-rich sequences that lack obvious secondary structure.

Rho factor is an essential transcription protein in prokaryotes.

Hairless

Hairless, also known as H, is a well-characterized Drosophila gene. Many mutations to hairless are embryonic lethal; however, there are several viable hairless mutants. Hairless is involved in the Notch signaling pathway in Drosophila, acting as a suppressor of Notch signaling.

General transcription factor

General transcription factors, also known as basal transcriptional factors, are a class of protein transcription factors that bind to specific sites on DNA to activate transcription. General transcription factors, RNA polymerase, and the mediator multiple protein complex constitute the basic transcriptional apparatus. General transcription factors are also intimately involved in the process of gene regulation, and most are required for life.

Eukaryote

A eukaryote is an organism whose cells contain a nucleus and other structures (organelles) enclosed within membranes. Eukaryotes are formally the taxon Eukarya or Eukaryota.

Insulator	An insulator is a genetic boundary element that blocks the interaction between enhancers and promoters. Insulators therefore determine the set of genes an enhancer can influence. The need for them arises where two adjacent genes on a chromosome have very different transcription patterns, and it is critical that the inducing or repressing mechanisms of one do not interfere with the neighbouring gene.
Minor	In law, a minor is a person under a certain age--usually the age of majority--which legally demarcates childhood from adulthood. The age depends upon jurisdiction and application, but is generally 18. Minor may also be used in contexts unconnected to the overall age of majority. For example, the drinking age in the United States is 21, and people below this age are sometimes called minors even if 18. The term underage often refers to those under the age of majority, but may also refer to persons under a certain age limit, such as the drinking age, smoking age, age of consent, marriageable age, driving age, voting age, etc.
Saga	Saga cheese is a mix of blue cheese and brie, originated in Denmark, a creamy, blue-veined cheese with a white-mould rind. Saga is a very mild blue-veined cheese. It comes with a delicate blue mold, that may not appear in other varieties of blue cheeses.
Forward genetics	Forward genetics encompasses several means of identifying the genotype that is responsible for a phenotype. Initially, this was done by generating random mutations in an organism, often with radiation or insertional mutagenesis (ex. Sleeping Beauty), and after subsequent breeding, isolating individuals with an aberrant phenotype.
Ferritin	Ferritin is a ubiquitous intracellular protein that stores iron and releases it in a controlled fashion. The amount of ferritin stored reflects the amount of iron stored. The protein is produced by almost all living organisms, including algae, bacteria, higher plants, and animals.
Genetics	Genetics, a discipline of biology, is the science of genes, heredity, and variation in living organisms. Genetics concerns the process of trait inheritance from parents to offspring, including the molecular structure and function of genes, gene behavior in the context of a cell or organism (e.g. dominance and epigenetics), gene distribution, and variation and change in populations (such as through Genome-Wide Association Studies). Given that genes are universal to living organisms, genetics can be applied to the study of all living systems; including bacteria, plants, animals, and humans.
Mediator	Mediator is a multiprotein complex that functions as a transcriptional coactivator in all eukaryotes. It was discovered by Roger D. Kornberg, winner of the 2006 Nobel Prize in Chemistry. It is also referred to in scientific literature as the Vitamin D Receptor Interacting Protein (DRIP) coactivator complex and the Thyroid Hormone Receptor-associated Proteins (TRAP).
Elongation factor	Elongation factors are a set of proteins that are used in protein synthesis in the cell.

In the ribosome, they facilitate translational elongation, from the formation of the first peptide bond to the formation of the last one.

Elongation is the most rapid step in translation:•in prokaryotes it proceeds at a rate of 15 to 20 amino acids added per second (about 60 nucleotides per second)•in eukaryotes the rate is about two amino acids per second.

Elongation factors play a role in orchestrating the events of this process, and in ensuring the 99.99% accuracy of translation at this speed.

FACT

FACT is a heterodimeric protein complex that affects eukaryotic RNA polymerase II (Pol II) transcription elongation both in vitro and in vivo. It was discovered in 1998 as a factor purified from human cells, consisting of 140 and 80 kilodalton (kDa) subunits, that was essential for productive in vitro Pol II transcription on a chromatinized DNA template.

The 140 kDa subunit is encoded by a human gene (SUPT16H) which is 36% identical to the S. cerevisiae gene Spt16 and the 80 kDa subunit is human SSRP1 (POB3 in S. cerevisiae).

Polyadenylation

Polyadenylation is the addition of a poly tail to an RNA molecule. The poly(A) tail consists of multiple adenosine monophosphates; in other words, it is a stretch of RNA that has only adenine bases. In eukaryotes, polyadenylation is part of the process that produces mature messenger RNA (mRNA) for translation.

Nucleosome

A nucleosome is the basic unit of DNA packaging in eukaryotes, consisting of a segment of DNA wound in sequence around eight histone protein cores. This structure is often compared to thread wrapped around a spool.

Nucleosomes form the fundamental repeating units of eukaryotic chromatin, which is used to pack the large eukaryotic genomes into the nucleus while still ensuring appropriate access to it (in mammalian cells approximately 2 m of linear DNA have to be packed into a nucleus of roughly 10 μm diameter).

1. In law, a _________ is a person under a certain age--usually the age of majority--which legally demarcates childhood from adulthood. The age depends upon jurisdiction and application, but is generally 18. _________ may also be used in contexts unconnected to the overall age of majority. For example, the drinking age in the United States is 21, and people below this age are sometimes called _________s even if 18. The term underage often refers to those under the age of majority, but may also refer to persons under a certain age limit, such as the drinking age, smoking age, age of consent, marriageable age, driving age, voting age, etc.

   a. Bairn
   b. Birth in Sri Lanka
   c. Chartier v. Chartier
   d. Minor

2. _________ is, in higher eukaryotes, the enzyme that only transcribes ribosomal RNA (but not 5S rRNA, which is synthesized by RNA Polymerase III), a type of RNA that accounts for over 50% of the total RNA synthesized in a cell.

   Pol I consists of 8-14 protein subunits (polypeptides). All 12 subunits have identical or related counterparts in Pol II and Pol III. rDNA transcription is confined to the nucleolus where several hundreds of copies of rRNA genes are present, arranged as tandem head-to-tail repeats.

   a. Bacterial transcription
   b. RNA polymerase I
   c. CAG promoter
   d. Cap analysis gene expression

3. The RNA _________ was the first of several types of synthetic ribozymes produced by in vitro evolution and selection techniques. They are an important class of ribozymes because they catalyze the assembly of RNA fragments into phosphodiester RNA polymers, a reaction required of all extant nucleic acid polymerases and thought to be required for any self-replicating molecule. Ideas that the origin of life may have involved the first self-replicating molecules being ribozymes are called RNA World hypotheses.

   a. Bacillaceae-1 RNA motif
   b. Bacillus-plasmid RNA motif
   c. Bacterial small RNA
   d. Ligase ribozyme

4. . _________ is an enzyme found in eukaryotic cells. It catalyzes the transcription of DNA to synthesize precursors of mRNA and most snRNA and microRNA. A 550 kDa complex of 12 subunits, RNAP II is the most studied type of RNA polymerase. A wide range of transcription factors are required for it to bind to upstream gene promoters and begin transcription.

   a. Bacterial transcription
   b. C1QL1
   c. RNA polymerase II

5. In anatomy, the _________ refers, in its most general of definitions, to the body minus the legs and arms. Functional movements are highly dependent on the _________, and lack of _________ development can result in a predisposition to injury. The major muscles of the _________ reside in the area of the belly and the mid and lower back (not the shoulders), and peripherally include the hips, the shoulders and the neck.

a. Balance
b. Core
c. Center of pressure
d. MF59

ANSWER KEY
11. Mechanisms of Transcription,

1. d
2. b
3. d
4. c
5. b

---

12. RNA Splicing,

CHAPTER OUTLINE: KEY TERMS, PEOPLE, PLACES, CONCEPTS

- Dihydrofolate reductase
- Exon
- Alternative splicing
- Group II intron
- Genome
- Genome size
- Circular DNA
- Exonic splicing enhancer
- Operon
- Trans-splicing
- Minor spliceosome
- Exon skipping
- Amino acid
- Gene
- DSCAM
- Exonic splicing silencer
- Family
- Ferritin
- Dosage compensation
- RNA polymerase
- Serine

12. RNA Splicing,

CHAPTER OUTLINE: KEY TERMS, PEOPLE, PLACES, CONCEPTS

- Protein
- Pluripotency
- Cell
- Exon shuffling
- Epidermal growth factor
- ADAR
- Adenosine
- RNA editing
- Deamination
- Guide RNA
- Insertion
- Nuclear pore
- Ramachandran plot

Dihydrofolate reductase	Dihydrofolate reductase, or DHFR, is an enzyme that reduces dihydrofolic acid to tetrahydrofolic acid, using NADPH as electron donor, which can be converted to the kinds of tetrahydrofolate cofactors used in 1-carbon transfer chemistry. In humans, the DHFR enzyme is encoded by the DHFR gene. It is found in the q11?q22 region of chromosome 5.
Exon	An exon is any nucleotide sequence encoded by a gene that remains present within the final mature RNA product of that gene after introns have been removed by RNA splicing. The term exon refers to both the DNA sequence within a gene and to the corresponding sequence in RNA transcripts. In RNA splicing, introns are removed and exons are covalently joined to one another as part of generating the mature messenger RNA or noncoding RNA product of a gene.
Alternative splicing	Alternative splicing is a regulated process during gene expression that results in a single gene coding for multiple proteins. In this process, particular exons of a gene may be included within, or excluded from, the final, processed messenger RNA (mRNA) produced from that gene. Consequently the proteins translated from alternatively spliced mRNAs will contain differences in their amino acid sequence and, often, in their biological functions .
Group II intron	Group II introns are a large class of self-catalytic ribozymes as well as mobile genetic element found within the genes of all three domains of life. Ribozyme activity (e.g., Self-splicing) can occur under high-salt conditions in vitro. However, assistance from proteins is required for in vivo splicing.
Genome	In modern molecular biology and genetics, the genome is the entirety of an organism's hereditary information. It is encoded either in DNA or, for many types of viruses, in RNA. The genome includes both the genes and the non-coding sequences of the DNA/RNA.
Genome size	Genome size is the total amount of DNA contained within one copy of a single genome. It is typically measured in terms of mass in picograms (trillionths (10^{-12}) of a gram, abbreviated pg) or less frequently in Daltons or as the total number of nucleotide base pairs typically in megabases (millions of base pairs, abbreviated Mb or Mbp). One picogram equals 978 megabases.
Circular DNA	Circular DNA is a form of DNA that is found in viruses, bacteria and archaea as well as in eukaryotic cells in the form of either mitochondrial DNA or plastid DNA. While the individual strands of a linear double helix represent two distinct and separable molecules, this need not be true for circular DNA.
Exonic splicing enhancer	An exonic splicing enhancer is a DNA sequence motif consisting of 6 bases within an exon that directs, or enhances, accurate splicing of hetero-nuclear RNA (hnRNA) or pre-mRNA into messenger RNA (mRNA).
Operon	In genetics, an operon is a functioning unit of genomic DNA containing a cluster of genes under the control of a single regulatory signal or promoter.

The genes are transcribed together into an mRNA strand and either translated together in the cytoplasm, or undergo trans-splicing to create monocistronic mRNAs that are translated separately, i.e. several strands of mRNA that each encode a single gene product. The result of this is that the genes contained in the operon are either expressed together or not at all.

Trans-splicing

Trans-splicing is a special form of RNA processing in eukaryotes where exons from two different primary RNA transcripts are joined end to end and ligated.

In contrast 'normal' splicing processes a single molecule. That is, trans-splicing results in an RNA transcript that came from multiple RNA polymerases on the genome.

Minor spliceosome

The minor spliceosome is a ribonucleoprotein complex that catalyses the removal of an atypical class of spliceosomal introns (U12-type) from eukaryotic messenger RNAs in plant, insects, vertebrates and some fungi (Rhizopus oryzae). This process is called noncanonical splicing, as opposed to U2-dependent canonical splicing. U12-type introns represent less than 1% of all introns in human cells.

Exon skipping

Exon skipping is a method used to cause cells to “skip” over faulty or misaligned sections of genetic code, leading to a truncated but still functional protein despite the genetic mutation.

Amino acid

Amino acids are biologically important organic compounds made from amine ($-NH_2$) and carboxylic acid ($-COOH$) functional groups, along with a side-chain specific to each amino acid. The key elements of an amino acid are carbon, hydrogen, oxygen, and nitrogen, though other elements are found in the side-chains of certain amino acids. About 500 amino acids are known and can be classified in many ways.

Gene

A gene is a molecular unit of heredity of a living organism. It is widely accepted by the scientific community as a name given to some stretches of deoxyribonucleic acids (DNA) and ribonucleic acids (RNA) that code for a polypeptide or for an RNA chain that has a function in the organism, though there still are controversies about what plays the role of the genetic material. Living beings depend on genes, as they specify all proteins and functional RNA chains.

DSCAM

DSCAM and Dscam are both abbreviations for DSCAM. The case difference between the two acronyms is significant as DSCAM refers to the gene that encodes for the Dscam protein.

Down Syndrome (DS), caused by trisomy 21, is the most common birth defect associated with mental retardation.

Exonic splicing silencer

An exonic splicing silencer is a small region of an exon that inhibits or silences splicing of the pre-mRNA.

Family	In biological classification, family isExample: Walnuts and hickories belong to Juglandaceae, the walnut family What does and does not belong to each family is determined by a taxonomist. Similarly for the question if a particular family should be recognized at all. Often there is no exact agreement, with different taxonomists each taking a different position.
Ferritin	Ferritin is a ubiquitous intracellular protein that stores iron and releases it in a controlled fashion. The amount of ferritin stored reflects the amount of iron stored. The protein is produced by almost all living organisms, including algae, bacteria, higher plants, and animals.
Dosage compensation	Dosage compensation is a hypothetical genetic regulatory mechanism which operates to equalize the phenotypic expression of characteristics determined by genes on the X chromosome so that they are equally expressed in the human XY male and the XX female. Dosage compensation may occur in other organisms like the fruit fly Drosophila melanogaster, the roundworm Caenorhabditis elegans and the plant White campion . Species can have different mechanisms of dosage compensation.
RNA polymerase	RNA polymerase, also known as DNA-dependent RNA polymerase, is an enzyme that produces RNA. In cells, RNAP is necessary for constructing RNA chains using DNA genes as templates, a process called transcription. RNA polymerase enzymes are essential to life and are found in all organisms and many viruses. In chemical terms, RNAP is a nucleotidyl transferase that polymerizes ribonucleotides at the 3' end of an RNA transcript.
Serine	Serine is an amino acid with the formula $HO_2CCH(NH_2)CH_2OH$. It is one of the proteinogenic amino acids. Its codons in the genetic code are UCU, UCC, UCA, UCG, AGU and AGC. By virtue of the hydroxyl group, serine is classified as a polar amino acid.
Protein	Proteins are large biological molecules consisting of one or more chains of amino acids. Proteins perform a vast array of functions within living organisms, including catalyzing metabolic reactions, replicating DNA, responding to stimuli, and transporting molecules from one location to another. Proteins differ from one another primarily in their sequence of amino acids, which is dictated by the nucleotide sequence of their genes, and which usually results in folding of the protein into a specific three-dimensional structure that determines its activity.
Pluripotency	The pluripotency of biological compounds describes the ability of certain substances to produce several distinct biological responses. For example, in immunology many cytokines are pluripotent, in that each of these compounds can activate specific behavior in some cell types and inhibit other behavior in other cell types.

12. RNA Splicing,

CHAPTER HIGHLIGHTS & NOTES: KEY TERMS, PEOPLE, PLACES, CONCEPTS

Cell	The cell is the basic structural, functional and biological unit of all known living organisms. Cells are the smallest unit of life that is classified as a living thing, and are often called the 'building blocks of life'. Cells consist of a protoplasm enclosed within a membrane, which contains many biomolecules such as proteins and nucleic acids.
Exon shuffling	Exon shuffling is a molecular mechanism for the formation of new genes. It is a process through which two or more exons from different genes can be brought together ectopically, or the same exon can be duplicated, to create a new exon-intron structure. There are different mechanisms through which exon shuffling occurs: transposon mediated exon shuffling, crossover during sexual recombination of parental genomes and illegitimate recombination.
Epidermal growth factor	Epidermal growth factor is a growth factor that stimulates cell growth, proliferation, and differentiation by binding to its receptor EGFR. Human Epidermal growth factor is a 6045-Da protein with 53 amino acid residues and three intramolecular disulfide bonds.
ADAR	Double-stranded RNA-specific adenosine deaminase is an enzyme that in humans is encoded by the ADAR gene . This gene encodes the enzyme responsible for RNA editing by site-specific deamination of adenosines. This enzyme destabilizes double stranded RNA through conversion of adenosine to inosine.
Adenosine	Adenosine is a purine nucleoside comprising a molecule of adenine attached to a ribose sugar molecule (ribofuranose) moiety via a ß-N_9-glycosidic bond. Adenosine plays an important role in biochemical processes, such as energy transfer--as adenosine triphosphate (ATP) and adenosine diphosphate (ADP)--as well as in signal transduction as cyclic adenosine monophosphate, cAMP. It is also an inhibitory neurotransmitter, believed to play a role in promoting sleep and suppressing arousal.
RNA editing	RNA editing is a molecular process through which some cells can make discrete changes to specific nucleotide sequences within a RNA molecule after it has been generated by RNA polymerase. RNA editing is relatively rare, and common forms of RNA processing (e.g. splicing, 5'-capping and 3'-polyadenylation) are not usually included as editing. Editing events may include the insertion, deletion, and base substitution of nucleotides within the edited RNA molecule.
Deamination	Deamination is the removal of an amine group from a molecule. Enzymes which catalyse this reaction are called deaminases.

CHAPTER HIGHLIGHTS & NOTES: KEY TERMS, PEOPLE, PLACES, CONCEPTS

Guide RNA	Guide RNAs are the RNAs that guide the insertion or deletion of uridine residues into mitochondrial mRNAs in kinetoplastid protists in a process known as RNA editing.
Insertion	In genetics, an insertion is the addition of one or more nucleotide base pairs into a DNA sequence. This can often happen in microsatellite regions due to the DNA polymerase slipping. Insertions can be anywhere in size from one base pair incorrectly inserted into a DNA sequence to a section of one chromosome inserted into another.
Nuclear pore	Nuclear pores are large protein complexes that cross the nuclear envelope, which is the double membrane surrounding the eukaryotic cell nucleus. There are about an average of 2000 nuclear pore complexes (NPCs), in the nuclear envelope of a vertebrate cell, but it varies depending on cell type and the stage in the life cycle. The proteins that make up the nuclear pore complex are known as nucleoporins.
Ramachandran plot	A Ramachandran plot, originally developed in 1963 by G. N. Ramachandran, C. Ramakrishnan, and V. Sasisekharan, is a way to visualize backbone dihedral angles ? against f of amino acid residues in protein structure. The figure at left illustrates the definition of the f and ? backbone dihedral angles (called f and f' by Ramachandran). The ? angle at the peptide bond is normally 180°, since the partial-double-bond character keeps the peptide planar.

CHAPTER QUIZ: KEY TERMS, PEOPLE, PLACES, CONCEPTS

1. _________, or DHFR, is an enzyme that reduces dihydrofolic acid to tetrahydrofolic acid, using NADPH as electron donor, which can be converted to the kinds of tetrahydrofolate cofactors used in 1-carbon transfer chemistry. In humans, the DHFR enzyme is encoded by the DHFR gene. It is found in the q11?q22 region of chromosome 5.

a. Bacterial glutathione transferase
b. Dihydrofolate reductase
c. Bisphosphoglycerate mutase
d. BRENDA

2. . _________, also known as DNA-dependent _________, is an enzyme that produces RNA. In cells, RNAP is necessary for constructing RNA chains using DNA genes as templates, a process called transcription. _________ enzymes are essential to life and are found in all organisms and many viruses. In chemical terms, RNAP is a nucleotidyl transferase that polymerizes ribonucleotides at the 3' end of an RNA transcript.

a. RNA polymerase
b. C1QL1
c. CAG promoter

3. _________ is a ubiquitous intracellular protein that stores iron and releases it in a controlled fashion. The amount of _________ stored reflects the amount of iron stored. The protein is produced by almost all living organisms, including algae, bacteria, higher plants, and animals.

a. Beta-2 transferrin
b. Ferritin
c. Biocrystallization
d. Biomarker

4. A _________, originally developed in 1963 by G. N. Ramachandran, C. Ramakrishnan, and V. Sasisekharan, is a way to visualize backbone dihedral angles ? against f of amino acid residues in protein structure. The figure at left illustrates the definition of the f and ? backbone dihedral angles (called f and f' by Ramachandran). The ? angle at the peptide bond is normally 180°, since the partial-double-bond character keeps the peptide planar.

a. Ramachandran plot
b. Bicinchoninic acid assay
c. Bioorthogonal chemical reporter
d. Biopanning

5. _________ is a special form of RNA processing in eukaryotes where exons from two different primary RNA transcripts are joined end to end and ligated.

In contrast 'normal' splicing processes a single molecule. That is, _________ results in an RNA transcript that came from multiple RNA polymerases on the genome.

a. Chimeric RNA
b. Circular RNA
c. Trans-splicing
d. Cis-regulatory element

ANSWER KEY
12. RNA Splicing,

1. b
2. a
3. b
4. a
5. c

13. Translation,

CHAPTER OUTLINE: KEY TERMS, PEOPLE, PLACES, CONCEPTS

- Cre recombinase
- Transfer RNA
- Translation
- Adaptor hypothesis
- Discovery
- Open reading frame
- Start codon
- Reading frame
- Stop codon
- DNA polymerase
- Eukaryotic translation
- Messenger RNA
- Prokaryotic translation
- DNA gyrase
- Shine-Dalgarno sequence
- Amino acid
- Tail
- 5-Methylcytosine
- Dihydrouridine
- Pseudouridine
- Uridine

13. Translation,

CHAPTER OUTLINE: KEY TERMS, PEOPLE, PLACES, CONCEPTS

- Adenylylation
- Aminoacyl-tRNA
- Ribosome
- Isoleucine
- Phenylalanine
- Proofreading
- Serine
- Tyrosine
- Valine
- Cysteine
- Transcription
- Peptidyl transferase
- RNA polymerase
- Association
- Dissociation
- Directionality
- Binding site
- Channel
- Methionine
- Recruitment
- Aminopeptidase

13. Translation,

CHAPTER OUTLINE: KEY TERMS, PEOPLE, PLACES, CONCEPTS

- Gene
- Eukaryote
- Ternary complex
- EF-Tu
- Elongation factor
- Accommodation
- Ribozyme
- EF-G
- EF-Ts
- Molecular mimicry
- Nucleosome
- Ribosome profiling
- MIMIC
- Recycling
- Bacteria
- Oskar
- Ferritin
- Marker gene
- Protein
- Stability

13. Translation,

Cre recombinase

Cre Recombinase is a tyrosine recombinase enzyme derived from the P1 Bacteriophage. The enzyme uses a topoisomerase I like mechanism to carry out site specific recombination events. The enzyme (38kDa) is a member of the Integrase family of site specific recombinase and it is known to catalyse the site specific recombination event between two DNA recognition sites (loxP sites).

Transfer RNA

A Transfer RNA is an adaptor molecule composed of RNA, typically 73 to 94 nucleotides in length, that serves as the physical link between the nucleotide sequence of nucleic acids (DNA and RNA) and the amino acid sequence of proteins. It does this by carrying an amino acid to the protein synthetic machinery of a cell (ribosome) as directed by a three-nucleotide sequence (codon) in a messenger RNA (mRNA). As such, tRNAs are a necessary component of protein translation, the biological synthesis of new proteins according to the genetic code.

Translation

In molecular biology and genetics, translation is the process in which cellular ribosomes create proteins. It is part of the process of gene expression. In translation, messenger RNA (mRNA) produced by transcription is decoded by a ribosome complex to produce a specific amino acid chain, or polypeptide, that will later fold into an active protein.

Adaptor hypothesis

The adaptor hypothesis is part of a scheme to explain how information encoded in DNA is used to specify the amino acid sequence of proteins. It was formulated by Francis Crick in the mid-1950s, together with the central dogma of molecular biology and the sequence hypothesis

Discovery

Discovery is the act of detecting something new, or something 'old' that had been unknown. With reference to science and academic disciplines, discovery is the observation of new phenomena, new actions, or new events and providing new reasoning to explain the knowledge gathered through such observations with previously acquired knowledge from abstract thought and everyday experiences. Visual discoveries are often called sightings.

Open reading frame

In molecular genetics, an open reading frame is the part of a reading frame that contains no stop codons. The transcription termination pause site is located after the Open reading frame, beyond the translation stop codon, because if transcription were to cease before the stop codon, an incomplete protein would be made during translation.

Normally, inserts which interrupt the reading frame of a subsequent region after the start codon cause frameshift mutation of the sequence and dislocate the sequences for stop codons.

Start codon

The Central dogma of molecular biology describes the process of translation of a gene to a protein. Specific sequences of DNA act as a template to synthesize mRNA.

The start codon is the first codon of a messenger RNA (mRNA) transcript translated by a ribosome.

Reading frame	In molecular biology, a reading frame is a way of dividing the sequence of nucleotides in a nucleic acid molecule into a set of consecutive, non-overlapping triplets. Where these triplets equate to amino acids or stop signals during translation, they are called codons. A single strand of a nucleic acid molecule has a phosphoryl end, (called the 5'-end) and a hydroxyl, or (3'-end).
Stop codon	In the genetic code, a stop codon is a nucleotide triplet within messenger RNA that signals a termination of translation. Proteins are based on polypeptides, which are unique sequences of amino acids. Most codons in messenger RNA (from DNA) correspond to the addition of an amino acid to a growing polypeptide chain, which may ultimately become a protein.
DNA polymerase	A DNA polymerase is a cellular or viral polymerase enzyme that synthesizes DNA molecules from their nucleotide building blocks. DNA polymerases are essential for DNA replication, and usually function in pairs while copying one double-stranded DNA molecule into two double-stranded DNAs in a process termed semiconservative DNA replication. DNA polymerases also play key roles in other processes within cells, including DNA repair, genetic recombination, reverse transcription, and the generation of antibody diversity via the specialized DNA polymerase, terminal deoxynucleotidyl transferase.
Eukaryotic translation	Eukaryotic translation is the process by which messenger RNA is translated into proteins in eukaryotes. It consists of initiation, elongation and termination.
Messenger RNA	Messenger RNA is a large family of RNA molecules that convey genetic information from DNA to the ribosome, where they specify the amino acid sequence of the protein products of gene expression. Following transcription of mRNA by RNA polymerase, the mRNA is translated into a polymer of amino acids: a protein, as summarized in the central dogma of molecular biology. As in DNA, mRNA genetic information is encoded in the sequence of nucleotides, which are arranged into codons consisting of three bases each.
Prokaryotic translation	Prokaryotic translation is the process by which messenger RNA is translated into proteins in prokaryotes.
DNA gyrase	DNA gyrase, often referred to simply as gyrase, is an enzyme that relieves strain while double-stranded DNA is being unwound by helicase. This causes negative supercoiling of the DNA. Bacterial DNA gyrase is the target of many antibiotics, including nalidixic acid, novobiocin, and ciprofloxacin.

13. Translation,

CHAPTER HIGHLIGHTS & NOTES: KEY TERMS, PEOPLE, PLACES, CONCEPTS

Shine-Dalgarno sequence	The Shine-Dalgarno sequence, proposed by Australian scientists John Shine (b. 1946) and Lynn Dalgarno (b. 1935), is a ribosomal binding site in prokaryotic mRNA, generally located around 8 bases upstream of the start codon AUG. The Shine-Dalgarno sequence exists both in bacteria and archaea, being also present in some chloroplast and mitochondrial transcripts. The six-base consensus sequence is AGGAGG; in Escherichia coli, for example, the sequence is AGGAGGU, while subsequence GAGG dominates in E. coli virus T4 early genes. Shine-Dalgarno sequence helps recruit the ribosome to the mRNA to initiate protein synthesis by aligning it with the start codon.
Amino acid	Amino acids are biologically important organic compounds made from amine ($-NH_2$) and carboxylic acid (-COOH) functional groups, along with a side-chain specific to each amino acid. The key elements of an amino acid are carbon, hydrogen, oxygen, and nitrogen, though other elements are found in the side-chains of certain amino acids. About 500 amino acids are known and can be classified in many ways.
Tail	The tail is the section at the rear end of an animal's body; in general, the term refers to a distinct, flexible appendage to the torso. It is the part of the body that corresponds roughly to the sacrum and coccyx in mammals, reptiles, and birds. While tails are primarily a feature of vertebrates, some invertebrates including scorpions and springtails, as well as snails and slugs, have tail-like appendages that are sometimes referred to as tails.
5-Methylcytosine	5-Methylcytosine is a methylated form of the DNA base cytosine that may be involved in the regulation of gene transcription. When cytosine is methylated, the DNA maintains the same sequence, but the expression of methylated genes can be altered (the study of this is part of the field of epigenetics). 5-Methylcytosine is incorporated in the nucleoside 5-methylcytidine.
Dihydrouridine	Dihydrouridine is a pyrimidine which is the result of adding two hydrogen atoms to a uridine, making it a fully saturated pyrimidine ring with no remaining double bonds. D is found in tRNA and rRNA molecules as a nucleoside; the corresponding nucleobase is 5,6-dihydrouracil. Because it is non-planar, D disturbs the stacking interactions in helices and destabilizes the RNA structure.
Pseudouridine	Pseudouridine is the C-glycoside isomer of the nucleoside uridine, and it is the most prevalent of the over one hundred different modified nucleosides found in RNA. ? is found in all species and in many classes of RNA except mRNA. ? is formed by enzymes called ? synthases, which post-transcriptionally isomerize specific uridine residues in RNA in a process termed pseudouridylation. It is commonly found in tRNA, associated with thymidine and cytosine in the T?C arm and is one of the invariant regions of tRNA.The function of it is not very clear, but it is expected to play a role in association with aminoacyl transferases during their interaction with tRNA, and hence in the initiation of translation.

Uridine

Uridine, a nucleoside, contains an uracil attached to a ribose ring via a ß-N_1-glycosidic bond.

If uracil is attached to a deoxyribose ring, it is known as a deoxyuridine.

Adenylylation

Adenylylation is a posttranslational modification that can occur to molecules such as tyrosine residues. Adenylylation involves a phosphodiester bond between a hydroxyl group of the molecule undergoing adenylylation and the phosphate group of the adenosine monophosphate nucleotide (i.e. adenylic acid).

The degree of adenylylation depends on the ratio of glutamine to a-ketoglutarate: The higher this ratio the more monomers are adenylylated, thereby producing lower activity of glutamine synthetase; the lower the ratio the less monomers are adenylated and the higher activity of glutamine synthetase.

Aminoacyl-tRNA

Aminoacyl-tRNA is tRNA to which its cognated amino acid is chemically bonded (charged). The aa-tRNA, along with some elongation factors, deliver the amino acid to the ribosome for incorporation into the polypeptide chain that is being produced. A specific cognate amino acid is charged or aminoacylated to each tRNA by aminoacyl tRNA synthetase.

Ribosome

The ribosome is a large and complex molecular machine, found within all living cells, that serves as the primary site of biological protein synthesis (translation). Ribosomes link amino acids together in the order specified by messenger RNA (mRNA) molecules. Ribosomes consist of two major subunits--the small ribosomal subunit reads the mRNA, while the large subunit joins amino acids to form a polypeptide chain.

Isoleucine

Isoleucine is an a-amino acid with the chemical formula $HO_2CCH(NH_2)CH(CH_3)CH_2CH_3$. It is an essential amino acid, which means that humans cannot synthesize it, so it must be ingested. Its codons are AUU, AUC and AUA.

With a hydrocarbon side chain, isoleucine is classified as a hydrophobic amino acid.

Phenylalanine

Phenylalanine is an a-amino acid with the formula $C_6H_5CH_2CH(NH_2)COOH$. This essential amino acid is classified as nonpolar because of the hydrophobic nature of the benzyl side chain. - Phenylalanine is an electrically neutral amino acid, one of the twenty common amino acids used to biochemically form proteins, coded for by DNA. The codons for -phenylalanine are UUU and UUC. Phenylalanine is a precursor for tyrosine, the monoamine signaling molecules dopamine, norepinephrine (noradrenaline), and epinephrine (adrenaline), and the skin pigment melanin.

Phenylalanine is found naturally in the breast milk of mammals.

13. Translation,

Proofreading

The term proofreading is used in genetics to refer to the error-correcting processes, first proposed by John Hopfield and Jacques Ninio, involved in DNA replication, immune system specificity, enzyme-substrate recognition among many other processes that require enhanced specificity. The proofreading mechanisms of Hopfield and Ninio are non-equilibrium active processes that consume ATP to enhance specificity of various biochemical reactions.

In bacteria, all three DNA polymerases (I, II, and III) have the ability to proofread, using 3'->5' exonuclease activity.

Serine

Serine is an amino acid with the formula $HO_2CCH(NH_2)CH_2OH$. It is one of the proteinogenic amino acids. Its codons in the genetic code are UCU, UCC, UCA, UCG, AGU and AGC. By virtue of the hydroxyl group, serine is classified as a polar amino acid.

Tyrosine

Tyrosine or 4-hydroxyphenylalanine, is one of the 20 amino acids that are used by cells to synthesize proteins. Its codons are UAC and UAU. It is a non-essential amino acid with a polar side group. The word 'tyrosine' is from the Greek tyri, meaning cheese, as it was first discovered in 1846 by German chemist Justus von Liebig in the protein casein from cheese.

Valine

Valine is an a-amino acid with the chemical formula $HO_2CCH(NH_2)CH(CH_3)_2$. -Valine is one of 20 proteinogenic amino acids. Its codons are GUU, GUC, GUA, and GUG. This essential amino acid is classified as nonpolar.

Cysteine

Cysteine is an a-amino acid with the chemical formula $HO_2CCH(NH_2)CH_2SH$. It is a semi-essential amino acid, which means that it can be biosynthesized in humans. The thiol side chain in cysteine often participates in enzymatic reactions, serving as a nucleophile. The thiol is susceptible to oxidization to give the disulfide derivative cystine, which serves an important structural role in many proteins.

Transcription

Transcription is the first step of gene expression, in which a particular segment of DNA is copied into RNA by the enzyme, RNA polymerase. Both RNA and DNA are nucleic acids, which use base pairs of nucleotides as a complementary language that can be converted back and forth from DNA to RNA by the action of the correct enzymes. During transcription, a DNA sequence is read by an RNA polymerase, which produces a complementary, antiparallel RNA strand.

Peptidyl transferase

The Peptidyl transferase is an aminoacyltransferase as well as the primary enzymatic function of the ribosome, which forms peptide bonds between adjacent amino acids using tRNAs during the translation process of protein biosynthesis.

Peptidyl transferase activity is carried out by the ribosome. Peptidyl transferase activity is not mediated by any ribosomal proteins but by ribosomal RNA (rRNA), a ribozyme.

RNA polymerase

RNA polymerase, also known as DNA-dependent RNA polymerase, is an enzyme that produces RNA. In cells, RNAP is necessary for constructing RNA chains using DNA genes as templates, a process called transcription. RNA polymerase enzymes are essential to life and are found in all organisms and many viruses. In chemical terms, RNAP is a nucleotidyl transferase that polymerizes ribonucleotides at the 3' end of an RNA transcript.

Association

In community ecology and phytosociology an association is a type of ecological community with a predictable species composition, consistent physiognomy which occurs in a particular habitat type. The term was first coined by Alexander von Humboldt and formalised by the International Botanical Congress in 1910.

An association can be viewed as a real, integrated entity shaped either by species interactions or by similar habitat requirements, or it can be viewed as merely a common point along a continuum.

Dissociation

In neuropsychology, dissociation involves identifying the neural substrate of a particular brain function through identification of case studies, neuroimaging, or neuropsychological testing.

Directionality

Directionality, in molecular biology and biochemistry, is the end-to-end chemical orientation of a single strand of nucleic acid. The chemical convention of naming carbon atoms in the nucleotide sugar-ring numerically gives rise to a 5'-end and a 3'-end (usually pronounced 'five prime end' and 'three prime end'). The relative positions of structures along a strand of nucleic acid, including genes and various protein binding sites, are usually noted as being either upstream (towards the 5'-end) or downstream (towards the 3'-end).

Binding site

In biochemistry, a binding site is a region on a protein, DNA, or RNA to which specific other molecules and ions--in this context collectively called ligands--form a chemical bond. An equilibrium exists between unbound ligands and bound ligands.

The term saturation refers to the fraction of total binding sites that are occupied at any given time.

Channel

In physical geography, a channel is a type of landform consisting of the outline of a path of relatively shallow and narrow body of fluid, most commonly the confine of a river, river delta or strait.

Channels can be either natural or human-made. A channel is typically outlined in terms of its bed and banks.

Methionine

Methionine is an a-amino acid with the chemical formula $HO_2CCH(NH_2)CH_2CH_2SCH_3$. This essential amino acid is classified as nonpolar. This amino-acid is coded by the initiation codon AUG which indicates mRNA's coding region where translation into protein begins.

Recruitment

In biology, recruitment occurs when juvenile organisms survive to be added to a population.

13. Translation,

CHAPTER HIGHLIGHTS & NOTES: KEY TERMS, PEOPLE, PLACES, CONCEPTS

Aminopeptidase	Aminopeptidases catalyze the cleavage of amino acids from the amino terminus of protein or peptide substrates. They are widely distributed throughout the animal and plant kingdoms and are found in many subcellular organelles, in cytoplasm, and as membrane components. Aminopeptidases are used in essential cellular functions.
Gene	A gene is a molecular unit of heredity of a living organism. It is widely accepted by the scientific community as a name given to some stretches of deoxyribonucleic acids (DNA) and ribonucleic acids (RNA) that code for a polypeptide or for an RNA chain that has a function in the organism, though there still are controversies about what plays the role of the genetic material. Living beings depend on genes, as they specify all proteins and functional RNA chains.
Eukaryote	A eukaryote is an organism whose cells contain a nucleus and other structures (organelles) enclosed within membranes. Eukaryotes are formally the taxon Eukarya or Eukaryota. The defining membrane-bound structure that sets eukaryotic cells apart from prokaryotic cells is the nucleus, or nuclear envelope, within which the genetic material is carried.
Ternary complex	A Ternary complex refers to a protein complex containing three different molecules which are bound together. In structural biology ternary complex can be used to describe a crystal containing a protein with two small molecules bound, for example cofactor and substrate; or a complex formed between two proteins and a single substrate. In Immunology, a ternary complex can refer to the MHC-Peptide-T-cell-receptor complex formed when T cells recognize epitopes of an antigen.
EF-Tu	EF-Tu is one of the prokaryotic elongation factors. Elongation factors are part of the mechanism that synthesizes new proteins by translation at the ribosome. Individual amino acid links are added to the protein chain by transfer RNA (t-RNA).
Elongation factor	Elongation factors are a set of proteins that are used in protein synthesis in the cell. In the ribosome, they facilitate translational elongation, from the formation of the first peptide bond to the formation of the last one. Elongation is the most rapid step in translation:•in prokaryotes it proceeds at a rate of 15 to 20 amino acids added per second (about 60 nucleotides per second)•in eukaryotes the rate is about two amino acids per second. Elongation factors play a role in orchestrating the events of this process, and in ensuring the 99.99% accuracy of translation at this speed.
Accommodation	Accommodation is the process by which the vertebrate eye changes optical power to maintain a clear image or focus on an object as its distance varies. Accommodation acts like a reflex, but can also be consciously controlled.

Ribozyme	A ribozyme is an RNA molecule that is capable of performing specific biochemical reactions, similar to the action of protein enzymes. The 1981 discovery of ribozymes demonstrated that RNA can be both genetic material (like DNA) and a biological catalyst (like protein enzymes), and contributed to the RNA world hypothesis, which suggests that RNA may have been important in the evolution of prebiotic self-replicating systems. Also termed catalytic RNA, ribozymes function within the ribosome (as part of the large subunit ribosomal RNA) to link amino acids during protein synthesis, and in a variety of RNA processing reactions, including RNA splicing, viral replication, and transfer RNA biosynthesis.
EF-G	EF-G or elongation factor G is one of the prokaryotic elongation factors.
EF-Ts	EF-Ts is one of the prokaryotic elongation factors. EF-Ts serves as the guanine nucleotide exchange factor for EF-Tu (elongation factor thermo unstable), catalyzing the release of guanosine diphosphate from EF-Tu. This enables EF-Tu to bind to a new guanosine triphosphate molecule, release EF-Ts, and go on to catalyze another aminoacyl tRNA addition.
Molecular mimicry	Molecular mimicry is defined as the theoretical possibility that sequence similarities between foreign and self-peptides are sufficient to result in the cross-activation of autoreactive T or B cells by pathogen-derived peptides. Despite the promiscuity of several peptide sequences which can be both foreign and self in nature, a single antibody or TCR (T cell receptor) can be activated by even a few crucial residues which stresses the importance of structural homology in the theory of molecular mimicry. Upon the activation of B or T cells, it is believed that these 'peptide mimic' specific T or B cells can cross-react with self-epitopes, thus leading to tissue pathology (autoimmunity).
Nucleosome	A nucleosome is the basic unit of DNA packaging in eukaryotes, consisting of a segment of DNA wound in sequence around eight histone protein cores. This structure is often compared to thread wrapped around a spool. Nucleosomes form the fundamental repeating units of eukaryotic chromatin, which is used to pack the large eukaryotic genomes into the nucleus while still ensuring appropriate access to it (in mammalian cells approximately 2 m of linear DNA have to be packed into a nucleus of roughly 10 µm diameter).
Ribosome profiling	Ribosome profiling is a technique that uses messenger RNA (mRNA) to determine what proteins are being translated. It produces a “global snapshot” of all the ribosomes active in a cell at a particular moment. Consequently, this enables researchers to identify the location of translation start sites, their distribution, and the speed of the translating ribosomes.

13. Translation,

CHAPTER HIGHLIGHTS & NOTES: KEY TERMS, PEOPLE, PLACES, CONCEPTS

MIMIC

MIMIC, or modular immune in vitro construct, is an artificial system imitating the human immune system. It has applications in vaccine development.

White blood cells, specifically peripheral blood mononuclear cells including T cells and B cells, from human donars are placed in standard tubes containing specially designed tissue constructs made out of collagen, where they develop into small but functioning immune systems.Up to ninety-six individual tubes can be carried on a plate the size of a deck of cards, allowing scientists to use cells from almost a hundred different donors at once.

Recycling

Recycling is a process to change materials into new products to prevent waste of potentially useful materials, reduce the consumption of fresh raw materials, reduce energy usage, reduce air pollution (from incineration) and water pollution (from landfilling) by reducing the need for 'conventional' waste disposal, and lower greenhouse gas emissions as compared to plastic production. Recycling is a key component of modern waste reduction and is the third component of the 'Reduce, Reuse, Recycle' waste hierarchy.

There are some ISO standards related to recycling such as ISO 15270:2008 for plastics waste and ISO 14001:2004 for environmental management control of recycling practice.

Bacteria

Bacteria constitute a large domain or kingdom of prokaryotic microorganisms. Typically a few micrometres in length, bacteria have a wide range of shapes, ranging from spheres to rods and spirals. Bacteria were among the first life forms to appear on Earth, and are present in most habitats on the planet.

Oskar

Oskar is a gene required for the development of the Drosophila embryo. It defines the posterior pole during early embryogenesis.

Ferritin

Ferritin is a ubiquitous intracellular protein that stores iron and releases it in a controlled fashion. The amount of ferritin stored reflects the amount of iron stored. The protein is produced by almost all living organisms, including algae, bacteria, higher plants, and animals.

Marker gene

A marker gene is a gene used in nuclear biology to determine if a nucleic acid sequence has been successfully inserted into an organism's DNA. There are two types of marker genes: a selectable marker and a marker for screening.

Protein

Proteins are large biological molecules consisting of one or more chains of amino acids. Proteins perform a vast array of functions within living organisms, including catalyzing metabolic reactions, replicating DNA, responding to stimuli, and transporting molecules from one location to another. Proteins differ from one another primarily in their sequence of amino acids, which is dictated by the nucleotide sequence of their genes, and which usually results in folding of the protein into a specific three-dimensional structure that determines its activity.

CHAPTER HIGHLIGHTS & NOTES: KEY TERMS, PEOPLE, PLACES, CONCEPTS

Stability	Stability, also known as algorithmic stability, is a notion in computational learning theory of how a machine learning algorithm is perturbed by small changes to its inputs. A stable learning algorithm is one for which the prediction does not change much when the training data is modified slightly. For instance, consider a machine learning algorithm that is being trained to recognize handwritten letters of the alphabet, using 1000 examples of handwritten letters and their labels ('A' to 'Z') as a training set.

CHAPTER QUIZ: KEY TERMS, PEOPLE, PLACES, CONCEPTS

1. _________ is one of the prokaryotic elongation factors. Elongation factors are part of the mechanism that synthesizes new proteins by translation at the ribosome. Individual amino acid links are added to the protein chain by transfer RNA (t-RNA).

a. Cucurmosin
b. Bacteremia
c. EF-Tu
d. Hypercalcaemia

2. _________ is a tyrosine recombinase enzyme derived from the P1 Bacteriophage. The enzyme uses a topoisomerase I like mechanism to carry out site specific recombination events. The enzyme (38kDa) is a member of the Integrase family of site specific recombinase and it is known to catalyse the site specific recombination event between two DNA recognition sites (loxP sites).

a. 2q37 monosomy
b. 5-HTTLPR
c. Cre recombinase
d. Backcrossing

3. _________ constitute a large domain or kingdom of prokaryotic microorganisms. Typically a few micrometres in length, _________ have a wide range of shapes, ranging from spheres to rods and spirals. _________ were among the first life forms to appear on Earth, and are present in most habitats on the planet.

a. Bacteria
b. Horizontal gene transfer
c. R-factor
d. Calicheamicin

4. . _________ is an a-amino acid with the chemical formula $HO_2CCH(NH_2)CH_2SH$. It is a semi-essential amino acid, which means that it can be biosynthesized in humans. The thiol side chain in _________ often participates in enzymatic reactions, serving as a nucleophile.

The thiol is susceptible to oxidization to give the disulfide derivative cystine, which serves an important structural role in many proteins.

a. 3-Hydroxyaspartic acid
b. Chaconine
c. Cysteine
d. Solamargine

5. A _________ is the basic unit of DNA packaging in eukaryotes, consisting of a segment of DNA wound in sequence around eight histone protein cores. This structure is often compared to thread wrapped around a spool.

_________s form the fundamental repeating units of eukaryotic chromatin, which is used to pack the large eukaryotic genomes into the nucleus while still ensuring appropriate access to it (in mammalian cells approximately 2 m of linear DNA have to be packed into a nucleus of roughly 10 μm diameter).

a. Nucleosome
b. Chromatin remodeling
c. DAnCER
d. Genomic imprinting

ANSWER KEY
13. Translation,

1. c
2. c
3. a
4. c
5. a

14. The Genetic Code,

CHAPTER OUTLINE: KEY TERMS, PEOPLE, PLACES, CONCEPTS

Degeneracy

Genetic code

Lesion

Genetics

Chromosome

Hot spot

Order

Transition

Transversion

Polynucleotide phosphorylase

Phenylalanine

Transfer RNA

Missense mutation

Nonsense mutation

Nonsense

Insect

Frameshift mutation

Limb

Prediction

Mutant

Mutation

14. The Genetic Code,

CHAPTER OUTLINE: KEY TERMS, PEOPLE, PLACES, CONCEPTS

Nonsense suppressor

Ribosome

Suppression

Candida albicans

CHAPTER HIGHLIGHTS & NOTES: KEY TERMS, PEOPLE, PLACES, CONCEPTS

Degeneracy	Within biological systems, degeneracy refers to circumstances where structurally dissimilar components/modules/pathways can perform similar functions under certain conditions, but perform distinct functions in other conditions. Degeneracy is thus a relational property that requires comparing the behaviour of two or more components. In particular, if degeneracy is present in a pair of components then there will exist conditions where the pair will appear functionally redundant but other conditions where they will appear functionally distinct.
Genetic code	The genetic code is the set of rules by which information encoded within genetic material is translated into proteins by living cells. Biological decoding is accomplished by the ribosome, which links amino acids in an order specified by mRNA, using transfer RNA (tRNA) molecules to carry amino acids and to read the mRNA three nucleotides at a time. The genetic code is highly similar among all organisms and can be expressed in a simple table with 64 entries.
Lesion	A lesion is any abnormality in the tissue of an organism, usually caused by disease or trauma. Lesion is derived from the Latin word laesio meaning injury.
Genetics	Genetics, a discipline of biology, is the science of genes, heredity, and variation in living organisms. Genetics concerns the process of trait inheritance from parents to offspring, including the molecular structure and function of genes, gene behavior in the context of a cell or organism (e.g. dominance and epigenetics), gene distribution, and variation and change in populations (such as through Genome-Wide Association Studies). Given that genes are universal to living organisms, genetics can be applied to the study of all living systems; including bacteria, plants, animals, and humans.
Chromosome	A chromosome is an organized structure of DNA, protein, and RNA found in cells. It is a single piece of coiled DNA containing many genes, regulatory elements and other nucleotide sequences.

Hot spot

In veterinary medicine, a 'hot spot' (or acute pyoderma, acute moist pyotraumatic dermatitis) is one of the many names for a raw, painful, irritated skin lesion that results in and worsens from a pet (such as a dog or a cat) constantly biting, scratching, chewing, and licking an area of its skin that is irritated or itchy. If it is covered by the dog's hair, the hair holds in the moisture and further irritates it.

It is a patch that appears suddenly and is often bright red, hairless, and scaly looking.

Order

In scientific classification used in biology, the order is•a taxonomic rank used in the classification of organisms. Other well-known ranks are life, domain, kingdom, phylum, class, family, genus, and species, with order fitting in between class and family. An immediately higher rank, superorder, may be added directly above order, while suborder would be a lower rank.•a taxonomic unit, a taxon, in that rank.

Transition

In genetics, a transition is a point mutation that changes a purine nucleotide to another purine or a pyrimidine nucleotide to another pyrimidine (T ? C). Approximately two out of three single nucleotide polymorphisms (SNPs) are transitions.

Transitions can be caused by oxidative deamination and tautomerization.

Transversion

In molecular biology, transversion refers to the substitution of a purine for a pyrimidine or vice versa. It can only be reversed by a spontaneous reversion. Because this type of mutation changes the chemical structure dramatically, the consequences of this change tend to be more drastic than those of transitions.

Polynucleotide phosphorylase

Polynucleotide Phosphorylase is a bifunctional enzyme with a phosphorolytic 3' to 5' exoribonuclease activity and a 3'-terminal oligonucleotide polymerase activity. That is, it dismantles the RNA chain starting at the 3' end and working toward the 5' end. It also synthesizes long, highly heteropolymeric tails in vivo.

Phenylalanine

Phenylalanine is an a-amino acid with the formula $C_6H_5CH_2CH(NH_2)COOH$. This essential amino acid is classified as nonpolar because of the hydrophobic nature of the benzyl side chain. -Phenylalanine is an electrically neutral amino acid, one of the twenty common amino acids used to biochemically form proteins, coded for by DNA. The codons for -phenylalanine are UUU and UUC. Phenylalanine is a precursor for tyrosine, the monoamine signaling molecules dopamine, norepinephrine (noradrenaline), and epinephrine (adrenaline), and the skin pigment melanin.

Phenylalanine is found naturally in the breast milk of mammals.

Transfer RNA

A Transfer RNA is an adaptor molecule composed of RNA, typically 73 to 94 nucleotides in length, that serves as the physical link between the nucleotide sequence of nucleic acids (DNA and RNA) and the amino acid sequence of proteins.

It does this by carrying an amino acid to the protein synthetic machinery of a cell (ribosome) as directed by a three-nucleotide sequence (codon) in a messenger RNA (mRNA). As such, tRNAs are a necessary component of protein translation, the biological synthesis of new proteins according to the genetic code.

Missense mutation

In genetics, a missense mutation is a point mutation in which a single nucleotide change results in a codon that codes for a different amino acid (mutations that change an amino acid to a stop codon are considered nonsense mutations, rather than missense mutations). This can render the resulting protein nonfunctional. Such mutations are responsible for diseases such as Epidermolysis bullosa, sickle-cell disease, and SOD1 mediated ALS (Boillée 2006, p. 39).

Nonsense mutation

In genetics, a nonsense mutation is a point mutation in a sequence of DNA that results in a premature stop codon, or a nonsense codon in the transcribed mRNA, and in a truncated, incomplete, and usually nonfunctional protein product. It differs from a missense mutation, which is a point mutation where a single nucleotide is changed to cause substitution of a different amino acid. Some genetic disorders, such as thalassemia and DMD, result from nonsense mutations.

Nonsense

Nonsense is a communication, via speech, writing, or any other symbolic system, that lacks any coherent meaning. Sometimes in ordinary usage, nonsense is synonymous with absurdity or the ridiculous. Many poets, novelists and songwriters have used nonsense in their works, often creating entire works using it for reasons ranging from pure comic amusement or satire, to illustrating a point about language or reasoning.

Insect

Insects (from Latin insectum, a calque of Greek ??t?µ?? [éntomon], 'cut into sections') are a class of invertebrates within the arthropod phylum that have a chitinous exoskeleton, a three-part body, three pairs of jointed legs, compound eyes and one pair of antennae. They are among the most diverse groups of animals on the planet, including more than a million described species and representing more than half of all known living organisms. The number of extant species is estimated at between six and ten million, and potentially represent over 90% of the differing animal life forms on Earth.

Frameshift mutation

A frameshift mutation is a genetic mutation caused by indels (insertions or deletions) of a number of nucleotides in a DNA sequence that is not divisible by three. Due to the triplet nature of gene expression by codons, the insertion or deletion can change the reading frame (the grouping of the codons), resulting in a completely different translation from the original. The earlier in the sequence the deletion or insertion occurs, the more altered the protein.

Limb

A limb, or extremity, is a jointed, or prehensile (as octopus tentacles or new world monkey tails), appendage of the human or other animal body. In the human body, the upper and lower limbs are commonly called the arms and the legs.

Prediction

A prediction or forecast is a statement about the way things will happen in the future, often but not always based on experience or knowledge. While there is much overlap between prediction and forecast, a prediction may be a statement that some outcome is expected, while a forecast is more specific, and may cover a range of possible outcomes.

Although guaranteed information about the future is in many cases impossible, prediction is necessary to allow plans to be made about possible developments; Howard H. Stevenson writes that prediction in business '... is at least two things: Important and hard.'

Mutant

In biology and especially genetics, a mutant is an individual, organism, or new genetic character, arising or resulting from an instance of mutation, which is a base-pair sequence change within the DNA of a gene or chromosome of an organism resulting in the creation of a new character or trait not found in the wild type. The natural occurrence of genetic mutations is integral to the process of evolution. The study of mutants is an integral part of biology; by understanding the effect that a mutation in a gene has, it is possible to establish the normal function of that gene.

Mutation

In genetics, a mutation is a change of the nucleotide sequence of the genome of an organism, virus, or extrachromosomal genetic element. Mutations result from unrepaired damage to DNA or to RNA genomes (typically caused by radiation or chemical mutagens), errors in the process of replication, or from the insertion or deletion of segments of DNA by mobile genetic elements. Mutations may or may not produce discernible changes in the observable characteristics (phenotype) of an organism.

Nonsense suppressor

A nonsense suppressor is a tRNA mutation that suppresses the protein truncation resulting from a nonsense mutation. The nonsense suppressor is a tRNA gene (from Escherichia coli) which has an anticodon mutated to recognize the nonsense (stop) codon.

As a result, when the ribosome reaches the codon in question, the nonsense suppressor will sometimes bind and incorporate its amino acid (instead of the regular release factor binding and causing termination), allowing translation to continue.

Ribosome

The ribosome is a large and complex molecular machine, found within all living cells, that serves as the primary site of biological protein synthesis (translation). Ribosomes link amino acids together in the order specified by messenger RNA (mRNA) molecules. Ribosomes consist of two major subunits--the small ribosomal subunit reads the mRNA, while the large subunit joins amino acids to form a polypeptide chain.

Suppression

Suppression of an eye is a subconscious adaptation by a person's brain to eliminate the symptoms of disorders of binocular vision such as strabismus, convergence insufficiency and aniseikonia. The brain can eliminate double vision by ignoring the images of one of the eyes. This can lead to Amblyopia.

14. The Genetic Code,

CHAPTER HIGHLIGHTS & NOTES: KEY TERMS, PEOPLE, PLACES, CONCEPTS

Candida albicans	Candida albicans is a diploid fungus that grows both as yeast and filamentous cells and a causal agent of opportunistic oral and genital infections in humans. RNA-binding protein Slr1 was recently discovered to play a role in instigating the hyphal formation and virulence in C. albicans. Systemic fungal infections (fungemias) including those by C. albicans have emerged as important causes of morbidity and mortality in immunocompromised patients (e.g., AIDS, cancer chemotherapy, organ or bone marrow transplantation).

CHAPTER QUIZ: KEY TERMS, PEOPLE, PLACES, CONCEPTS

1. In biology and especially genetics, a _________ is an individual, organism, or new genetic character, arising or resulting from an instance of mutation, which is a base-pair sequence change within the DNA of a gene or chromosome of an organism resulting in the creation of a new character or trait not found in the wild type. The natural occurrence of genetic mutations is integral to the process of evolution. The study of _________s is an integral part of biology; by understanding the effect that a mutation in a gene has, it is possible to establish the normal function of that gene.

   a. Chromosomal polymorphism
   b. Cleft chin
   c. Codominance
   d. Mutant

2. _________ is an a-amino acid with the formula $C_6H_5CH_2CH(NH_2)COOH$. This essential amino acid is classified as nonpolar because of the hydrophobic nature of the benzyl side chain. -_________ is an electrically neutral amino acid, one of the twenty common amino acids used to biochemically form proteins, coded for by DNA. The codons for - _________ are UUU and UUC. _________ is a precursor for tyrosine, the monoamine signaling molecules dopamine, norepinephrine (noradrenaline), and epinephrine (adrenaline), and the skin pigment melanin.

   _________ is found naturally in the breast milk of mammals.

   a. Cysteine
   b. Glutamine
   c. Phenylalanine
   d. Methionine

3. . _________ is a bifunctional enzyme with a phosphorolytic 3' to 5' exoribonuclease activity and a 3'-terminal oligonucleotide polymerase activity. That is, it dismantles the RNA chain starting at the 3' end and working toward the 5' end. It also synthesizes long, highly heteropolymeric tails in vivo.

   a. 2010107G12Rik
   b. 24-dehydrocholesterol reductase

c. 3110001I22Rik
d. Polynucleotide phosphorylase

4. Within biological systems, _________ refers to circumstances where structurally dissimilar components/modules/pathways can perform similar functions under certain conditions, but perform distinct functions in other conditions. _________ is thus a relational property that requires comparing the behaviour of two or more components. In particular, if _________ is present in a pair of components then there will exist conditions where the pair will appear functionally redundant but other conditions where they will appear functionally distinct.

   a. Cursorial
   b. Kleine Feldhofer Grotte
   c. Neanderthal anatomy
   d. Degeneracy

5. The _________ is the set of rules by which information encoded within genetic material is translated into proteins by living cells. Biological decoding is accomplished by the ribosome, which links amino acids in an order specified by mRNA, using transfer RNA (tRNA) molecules to carry amino acids and to read the mRNA three nucleotides at a time. The _________ is highly similar among all organisms and can be expressed in a simple table with 64 entries.

   a. Bacterial one-hybrid system
   b. Baek Sung-hee
   c. Biopolymer
   d. Genetic code

ANSWER KEY
14. The Genetic Code,

1. d
2. c
3. d
4. d
5. d

15. The Origin and Early Evolution of Life,

CHAPTER OUTLINE: KEY TERMS, PEOPLE, PLACES, CONCEPTS

- Evolution
- Origin
- Cytokinesis
- Darwin
- Mycoplasma
- Saccharomyces cerevisiae
- Self-replication
- Clay
- Murchison meteorite
- RNA world hypothesis
- RNA polymerase
- Discovery
- Ligase ribozyme
- Lipid
- Life

Evolution	Evolution is a 2001 documentary series by the American broadcaster Public Broadcasting Service and WGBH on evolutionary biology. The spokespeople for the series were Jane Goodall (overall spokesperson), Kenneth R. Miller and Stephen Jay Gould (science spokespeople), Eugenie C. Scott (education spokesperson), Arthur Peacocke and Arnold Thomas (religious spokespeople). The series was narrated by the Irish actor Liam Neeson.
Origin	The anatomical origin is a concept used when describing muscles, tendons, ligaments, nerves, and blood and lymph vessels. While it often has a slightly different meaning depending on which kind of origin is referred to, it is generally used to explain the relative location of the anatomical structure in question. It is not to be understood in a temporal/ontogenetical sense.
Cytokinesis	Cytokinesis (from the greek cyto- and kinesis (motion, movement)) is the process in which the cytoplasm of a single eukaryotic cell is divided to form two daughter cells. It usually initiates during the late stages of mitosis, and sometimes meiosis, splitting a mitotic cell in two, to ensure that chromosome number is maintained from one generation to the next. In animal cells, one notable exception to the normal process of cytokinesis is oogenesis (the creation of an ovum in the ovarian follicle of the ovary), where the ovum takes almost all the cytoplasm and organelles, leaving very little for the resulting polar bodies, which then die.
Darwin	The darwin is a unit of evolutionary change, defined by J.B.S. Haldane in 1949. One darwin is defined to be an e-fold (about 2.718) change in a trait over one million years. Haldane named the unit after Charles Darwin.
Mycoplasma	Mycoplasma refers to a genus of bacteria that lack a cell wall. Without a cell wall, they are unaffected by many common antibiotics such as penicillin or other beta-lactam antibiotics that target cell wall synthesis. They can be parasitic or saprotrophic.
Saccharomyces cerevisiae	Saccharomyces cerevisiae is a species of yeast. It is perhaps the most useful yeast, having been instrumental to winemaking, baking and brewing since ancient times. It is believed that it was originally isolated from the skin of grapes .
Self-replication	Self-replication is any behavior of a dynamical system that yields construction of an identical copy of itself. Biological cells, given suitable environments, reproduce by cell division. During cell division, DNA is replicated and can be transmitted to offspring during reproduction.
Clay	Clay is a general term including many combinations of one or more clay minerals with traces of metal oxides and organic matter. Geologic clay deposits are mostly composed of phyllosilicate minerals containing variable amounts of water trapped in the mineral structure.
Murchison meteorite	The Murchison meteorite is named after Murchison, Victoria, in Australia.

15. The Origin and Early Evolution of Life,

CHAPTER HIGHLIGHTS & NOTES: KEY TERMS, PEOPLE, PLACES, CONCEPTS

RNA world hypothesis	The RNA world hypothesis proposes that self-replicating ribonucleic acid molecules were precursors to current life, which is based on deoxyribonucleic acid (DNA), RNA and proteins. RNA stores genetic information like DNA, and catalyzes chemical reactions like an enzyme protein. It may, therefore, have played a major step in the evolution of cellular life.
RNA polymerase	RNA polymerase, also known as DNA-dependent RNA polymerase, is an enzyme that produces RNA. In cells, RNAP is necessary for constructing RNA chains using DNA genes as templates, a process called transcription. RNA polymerase enzymes are essential to life and are found in all organisms and many viruses. In chemical terms, RNAP is a nucleotidyl transferase that polymerizes ribonucleotides at the 3' end of an RNA transcript.
Discovery	Discovery is the act of detecting something new, or something 'old' that had been unknown. With reference to science and academic disciplines, discovery is the observation of new phenomena, new actions, or new events and providing new reasoning to explain the knowledge gathered through such observations with previously acquired knowledge from abstract thought and everyday experiences. Visual discoveries are often called sightings.
Ligase ribozyme	The RNA Ligase ribozyme was the first of several types of synthetic ribozymes produced by in vitro evolution and selection techniques. They are an important class of ribozymes because they catalyze the assembly of RNA fragments into phosphodiester RNA polymers, a reaction required of all extant nucleic acid polymerases and thought to be required for any self-replicating molecule. Ideas that the origin of life may have involved the first self-replicating molecules being ribozymes are called RNA World hypotheses.
Lipid	Lipids are a group of naturally occurring molecules that include fats, waxes, sterols, fat-soluble vitamins, monoglycerides, diglycerides, triglycerides, phospholipids, and others. The main biological functions of lipids include storing energy, signaling, and acting as structural components of cell membranes. Lipids have applications in the cosmetic and food industries as well as in nanotechnology.
Life	Life is a characteristic that distinguishes objects that have signaling and self-sustaining processes from those that do not, either because such functions have ceased, or else because they lack such functions and are classified as inanimate. Biology is the science concerned with the study of life. Any contiguous living system is called an organism.

1. _________ is any behavior of a dynamical system that yields construction of an identical copy of itself. Biological cells, given suitable environments, reproduce by cell division. During cell division, DNA is replicated and can be transmitted to offspring during reproduction.

   a. Self-replication
   b. Biochemical cascade
   c. Biocommunication
   d. Bioconjugation

2. The RNA _________ was the first of several types of synthetic ribozymes produced by in vitro evolution and selection techniques. They are an important class of ribozymes because they catalyze the assembly of RNA fragments into phosphodiester RNA polymers, a reaction required of all extant nucleic acid polymerases and thought to be required for any self-replicating molecule. Ideas that the origin of life may have involved the first self-replicating molecules being ribozymes are called RNA World hypotheses.

   a. Bacillaceae-1 RNA motif
   b. Bacillus-plasmid RNA motif
   c. Bacterial small RNA
   d. Ligase ribozyme

3. _________ is a characteristic that distinguishes objects that have signaling and self-sustaining processes from those that do not, either because such functions have ceased, or else because they lack such functions and are classified as inanimate. Biology is the science concerned with the study of _________.

   Any contiguous living system is called an organism.

   a. Biological system
   b. Biosphere
   c. Life
   d. Developmental systems theory

4. _________ is a 2001 documentary series by the American broadcaster Public Broadcasting Service and WGBH on evolutionary biology.

   The spokespeople for the series were Jane Goodall (overall spokesperson), Kenneth R. Miller and Stephen Jay Gould (science spokespeople), Eugenie C. Scott (education spokesperson), Arthur Peacocke and Arnold Thomas (religious spokespeople). The series was narrated by the Irish actor Liam Neeson.

   a. Biological dispersal
   b. Cellularization
   c. Evolution
   d. Gordo

5. The anatomical _________ is a concept used when describing muscles, tendons, ligaments, nerves, and blood and lymph vessels. While it often has a slightly different meaning depending on which kind of _________ is referred to, it is generally used to explain the relative location of the anatomical structure in question. It is not to be understood in a temporal/ontogenetical sense.

   a. Origin
   b. Basion
   c. Body orifice
   d. Canal

ANSWER KEY
15. The Origin and Early Evolution of Life,

---

1. a
2. d
3. c
4. c
5. a

---

16. Transcriptional Regulation in Prokaryotes,

CHAPTER OUTLINE: KEY TERMS, PEOPLE, PLACES, CONCEPTS

- Transcriptional regulation
- Snail
- Promoter
- Transcription
- Basal
- Edman degradation
- RNA polymerase
- Recruitment
- Cooperative binding
- Ligase ribozyme
- Operator
- Polymerase
- Activator
- Allosteric regulation
- Gene
- Antitermination
- Lactose
- Lactose permease
- Glucose
- Candida albicans
- Binding site

16. Transcriptional Regulation in Prokaryotes,

CHAPTER OUTLINE: KEY TERMS, PEOPLE, PLACES, CONCEPTS

Lac operon

Mutant

Operon

Logic

Allolactose

Candida

Protein

Heat shock

Infection

Bacteriophage

Arabinose

Expression vector

Quorum sensing

Prophage

Evolution

Gene expression

Regulation of gene expression

Chromosome segregation

Function

Cleavage

SOS response

CHAPTER OUTLINE: KEY TERMS, PEOPLE, PLACES, CONCEPTS

Multiplicity of infection

Retinitis pigmentosa

CHAPTER HIGHLIGHTS & NOTES: KEY TERMS, PEOPLE, PLACES, CONCEPTS

Transcriptional regulation	Transcriptional regulation is the change in gene expression levels by altering transcription rates.
Snail	Snail is a common name that is applied most often to land snails, terrestrial pulmonate gastropod molluscs. However, the common name 'snail' is also applied to most of the members of the molluscan class Gastropoda that have a coiled shell that is large enough for the animal to retract completely into. When the word 'snail' is used in this most general sense, it includes not just land snails but also thousands of species of sea snails and freshwater snails.
Promoter	In genetics, a promoter is a region of DNA that initiates transcription of a particular gene. Promoters are located near the genes they transcribe, on the same strand and upstream on the DNA (towards the 3' region of the anti-sense strand, also called template strand and non-coding strand). Promoters can be about 100-1000 base pairs long.
Transcription	Transcription is the first step of gene expression, in which a particular segment of DNA is copied into RNA by the enzyme, RNA polymerase. Both RNA and DNA are nucleic acids, which use base pairs of nucleotides as a complementary language that can be converted back and forth from DNA to RNA by the action of the correct enzymes. During transcription, a DNA sequence is read by an RNA polymerase, which produces a complementary, antiparallel RNA strand.
Basal	In phylogenetics, a basal clade is the earliest clade to branch in a larger clade; it appears at the base of a cladogram. A basal group forms an outgroup to the rest of the clade, such as in the following example: The word 'basal' is preferred to the term 'primitive', which may carry false connotations of inferiority or a lack of complexity. The term basal can only be correctly applied to clades of organisms, not to individual traits possessed by the organisms--although it can be misused in this manner in technical literature.

16. Transcriptional Regulation in Prokaryotes,

CHAPTER HIGHLIGHTS & NOTES: KEY TERMS, PEOPLE, PLACES, CONCEPTS

Edman degradation	Edman degradation, developed by Pehr Edman, is a method of sequencing amino acids in a peptide. In this method, the amino-terminal residue is labeled and cleaved from the peptide without disrupting the peptide bonds between other amino acid residues.
RNA polymerase	RNA polymerase, also known as DNA-dependent RNA polymerase, is an enzyme that produces RNA. In cells, RNAP is necessary for constructing RNA chains using DNA genes as templates, a process called transcription. RNA polymerase enzymes are essential to life and are found in all organisms and many viruses. In chemical terms, RNAP is a nucleotidyl transferase that polymerizes ribonucleotides at the 3' end of an RNA transcript.
Recruitment	In biology, recruitment occurs when juvenile organisms survive to be added to a population. The term is generally used to refer to a stage whereby the organisms are settled and able to be detected by an observer.
Cooperative binding	Molecular binding is an interaction between molecules that results in a stable association between those molecules. Cooperative binding occurs if the number of binding sites of a macromolecule that are occupied by a specific type of ligand is a non-linear function of this ligand's concentration. This can be due, for instance, to an affinity for the ligand that depends on the amount of ligand bound.
Ligase ribozyme	The RNA Ligase ribozyme was the first of several types of synthetic ribozymes produced by in vitro evolution and selection techniques. They are an important class of ribozymes because they catalyze the assembly of RNA fragments into phosphodiester RNA polymers, a reaction required of all extant nucleic acid polymerases and thought to be required for any self-replicating molecule. Ideas that the origin of life may have involved the first self-replicating molecules being ribozymes are called RNA World hypotheses.
Operator	In genetics, an operator is a segment of DNA to which a transcription factor protein binds. It is classically defined in the lac operon as a segment between the promoter and the genes of the operon. In the case of a repressor, the repressor protein physically obstructs the RNA polymerase from transcribing the genes.
Polymerase	A polymerase is an enzyme whose central biological function is the synthesis of polymers of nucleic acids. DNA polymerase and RNA polymerase are used to assemble DNA and RNA molecules, respectively, generally by copying a DNA or RNA template strand using base-pairing interactions. It is an accident of history that the enzymes responsible for the generation of other biopolymers are not also referred to as polymerases.
Activator	A transcriptional activator is a protein that increases gene transcription of a gene or set of genes. Most activators are DNA-binding proteins.

Allosteric regulation	In biochemistry, allosteric regulation is the regulation of an enzyme or other protein by binding an effector molecule at the protein's allosteric site . Effectors that enhance the protein's activity are referred to as allosteric activators, whereas those that decrease the protein's activity are called allosteric inhibitors. The term allostery comes from the Greek allos (?????), 'other', and stereos (ste?e??), 'solid (object)', in reference to the fact that the regulatory site of an allosteric protein is physically distinct from its active site.
Gene	A gene is a molecular unit of heredity of a living organism. It is widely accepted by the scientific community as a name given to some stretches of deoxyribonucleic acids (DNA) and ribonucleic acids (RNA) that code for a polypeptide or for an RNA chain that has a function in the organism, though there still are controversies about what plays the role of the genetic material. Living beings depend on genes, as they specify all proteins and functional RNA chains.
Antitermination	Antitermination is the prokaryotic cell's aid to fix premature termination of RNA synthesis during the transcription of RNA. It occurs when the RNA polymerase ignores the termination signal, and it provides a mechanism whereby one or more genes at the end of an operon can be switched either on or off, depending on the polymerase either recognizing or not recognizing the termination signal. Antitermination is used by some phages to regulate progression from one stage of gene expression to the next. The lambda gene N, codes for an antitermination protein (pN) that is necessary to allow RNA polymerase to read through the terminators located at the ends of the immediate early genes.
Lactose	Lactose is a disaccharide sugar derived from galactose and glucose that is found in milk. Lactose makes up around 0~8% of milk (by weight), although the amount varies among species and individuals. It is extracted from sweet or sour whey.
Lactose permease	Lactose permease is a membrane protein which is a member of the major facilitator superfamily. Lactose permease can be classified as a symporter, which uses the gradient of H+ towards the cell to transport lactose in the same direction into the cell. The protein has twelve transmembrane helices and exhibits an internal two-fold symmetry, relating the N-terminal six helices onto the C-terminal helices.
Glucose	Glucose, meaning 'sweet'. The suffix '-ose' denotes a sugar.
Candida albicans	Candida albicans is a diploid fungus that grows both as yeast and filamentous cells and a causal agent of opportunistic oral and genital infections in humans. RNA-binding protein Slr1 was recently discovered to play a role in instigating the hyphal formation and virulence in C. albicans. Systemic fungal infections (fungemias) including those by C. albicans have emerged as important causes of morbidity and mortality in immunocompromised patients (e.g., AIDS, cancer chemotherapy, organ or bone marrow transplantation).

16. Transcriptional Regulation in Prokaryotes,

CHAPTER HIGHLIGHTS & NOTES: KEY TERMS, PEOPLE, PLACES, CONCEPTS

Binding site

In biochemistry, a binding site is a region on a protein, DNA, or RNA to which specific other molecules and ions--in this context collectively called ligands--form a chemical bond. An equilibrium exists between unbound ligands and bound ligands.

The term saturation refers to the fraction of total binding sites that are occupied at any given time.

Lac operon

The lac operon is an operon required for the transport and metabolism of lactose in Escherichia coli and some other enteric bacteria. It consists of three adjacent structural genes, lacZ, lacY, and lacA. The genes encode ß-galactosidase, lactose permease, and thiogalactoside transacetylase (or galactoside O-acetyltransferase), respectively.

In its natural environment, the lac operon allows for the effective digestion of lactose.

Mutant

In biology and especially genetics, a mutant is an individual, organism, or new genetic character, arising or resulting from an instance of mutation, which is a base-pair sequence change within the DNA of a gene or chromosome of an organism resulting in the creation of a new character or trait not found in the wild type. The natural occurrence of genetic mutations is integral to the process of evolution. The study of mutants is an integral part of biology; by understanding the effect that a mutation in a gene has, it is possible to establish the normal function of that gene.

Operon

In genetics, an operon is a functioning unit of genomic DNA containing a cluster of genes under the control of a single regulatory signal or promoter. The genes are transcribed together into an mRNA strand and either translated together in the cytoplasm, or undergo trans-splicing to create monocistronic mRNAs that are translated separately, i.e. several strands of mRNA that each encode a single gene product. The result of this is that the genes contained in the operon are either expressed together or not at all.

Logic

Logic has two meanings: first, it describes the use of valid reasoning in some activity; second, it names the normative study of reasoning or a branch thereof. In the latter sense, it features most prominently in the subjects of philosophy, mathematics, and computer science.

Logic was studied in several ancient civilizations, including India, China, Persia and Greece.

Allolactose

Allolactose is a disaccharide similar to lactose. It consists of the monosaccharides -galactose and -glucose linked through a ß1-6 glycosidic linkage instead of the ß1-4 linkage of lactose. It may arise from the occasional transglycosylation of lactose by ß-galactosidase.

Candida

Candida is a genus of yeasts and is currently the most common cause of fungal infections worldwide. Many species are harmless commensals or endosymbionts of hosts including humans; however, when mucosal barriers are disrupted or the immune system is compromised they can invade and cause disease.

Protein	Proteins are large biological molecules consisting of one or more chains of amino acids. Proteins perform a vast array of functions within living organisms, including catalyzing metabolic reactions, replicating DNA, responding to stimuli, and transporting molecules from one location to another. Proteins differ from one another primarily in their sequence of amino acids, which is dictated by the nucleotide sequence of their genes, and which usually results in folding of the protein into a specific three-dimensional structure that determines its activity.
Heat shock	In biochemistry, heat shock is the effect of subjecting a cell to a higher temperature than that of the ideal body temperature of the organism from which the cell line was derived.
Infection	Infection is the invasion of a host organism's bodily tissues by disease-causing organisms, their multiplication, and the reaction of host tissues to these organisms and the toxins they produce. Infections are caused by infectious agents such as viruses, viroids, and prions, microorganisms such as bacteria, nematodes such as roundworms and pinworms, arthropods such as ticks, mites, fleas, and lice, fungi such as ringworm, and other macroparasites such as tapeworms. Hosts can fight infections using their immune system.
Bacteriophage	A bacteriophage is a virus that infects and replicates within bacteria. The term is derived from 'bacteria' and the Greek fa?e?? phagein 'to devour'. Bacteriophages are composed of proteins that encapsulate a DNA or RNA genome, and may have relatively simple or elaborate structures.
Arabinose	Arabinose is an aldopentose - a monosaccharide containing five carbon atoms, and including an aldehyde functional group. For biosynthetic reasons, most saccharides are almost always more abundant in nature as the '-form, or structurally analogous to -glyceraldehyde. However, -arabinose is in fact more common than -arabinose in nature and is found in nature as a component of biopolymers such as hemicellulose and pectin.
Expression vector	An expression vector, otherwise known as an expression construct, is usually a plasmid or virus designed for protein expression in cells. The vector is used to introduce a specific gene into a target cell, and can commandeer the cell's mechanism for protein synthesis to produce the protein encoded by the gene. The plasmid is engineered to contain regulatory sequences that act as enhancer and promoter regions and lead to efficient transcription of the gene carried on the expression vector.
Quorum sensing	Quorum sensing is a system of stimulus and response correlated to population density. Many species of bacteria use quorum sensing to coordinate gene expression according to the density of their local population. In similar fashion, some social insects use quorum sensing to determine where to nest.

16. Transcriptional Regulation in Prokaryotes,

Prophage

A prophage is a phage genome inserted and integrated into the circular bacterial DNA chromosome or existing as an extrachromosomal plasmid. This is a latent form of a bacteriophage, in which the viral genes are present in the bacterium without causing disruption of the bacterial cell.

Upon detection of host cell damage, such as UV light or certain chemicals, the prophage is excised from the bacterial chromosome in a process called prophage induction.

Evolution

Evolution is a 2001 documentary series by the American broadcaster Public Broadcasting Service and WGBH on evolutionary biology.

The spokespeople for the series were Jane Goodall (overall spokesperson), Kenneth R. Miller and Stephen Jay Gould (science spokespeople), Eugenie C. Scott (education spokesperson), Arthur Peacocke and Arnold Thomas (religious spokespeople). The series was narrated by the Irish actor Liam Neeson.

Gene expression

Gene expression is the process by which information from a gene is used in the synthesis of a functional gene product. These products are often proteins, but in non-protein coding genes such as ribosomal RNA (rRNA), transfer RNA (tRNA) or small nuclear RNA (snRNA) genes, the product is a functional RNA. The process of gene expression is used by all known life - eukaryotes (including multicellular organisms), prokaryotes (bacteria and archaea), possibly induced by viruses - to generate the macromolecular machinery for life. Several steps in the gene expression process may be modulated, including the transcription, RNA splicing, translation, and post-translational modification of a protein.

Regulation of gene expression

Regulation of gene expression includes a wide range of mechanisms that are used by cells to increase or decrease the production of specific gene products (protein or RNA), and is informally termed gene regulation. Sophisticated programs of gene expression are widely observed in biology, for example to trigger developmental pathways, respond to environmental stimuli, or adapt to new food sources. Virtually any step of gene expression can be modulated, from transcriptional initiation, to RNA processing, and to the post-translational modification of a protein.

Chromosome segregation

Chromosome segregation is a step in cell reproduction or division, where chromosomes pair off with their similar homologous chromosome. In mitosis, a complete copy of each one is made. In meiosis, one chromosome from each pair migrates to opposite ends of the cell and the genes are split to make a gamete.

Function

A function is the reason some object or process occurred in a system that evolved through a process of selection or Natural selection. Thus, function refers forward from the object or process, along some chain of causation, to the goal or success. Compare this to the mechanism of the object or process, which looks backward along some chain of causation, explaining how the feature occurred.

CHAPTER HIGHLIGHTS & NOTES: KEY TERMS, PEOPLE, PLACES, CONCEPTS

Cleavage	Cleavage, anatomically known as the intermammary cleft or the intermammary sulcus, is the space between a woman's breasts lying over the sternum. In popular culture, it is often defined by garments with low necklines, like ball gowns, evening gowns, lingerie and swimwear that expose or highlight cleavage. Most people in Western culture, both male and female, consider breasts an important aspect of femininity and many women use cleavage to enhance their physical and sexual attractiveness and to improve their sense of femininity.
SOS response	The SOS response is a global response to DNA damage in which the cell cycle is arrested and DNA repair and mutagenesis are induced. The system involves the RecA protein (Rad51 in eukaryotes). The RecA protein, stimulated by single-stranded DNA, is involved in the inactivation of the LexA repressor thereby inducing the response.
Multiplicity of infection	In virology, the multiplicity of infection is the ratio of infectious agents to infection targets (e.g. cell). For example, when referring to a group of cells inoculated with infectious virus particles, the multiplicity of infection or Multiplicity of infection is the ratio of the number of infectious virus particles to the number of target cells present in a defined space.
Retinitis pigmentosa	Retinitis pigmentosa is an inherited, degenerative eye disease that causes severe vision impairment and often blindness. The progress of RP is not consistent. Some people will exhibit symptoms from infancy, others may not notice symptoms until later in life.

CHAPTER QUIZ: KEY TERMS, PEOPLE, PLACES, CONCEPTS

1. _________ is a 2001 documentary series by the American broadcaster Public Broadcasting Service and WGBH on evolutionary biology.

   The spokespeople for the series were Jane Goodall (overall spokesperson), Kenneth R. Miller and Stephen Jay Gould (science spokespeople), Eugenie C. Scott (education spokesperson), Arthur Peacocke and Arnold Thomas (religious spokespeople). The series was narrated by the Irish actor Liam Neeson.

   a. Evolution
   b. Cellularization
   c. Decellularization
   d. Gordo

2. . _________ is a disaccharide similar to lactose. It consists of the monosaccharides -galactose and -glucose linked through a ß1-6 glycosidic linkage instead of the ß1-4 linkage of lactose.

It may arise from the occasional transglycosylation of lactose by ß-galactosidase.

a. Bowel infarction
b. Cardia
c. Allolactose
d. Coelomic epithelium

3. A _________ is the reason some object or process occurred in a system that evolved through a process of selection or Natural selection. Thus, _________ refers forward from the object or process, along some chain of causation, to the goal or success. Compare this to the mechanism of the object or process, which looks backward along some chain of causation, explaining how the feature occurred.

a. Function
b. Biodilution
c. Biodiversity
d. Biofact

4. _________ includes a wide range of mechanisms that are used by cells to increase or decrease the production of specific gene products (protein or RNA), and is informally termed gene regulation. Sophisticated programs of gene expression are widely observed in biology, for example to trigger developmental pathways, respond to environmental stimuli, or adapt to new food sources. Virtually any step of gene expression can be modulated, from transcriptional initiation, to RNA processing, and to the post-translational modification of a protein.

a. Binding site
b. Regulation of gene expression
c. Catabolite activator protein
d. CccDNA

5. _________ is a disaccharide sugar derived from ga_________ and glucose that is found in milk. _________ makes up around 0~8% of milk (by weight), although the amount varies among species and individuals. It is extracted from sweet or sour whey.

a. Cellobiose
b. Gentiobiose
c. Kojibiose
d. Lactose

ANSWER KEY
16. Transcriptional Regulation in Prokaryotes,

1. a
2. c
3. a
4. b
5. d

You can take the complete Chapter Practice Test

for 16. Transcriptional Regulation in Prokaryotes,
on all key terms, persons, places, and concepts.

Online 99 Cents

http://www.JustTheFacts101.com

17. Transcriptional Regulation in Eukaryotes,

CHAPTER OUTLINE: KEY TERMS, PEOPLE, PLACES, CONCEPTS

- DNA replication
- Eukaryote
- Transcriptional regulation
- Gene silencing
- Insulator
- DNA-binding domain
- Activator
- Leucine zipper
- Zinc finger
- HMG protein
- Gene
- Chromatin
- Chromatin immunoprecipitation
- Immunoprecipitation
- Histone acetyltransferase
- Nucleosome
- Recruitment
- Bromodomain
- RNA polymerase
- Saga
- Elongation factor

17. Transcriptional Regulation in Eukaryotes,

CHAPTER OUTLINE: KEY TERMS, PEOPLE, PLACES, CONCEPTS

- Ligase ribozyme
- Phosphorylation
- Ferritin
- Promoter
- Cohesin
- Enhancer
- Heterochromatin
- Locus control region
- Blue
- Cooperative binding
- Coactivator
- Evolution
- Histone
- Protein
- Signal transduction
- Cell surface receptor
- Genetic code
- Centromere
- Euchromatin
- Histone methyltransferase
- RNA interference

17. Transcriptional Regulation in Eukaryotes,

CHAPTER OUTLINE: KEY TERMS, PEOPLE, PLACES, CONCEPTS

- Yeast
- Hox gene
- Variegation
- White
- Methylation
- Mutation
- DNA methylation
- Imprinting
- Growth factor
- Chromosome segregation
- Inheritance

CHAPTER HIGHLIGHTS & NOTES: KEY TERMS, PEOPLE, PLACES, CONCEPTS

DNA replication	DNA replication is the process of producing two identical copies from one original DNA molecule. This biological process occurs in all living organisms and is the basis for biological inheritance. DNA is composed of two strands and each strand of the original DNA molecule serves as template for the production of the complementary strand, a process referred to as semiconservative replication.
Eukaryote	A eukaryote is an organism whose cells contain a nucleus and other structures (organelles) enclosed within membranes. Eukaryotes are formally the taxon Eukarya or Eukaryota. The defining membrane-bound structure that sets eukaryotic cells apart from prokaryotic cells is the nucleus, or nuclear envelope, within which the genetic material is carried.

17. Transcriptional Regulation in Eukaryotes,

CHAPTER HIGHLIGHTS & NOTES: KEY TERMS, PEOPLE, PLACES, CONCEPTS

Gene silencing
Gene silencing is a general term describing epigenetic processes of gene regulation. The term gene silencing is generally used to describe the 'switching off' of a gene by a mechanism other than genetic modification. That is, a gene which would be expressed ('turned on') under normal circumstances is switched off by machinery in the cell.

Insulator
An insulator is a genetic boundary element that blocks the interaction between enhancers and promoters. Insulators therefore determine the set of genes an enhancer can influence. The need for them arises where two adjacent genes on a chromosome have very different transcription patterns, and it is critical that the inducing or repressing mechanisms of one do not interfere with the neighbouring gene.

DNA-binding domain
A DNA-binding domain is an independently folded protein domain that contains at least one motif that recognizes double- or single-stranded DNA. A DNA binding domain can recognize a specific DNA sequence (a recognition sequence) or have a general affinity to DNA. Some DNA-binding domains may also include nucleic acids in their folded structure.

Activator
A transcriptional activator is a protein that increases gene transcription of a gene or set of genes.

Most activators are DNA-binding proteins.

Most activators function by binding sequence-specifically to a DNA site located in or near a promoter and making protein-protein interactions with the general transcription machinery, thereby facilitating the binding of the general transcription machinery to the promoter.

Leucine zipper
A leucine zipper, aka leucine scissors, is a common three-dimensional structural motif in proteins. These motifs are usually found as part of a DNA-binding domain in various transcription factors, and are therefore involved in regulating gene expression. Leucine zippers are found in both eukaryotic and prokaryotic regulatory proteins, but are mainly a feature of eukaryotes.

Zinc finger
A zinc finger is a small protein structural motif that is characterized by the coordination of one or more zinc ions in order to stabilize the fold. Originally coined to describe the finger-like appearance of a hypothesized structure from Xenopus laevis transcription factor IIIA, the zinc finger name has now come to encompass a wide variety of differing protein structures.

Proteins that contain zinc fingers (zinc finger proteins) are classified into several different structural families.

HMG protein
An HMG protein is a protein involved with chromatin structure. They endow the chromosome with nuclease sensitivity. They also recruit transcription factors to bind to enhancers.

Gene
A gene is a molecular unit of heredity of a living organism.

It is widely accepted by the scientific community as a name given to some stretches of deoxyribonucleic acids (DNA) and ribonucleic acids (RNA) that code for a polypeptide or for an RNA chain that has a function in the organism, though there still are controversies about what plays the role of the genetic material. Living beings depend on genes, as they specify all proteins and functional RNA chains.

Chromatin — Chromatin is the combination of DNA and proteins that make up the contents of the nucleus of a cell. The primary functions of chromatin are 1) to package DNA into a smaller volume to fit in the cell, 2) to strengthen the DNA to allow mitosis, 3) to prevent DNA damage, and 4) to control gene expression and DNA replication. The primary protein components of chromatin are histones that compact the DNA. Chromatin is only found in eukaryotic cells: prokaryotic cells have a very different organization of their DNA which is referred to as a genophore (a chromosome without chromatin).

Chromatin immunoprecipitation — Chromatin Immunoprecipitation is a type of immunoprecipitation experimental technique used to investigate the interaction between proteins and DNA in the cell. It aims to determine whether specific proteins are associated with specific genomic regions, such as transcription factors on promoters or other DNA binding sites, and possibly defining cistromes. ChIP also aims to determine the specific location in the genome that various histone modifications are associated with, indicating the target of the histone modifiers.

Immunoprecipitation — Immunoprecipitation is the technique of precipitating a protein antigen out of solution using an antibody that specifically binds to that particular protein. This process can be used to isolate and concentrate a particular protein from a sample containing many thousands of different proteins. Immunoprecipitation requires that the antibody be coupled to a solid substrate at some point in the procedure.

Histone acetyltransferase — Histone acetyltransferases are enzymes that acetylate conserved lysine amino acids on histone proteins by transferring an acetyl group from acetyl CoA to form e-N-acetyllysine. DNA is wrapped around histones, and by transferring an acetyl group to the histones, genes can be turned on and off. Histone acetylation increases gene expression.

Nucleosome — A nucleosome is the basic unit of DNA packaging in eukaryotes, consisting of a segment of DNA wound in sequence around eight histone protein cores. This structure is often compared to thread wrapped around a spool.

Nucleosomes form the fundamental repeating units of eukaryotic chromatin, which is used to pack the large eukaryotic genomes into the nucleus while still ensuring appropriate access to it (in mammalian cells approximately 2 m of linear DNA have to be packed into a nucleus of roughly 10 μm diameter).

Recruitment — In biology, recruitment occurs when juvenile organisms survive to be added to a population.

17. Transcriptional Regulation in Eukaryotes,

CHAPTER HIGHLIGHTS & NOTES: KEY TERMS, PEOPLE, PLACES, CONCEPTS

Bromodomain	A bromodomain is a protein domain that recognizes acetylated lysine residues such as those on the N-terminal tails of histones. This recognition is often a prerequisite for protein-histone association and chromatin remodeling. The domain itself adopts an all-a protein fold, a bundle of four alpha helices.
RNA polymerase	RNA polymerase, also known as DNA-dependent RNA polymerase, is an enzyme that produces RNA. In cells, RNAP is necessary for constructing RNA chains using DNA genes as templates, a process called transcription. RNA polymerase enzymes are essential to life and are found in all organisms and many viruses. In chemical terms, RNAP is a nucleotidyl transferase that polymerizes ribonucleotides at the 3' end of an RNA transcript.
Saga	Saga cheese is a mix of blue cheese and brie, originated in Denmark, a creamy, blue-veined cheese with a white-mould rind. Saga is a very mild blue-veined cheese. It comes with a delicate blue mold, that may not appear in other varieties of blue cheeses.
Elongation factor	Elongation factors are a set of proteins that are used in protein synthesis in the cell. In the ribosome, they facilitate translational elongation, from the formation of the first peptide bond to the formation of the last one. Elongation is the most rapid step in translation:•in prokaryotes it proceeds at a rate of 15 to 20 amino acids added per second (about 60 nucleotides per second)•in eukaryotes the rate is about two amino acids per second. Elongation factors play a role in orchestrating the events of this process, and in ensuring the 99.99% accuracy of translation at this speed.
Ligase ribozyme	The RNA Ligase ribozyme was the first of several types of synthetic ribozymes produced by in vitro evolution and selection techniques. They are an important class of ribozymes because they catalyze the assembly of RNA fragments into phosphodiester RNA polymers, a reaction required of all extant nucleic acid polymerases and thought to be required for any self-replicating molecule. Ideas that the origin of life may have involved the first self-replicating molecules being ribozymes are called RNA World hypotheses.
Phosphorylation	Phosphorylation is the addition of a phosphate group to a protein or other organic molecule . Phosphorylation turns many protein enzymes on and off, thereby altering their function and activity. Protein phosphorylation is one type of post-translational modification.
Ferritin	Ferritin is a ubiquitous intracellular protein that stores iron and releases it in a controlled fashion. The amount of ferritin stored reflects the amount of iron stored. The protein is produced by almost all living organisms, including algae, bacteria, higher plants, and animals.
Promoter	In genetics, a promoter is a region of DNA that initiates transcription of a particular gene.

Promoters are located near the genes they transcribe, on the same strand and upstream on the DNA (towards the 3' region of the anti-sense strand, also called template strand and non-coding strand). Promoters can be about 100-1000 base pairs long.

Cohesin

Cohesin is a protein complex that regulates the separation of sister chromatids during cell division, either mitosis or meiosis.

Enhancer

In genetics, an enhancer is a short region of DNA that can be bound with proteins to enhance transcription levels of genes (hence the name) in a gene cluster. While enhancers are usually cis-acting, an enhancer does not need to be particularly close to the genes it acts on, and sometimes need not be located on the same chromosome.

Heterochromatin

Heterochromatin is a tightly packed form of DNA, which comes in different varieties. These varieties lie on a continuum between the two extremes of constitutive and facultative heterochromatin. Both play a role in the expression of genes, where constitutive heterochromatin can affect the genes near them (position-effect variegation) and where facultative heterochromatin is the result of genes that are silenced through a mechanism such as histone methylation or siRNA through RNAi.

Locus control region

Locus control regions are defined by their ability to enhance the expression of linked genes to physiological levels in a tissue-specific and copy number-dependent manner at ectopic chromatin sites. The concept derives from the idea that developmental and cell lineage-specific regulation of gene expression relies not only on gene-proximal elements such as promoters, enhancers, and silencers, but also on long-range interactions of various cis-regulatory elements and dynamic chromatin alterations.

The Locus control region was identified over 20 years ago.

Blue

Blue was a white Bull Terrier owned by hockey commentator Don Cherry. Blue was reportedly a gift from the members of the Boston Bruins when Cherry was their head coach from 1974 to 1979. The original Blue, who died in 1989, was actually a female. Cherry has since owned other white bull terriers, all of which were named Blue.

Cooperative binding

Molecular binding is an interaction between molecules that results in a stable association between those molecules. Cooperative binding occurs if the number of binding sites of a macromolecule that are occupied by a specific type of ligand is a non-linear function of this ligand's concentration. This can be due, for instance, to an affinity for the ligand that depends on the amount of ligand bound.

Coactivator

A coactivator is a protein that increases gene expression by binding to an activator which contains a DNA binding domain. The coactivator is unable to bind DNA by itself.

17. Transcriptional Regulation in Eukaryotes,

CHAPTER HIGHLIGHTS & NOTES: KEY TERMS, PEOPLE, PLACES, CONCEPTS

Evolution	Evolution is a 2001 documentary series by the American broadcaster Public Broadcasting Service and WGBH on evolutionary biology. The spokespeople for the series were Jane Goodall (overall spokesperson), Kenneth R. Miller and Stephen Jay Gould (science spokespeople), Eugenie C. Scott (education spokesperson), Arthur Peacocke and Arnold Thomas (religious spokespeople). The series was narrated by the Irish actor Liam Neeson.
Histone	In biology, histones are highly alkaline proteins found in eukaryotic cell nuclei that package and order the DNA into structural units called nucleosomes. They are the chief protein components of chromatin, acting as spools around which DNA winds, and play a role in gene regulation. Without histones, the unwound DNA in chromosomes would be very long (a length to width ratio of more than 10 million to 1 in human DNA).
Protein	Proteins are large biological molecules consisting of one or more chains of amino acids. Proteins perform a vast array of functions within living organisms, including catalyzing metabolic reactions, replicating DNA, responding to stimuli, and transporting molecules from one location to another. Proteins differ from one another primarily in their sequence of amino acids, which is dictated by the nucleotide sequence of their genes, and which usually results in folding of the protein into a specific three-dimensional structure that determines its activity.
Signal transduction	Signal transduction occurs when an extracellular signaling molecule activates a cell surface receptor. In turn, this receptor alters intracellular molecules creating a response. There are two stages in this process:•A signaling molecule activates a specific receptor protein on the cell membrane.•A second messenger transmits the signal into the cell, eliciting a physiological response. In either step, the signal can be amplified.
Cell surface receptor	Cell surface receptors are specialized integral membrane proteins that take part in communication between the cell and the outside world. Extracellular signaling molecules (usually hormones, neurotransmitters, cytokines, growth factors or cell recognition molecules) attach to the receptor, triggering changes in the function of the cell. This process is called signal transduction: The binding initiates a chemical change on the intracellular side of the membrane.
Genetic code	The genetic code is the set of rules by which information encoded within genetic material is translated into proteins by living cells. Biological decoding is accomplished by the ribosome, which links amino acids in an order specified by mRNA, using transfer RNA (tRNA) molecules to carry amino acids and to read the mRNA three nucleotides at a time. The genetic code is highly similar among all organisms and can be expressed in a simple table with 64 entries.
Centromere	The centromere is the part of a chromosome that links sister chromatids.

During mitosis, spindle fibers attach to the centromere via the kinetochore. Centromeres were first defined as genetic loci that direct the behavior of chromosomes.

Euchromatin: Euchromatin is a lightly packed form of chromatin that is rich in gene concentration, and is often (but not always) under active transcription. Euchromatin comprises the most active portion of the genome within the cell nucleus. 92% of the human genome is euchromatic.

Histone methyltransferase: Histone methyltransferases are histone-modifying enzymes, (including histone-lysine N-methyltransferase and histone-arginine N-methyltransferase), that catalyze the transfer of one, two, or three methyl groups to lysine and arginine residues of histone proteins. The attachment of methyl groups occurs predominantly at specific lysine or arginine residues on histones H3 and H4. Two major types of histone methyltranferases exist, lysine-specific (which can be SET (Su(var)3-9, Enhancer of Zeste, Trithorax) domain containing or non-SET domain containing) and arginine-specific. In both types of histone methyltransferases, cofactor S-Adenosyl methionine (SAM) serves as a cofactor and methyl donor group.

RNA interference: RNA interference also called post transcriptional gene silencing (PTGS), is a biological process in which RNA molecules inhibit gene expression, typically by causing the destruction of specific mRNA molecules. Historically, it was known by other names, including co-suppression, post transcriptional gene silencing (PTGS), and quelling. Only after these apparently unrelated processes were fully understood did it become clear that they all described the RNAi phenomenon.

Yeast: Yeasts are eukaryotic microorganisms classified in the kingdom Fungi, with 1,500 species currently described . Yeasts are unicellular, although some species with yeast forms may become multicellular through the formation of strings of connected budding cells known as pseudohyphae, or false hyphae, as seen in most molds. Yeast size can vary greatly depending on the species, typically measuring 3-4 µm in diameter, although some yeasts can reach over 40 µm.

Hox gene: Hox genes are a group of related genes that control the body plan of the embryo along the anterior-posterior (head-tail) axis. After the embryonic segments have formed, the Hox proteins determine the type of segment structures (e.g. legs, antennae, and wings in fruit flies or the different vertebrate ribs in humans) that will form on a given segment. Hox proteins thus confer segmental identity, but do not form the actual segments themselves

Hox genes are defined as having the following properties:•their protein product is a transcription factor•they contain a DNA sequence known as the homeobox•in many animals, the organization of the Hox genes on the chromosome is the same as the order of their expression along the anterior-posterior axis of the developing animal, and are thus said to display colinearity..

Variegation: Variegation is the appearance of differently coloured zones in the leaves, and sometimes the stems, of plants. This may be due to a number of causes.

17. Transcriptional Regulation in Eukaryotes,

CHAPTER HIGHLIGHTS & NOTES: KEY TERMS, PEOPLE, PLACES, CONCEPTS

White	White Gene, abbreviated w, was the first sex-linked mutation ever discovered in the fruit fly Drosophila melanogaster. In 1910 Thomas Hunt Morgan and Lilian Vaughan Morgan collected a single male white-eyed mutant from a population of Drosophila melanogaster fruit flies, which usually have dark brick red eyes. Upon crossing this male with wild-type female flies, they found that the offspring did not conform to the expectations of Mendelian inheritance.
Methylation	In the chemical sciences, methylation denotes the addition of a methyl group to a substrate or the substitution of an atom or group by a methyl group. Methylation is a form of alkylation with a methyl group, rather than a larger carbon chain, replacing a hydrogen atom. These terms are commonly used in chemistry, biochemistry, soil science, and the biological sciences.
Mutation	In genetics, a mutation is a change of the nucleotide sequence of the genome of an organism, virus, or extrachromosomal genetic element. Mutations result from unrepaired damage to DNA or to RNA genomes (typically caused by radiation or chemical mutagens), errors in the process of replication, or from the insertion or deletion of segments of DNA by mobile genetic elements. Mutations may or may not produce discernible changes in the observable characteristics (phenotype) of an organism.
DNA methylation	DNA methylation is a biochemical process involving the addition of a methyl group to the cytosine or adenine DNA nucleotides. DNA methylation stably alters the expression of genes in cells as cells divide and differentiate from embryonic stem cells into specific tissues. The resulting change is normally permanent and unidirectional, preventing one organism from reverting to a stem cell or converting into another type of tissue.
Imprinting	Imprinting is the term used in psychology and ethology to describe any kind of phase-sensitive learning that is rapid and apparently independent of the consequences of behavior. It was first used to describe situations in which an animal or person learns the characteristics of some stimulus, which is therefore said to be 'imprinted' onto the subject. Imprinting is hypothesized to have a critical period.
Growth factor	A growth factor is a naturally occurring substance capable of stimulating cellular growth, proliferation and cellular differentiation. Usually it is a protein or a steroid hormone. Growth factors are important for regulating a variety of cellular processes.
Chromosome segregation	Chromosome segregation is a step in cell reproduction or division, where chromosomes pair off with their similar homologous chromosome. In mitosis, a complete copy of each one is made. In meiosis, one chromosome from each pair migrates to opposite ends of the cell and the genes are split to make a gamete.

1. A _________ is an independently folded protein domain that contains at least one motif that recognizes double- or single-stranded DNA. A DNA binding domain can recognize a specific DNA sequence (a recognition sequence) or have a general affinity to DNA. Some _________s may also include nucleic acids in their folded structure.

   a. Bacterial one-hybrid system
   b. DNA-binding domain
   c. Biopolymer
   d. Biopunk

2. _________, also known as DNA-dependent _________, is an enzyme that produces RNA. In cells, RNAP is necessary for constructing RNA chains using DNA genes as templates, a process called transcription. _________ enzymes are essential to life and are found in all organisms and many viruses. In chemical terms, RNAP is a nucleotidyl transferase that polymerizes ribonucleotides at the 3' end of an RNA transcript.

   a. Bacterial transcription
   b. RNA polymerase
   c. CAG promoter
   d. Cap analysis gene expression

3. In biology, _________ occurs when juvenile organisms survive to be added to a population. The term is generally used to refer to a stage whereby the organisms are settled and able to be detected by an observer.

   a. Biotope
   b. Recruitment
   c. Box-Ironbark forest
   d. Coral reef

4. The _________ is the set of rules by which information encoded within genetic material is translated into proteins by living cells. Biological decoding is accomplished by the ribosome, which links amino acids in an order specified by mRNA, using transfer RNA (tRNA) molecules to carry amino acids and to read the mRNA three nucleotides at a time. The _________ is highly similar among all organisms and can be expressed in a simple table with 64 entries.

   a. Bacterial one-hybrid system
   b. Baek Sung-hee
   c. Biopolymer
   d. Genetic code

5. . _________ is the process of producing two identical copies from one original DNA molecule. This biological process occurs in all living organisms and is the basis for biological inheritance. DNA is composed of two strands and each strand of the original DNA molecule serves as template for the production of the complementary strand, a process referred to as semiconservative replication.

   a. Cationic liposome
   b. 23andMe

c. DNA replication

d. Biodistribution

ANSWER KEY
17. Transcriptional Regulation in Eukaryotes,

1. b
2. b
3. b
4. d
5. c

---

18. Regulatory RNAs,

CHAPTER OUTLINE: KEY TERMS, PEOPLE, PLACES, CONCEPTS

- Bacteria
- Antisense RNA
- Hfq protein
- Riboswitch
- RNA polymerase
- Neurospora crassa
- Transfer RNA
- CRISPR
- Virulence
- Gene
- DNA polymerase
- Eukaryote
- MicroRNA
- RNA interference
- Guide RNA
- RNA-induced silencing complex
- RNAI
- Schizosaccharomyces
- Schizosaccharomyces pombe
- Discovery
- Lesion

18. Regulatory RNAs,

CHAPTER OUTLINE: KEY TERMS, PEOPLE, PLACES, CONCEPTS

Dicer

Drosha

Pasha

Argonaute

Gene silencing

Modifications

DNA replication

Evolution

Potato virus Y

Gene expression

HOTAIR

Long non-coding RNA

X-inactivation

Non-coding RNA

Dosage compensation

RNA editing

Tsix

Trp operon

Bacteria	Bacteria constitute a large domain or kingdom of prokaryotic microorganisms. Typically a few micrometres in length, bacteria have a wide range of shapes, ranging from spheres to rods and spirals. Bacteria were among the first life forms to appear on Earth, and are present in most habitats on the planet.
Antisense RNA	Antisense RNA is a single-stranded RNA that is complementary to a messenger RNA (mRNA) strand transcribed within a cell. Some authors have used the term micRNA (mRNA-interfering complementary RNA) to refer to these RNAs but it is not widely used. Antisense RNA may be introduced into a cell to inhibit translation of a complementary mRNA by base pairing to it and physically obstructing the translation machinery.
Hfq protein	The Hfq protein encoded by the hfq gene was discovered in 1968 as an Escherichia. coli host factor that was essential for replication of the bacteriophage Qß. It is now clear that Hfq is an abundant bacterial RNA binding protein which has many important physiological roles.
Riboswitch	In molecular biology, a riboswitch is a regulatory segment of a messenger RNA molecule that binds a small molecule, resulting in a change in production of the proteins encoded by the mRNA. Thus, an mRNA that contains a riboswitch is directly involved in regulating its own activity, in response to the concentrations of its effector molecule. The discovery that modern organisms use RNA to bind small molecules, and discriminate against closely related analogs, expanded the known natural capabilities of RNA beyond its ability to code for proteins, catalyze reactions, or to bind other RNA or protein macromolecules. Most known riboswitches occur in bacteria, but functional riboswitches of one type (the TPP riboswitch) have been discovered in plants and certain fungi.
RNA polymerase	RNA polymerase, also known as DNA-dependent RNA polymerase, is an enzyme that produces RNA. In cells, RNAP is necessary for constructing RNA chains using DNA genes as templates, a process called transcription. RNA polymerase enzymes are essential to life and are found in all organisms and many viruses. In chemical terms, RNAP is a nucleotidyl transferase that polymerizes ribonucleotides at the 3' end of an RNA transcript.
Neurospora crassa	Neurospora crassa is a type of red bread mould of the phylum Ascomycota. The genus name, meaning 'nerve spore' refers to the characteristic striations on the spores. The first published account of this fungus was from an infestation of French bakeries in 1843.
Transfer RNA	A Transfer RNA is an adaptor molecule composed of RNA, typically 73 to 94 nucleotides in length, that serves as the physical link between the nucleotide sequence of nucleic acids (DNA and RNA) and the amino acid sequence of proteins. It does this by carrying an amino acid to the protein synthetic machinery of a cell (ribosome) as directed by a three-nucleotide sequence (codon) in a messenger RNA (mRNA).

18. Regulatory RNAs,

CHAPTER HIGHLIGHTS & NOTES: KEY TERMS, PEOPLE, PLACES, CONCEPTS

CRISPR	CRISPRs are loci containing multiple short direct repeats that are found in the genomes of approximately 40% of sequenced bacteria and 90% of sequenced archaea. CRISPR functions as a prokaryotic immune system, in that it confers resistance to exogenous genetic elements such as plasmids and phages. The CRISPR system provides a form of acquired immunity.
Virulence	Virulence is, by MeSH definition, the degree of pathogenicity within a group or species of parasites as indicated by case fatality rates and/or the ability of the organism to invade the tissues of the host. The pathogenicity of an organism - its ability to cause disease - is determined by its virulence factors. The noun virulence derives from the adjective virulent.
Gene	A gene is a molecular unit of heredity of a living organism. It is widely accepted by the scientific community as a name given to some stretches of deoxyribonucleic acids (DNA) and ribonucleic acids (RNA) that code for a polypeptide or for an RNA chain that has a function in the organism, though there still are controversies about what plays the role of the genetic material. Living beings depend on genes, as they specify all proteins and functional RNA chains.
DNA polymerase	A DNA polymerase is a cellular or viral polymerase enzyme that synthesizes DNA molecules from their nucleotide building blocks. DNA polymerases are essential for DNA replication, and usually function in pairs while copying one double-stranded DNA molecule into two double-stranded DNAs in a process termed semiconservative DNA replication. DNA polymerases also play key roles in other processes within cells, including DNA repair, genetic recombination, reverse transcription, and the generation of antibody diversity via the specialized DNA polymerase, terminal deoxynucleotidyl transferase.
Eukaryote	A eukaryote is an organism whose cells contain a nucleus and other structures (organelles) enclosed within membranes. Eukaryotes are formally the taxon Eukarya or Eukaryota. The defining membrane-bound structure that sets eukaryotic cells apart from prokaryotic cells is the nucleus, or nuclear envelope, within which the genetic material is carried.
MicroRNA	A microRNA is a small non-coding RNA molecule (ca. 22 nucleotides) found in plants and animals, which functions in transcriptional and post-transcriptional regulation of gene expression. Encoded by eukaryotic nuclear DNA, miRNAs function via base-pairing with complementary sequences within mRNA molecules, usually resulting in gene silencing via translational repression or target degradation. The human genome may encode over 1000 miRNAs, which may target about 60% of mammalian genes and are abundant in many human cell types.
RNA interference	RNA interference also called post transcriptional gene silencing (PTGS), is a biological process in which RNA molecules inhibit gene expression, typically by causing the destruction of specific mRNA molecules. Historically, it was known by other names, including co-suppression, post transcriptional gene silencing (PTGS), and quelling. Only after these apparently unrelated processes were fully understood did it become clear that they all described the RNAi phenomenon.

RNA-induced silencing complex	The RNA-induced silencing complex, or RNA induced silencing complex, is a multiprotein complex that incorporates one strand of a small interfering RNA or microRNA (miRNA). RNA induced silencing complex uses the siRNA or miRNA as a template for recognizing complementary mRNA. When it finds a complementary strand, it activates RNase and cleaves the RNA. This process is important both in gene regulation by microRNAs and in defense against viral infections, which often use double-stranded RNA as an infectious vector.
RNAI	RNAI is a non-coding RNA that is an antisense repressor of the replication of some E. coli plasmids, including ColE1. Plasmid replication is usually initiated by RNAII, which acts as a primer by binding to its template DNA. The complementary RNAI binds RNAII prohibiting it from its initiation role. The rate of degradation of RNAI is therefore a major factor in control of plasmid replication. This rate of degradation is aided by the pcnB (plasmid copy number B) gene product, which polyadenylates the 3' end of RNAI targeting it for degradation by PNPase.
Schizosaccharomyces	Schizosaccharomyces is a genus of fission yeasts. The most well-studied species is S. pombe. At present four Schizosaccharomyces species have been described (S. pombe, S. japonicus, S. octosporus and S. cryophilus).
Schizosaccharomyces pombe	Schizosaccharomyces pombe, also called 'fission yeast', is a species of yeast. It is used as a model organism in molecular and cell biology. It is a unicellular eukaryote, whose cells are rod-shaped.
Discovery	Discovery is the act of detecting something new, or something 'old' that had been unknown. With reference to science and academic disciplines, discovery is the observation of new phenomena, new actions, or new events and providing new reasoning to explain the knowledge gathered through such observations with previously acquired knowledge from abstract thought and everyday experiences. Visual discoveries are often called sightings.
Lesion	A lesion is any abnormality in the tissue of an organism, usually caused by disease or trauma. Lesion is derived from the Latin word laesio meaning injury.
Dicer	Dicer is an endoribonuclease in the RNase III family that cleaves double-stranded RNA and pre-microRNA (miRNA) into short double-stranded RNA fragments about 20-25 base pairs long, with a two-base overhang on the 3' end. Dicer contains two RNase III domains and one PAZ domain; the distance between these two regions of the molecule is determined by the length and angle of the connector helix and influences the length of the siRNAs it produces. Dicers interact with several partner proteins (TRBP in humans, R2D2, Loqs in Drosophila).
Drosha	Drosha is a Class 2 RNase III enzyme responsible for initiating the processing of microRNA, or short RNA molecules naturally expressed by the cell that regulate a wide variety of other genes by interacting with the RNA-induced silencing complex (RISC) to induce cleavage of complementary messenger RNA (mRNA) as part of the RNAi pathway.

A microRNA molecule is synthesized as a long RNA primary transcript known as a pri-miRNA, which is cleaved by Drosha to produce a characteristic stem-loop structure of about 70 base pairs long, known as a pre-miRNA. Drosha exists as part of a protein complex called the Microprocessor complex, which also contains the double-stranded RNA binding protein Pasha (also called DGCR8), which is essential for Drosha activity and is capable of binding single-stranded fragments of the pri-miRNA that are required for proper processing. Human Drosha was cloned in 2000, when it was identified as a nuclear dsRNA ribonuclease involved in the processing of ribosomal RNA precursors.

Pasha

Pasha, also known as DGCR8 in vertebrates, is a protein localized to the cell nucleus that is required for microRNA processing. It binds to Drosha, an RNase III enzyme, to form the Microprocessor complex that cleaves a primary transcript known as pri-miRNA to a characteristic stem-loop structure known as a pre-miRNA, which is then further processed to miRNA fragments by the enzyme Dicer. Pasha contains an RNA-binding domain and is thought to bind pri-miRNA to stabilize it for processing by Drosha.

Argonaute

Argonaute proteins are the catalytic components of the RNA-induced silencing complex, the protein complex responsible for the gene silencing phenomenon known as RNA interference (RNAi). Argonaute proteins bind different classes of small non-coding RNAs, including microRNAs (miRNAs), small interfering RNAs (siRNAs) and Piwi-interacting RNAs (piRNAs). Small RNAs guide Argonaute proteins to their specific targets through sequence complementarity, which typically leads to silencing of the target.

Gene silencing

Gene silencing is a general term describing epigenetic processes of gene regulation. The term gene silencing is generally used to describe the 'switching off' of a gene by a mechanism other than genetic modification. That is, a gene which would be expressed ('turned on') under normal circumstances is switched off by machinery in the cell.

Modifications

In opposition to mutations, modifications are included in the band width of the genome of an individual creature. Modifications are dependent on the plentifulness of the substrate, light, warmths, stress, training, and so on.

A modification is a change in the physical appearance of an organism (phenotype) caused by environmental factors.

DNA replication

DNA replication is the process of producing two identical copies from one original DNA molecule. This biological process occurs in all living organisms and is the basis for biological inheritance. DNA is composed of two strands and each strand of the original DNA molecule serves as template for the production of the complementary strand, a process referred to as semiconservative replication.

Evolution	Evolution is a 2001 documentary series by the American broadcaster Public Broadcasting Service and WGBH on evolutionary biology. The spokespeople for the series were Jane Goodall (overall spokesperson), Kenneth R. Miller and Stephen Jay Gould (science spokespeople), Eugenie C. Scott (education spokesperson), Arthur Peacocke and Arnold Thomas (religious spokespeople). The series was narrated by the Irish actor Liam Neeson.
Potato virus Y	Potato virus Y is a plant pathogenic virus of the family Potyviridae, and one of the most important plant viruses affecting potato production. Potato virus Y infection of potato plants results in a variety of symptoms depending on the viral strain. The mildest of these symptoms is production loss, but the most detrimental is 'potato tuber necrotic ringspot disease' (PTNRD).
Gene expression	Gene expression is the process by which information from a gene is used in the synthesis of a functional gene product. These products are often proteins, but in non-protein coding genes such as ribosomal RNA (rRNA), transfer RNA (tRNA) or small nuclear RNA (snRNA) genes, the product is a functional RNA. The process of gene expression is used by all known life - eukaryotes (including multicellular organisms), prokaryotes (bacteria and archaea), possibly induced by viruses - to generate the macromolecular machinery for life. Several steps in the gene expression process may be modulated, including the transcription, RNA splicing, translation, and post-translational modification of a protein.
HOTAIR	HOTAIR is a human gene located on chromosome 12. It is the first example of an RNA expressed on one chromosome that has been found to influence transcription on another chromosome.
Long non-coding RNA	Long non-coding RNAs are non-protein coding transcripts longer than 200 nucleotides (Perkel 2013). This somewhat arbitrary limit distinguishes long ncRNAs from small regulatory RNAs such as microRNAs (miRNAs), short interfering RNAs (siRNAs), Piwi-interacting RNAs (piRNAs), small nucleolar RNAs (snoRNAs), and other short RNAs (Ma 2013).
X-inactivation	X-inactivation is a process by which one of the two copies of the X chromosome present in female mammals is inactivated. The inactive X chromosome is silenced by it being packaged in such a way that it has a transcriptionally inactive structure called heterochromatin. As female mammals have two X chromosomes, X-inactivation prevents them from having twice as many X chromosome gene products as males, which only possess a single copy of the X chromosome .
Non-coding RNA	A non-coding RNA is a functional RNA molecule that is not translated into a protein. Less-frequently used synonyms are non-protein-coding RNA (npcRNA), non-messenger RNA (nmRNA) and functional RNA (fRNA). The term small RNA (sRNA) is often used for short bacterial ncRNAs.

18. Regulatory RNAs,

CHAPTER HIGHLIGHTS & NOTES: KEY TERMS, PEOPLE, PLACES, CONCEPTS

Dosage compensation	Dosage compensation is a hypothetical genetic regulatory mechanism which operates to equalize the phenotypic expression of characteristics determined by genes on the X chromosome so that they are equally expressed in the human XY male and the XX female. Dosage compensation may occur in other organisms like the fruit fly Drosophila melanogaster, the roundworm Caenorhabditis elegans and the plant White campion . Species can have different mechanisms of dosage compensation.
RNA editing	RNA editing is a molecular process through which some cells can make discrete changes to specific nucleotide sequences within a RNA molecule after it has been generated by RNA polymerase. RNA editing is relatively rare, and common forms of RNA processing (e.g. splicing, 5'-capping and 3'-polyadenylation) are not usually included as editing. Editing events may include the insertion, deletion, and base substitution of nucleotides within the edited RNA molecule.
Tsix	Tsix is a gene that functions as the antisense to the Xist gene during X chromosome inactivation. Tsix controls X chromosome inactivation by preventing the accumulation of Xist on one female X chromosome to maintain the active euchromatic state of the chosen chromosome. This gene is only active in mice, although both bovine and humans have an inactive version of this gene.
Trp operon	Trp operon is an operon -- a group of genes that are used, or transcribed, together -- that codes for the components for production of tryptophan. The Trp operon is present in many bacteria, but was first characterized in Escherichia coli. It is regulated so that when tryptophan is present in the environment, it is not used.

CHAPTER QUIZ: KEY TERMS, PEOPLE, PLACES, CONCEPTS

1. . _________ is a single-stranded RNA that is complementary to a messenger RNA (mRNA) strand transcribed within a cell. Some authors have used the term micRNA (mRNA-interfering complementary RNA) to refer to these RNAs but it is not widely used.

   _________ may be introduced into a cell to inhibit translation of a complementary mRNA by base pairing to it and physically obstructing the translation machinery.

   a. Kleine Feldhofer Grotte
   b. Neanderthal anatomy
   c. Antisense RNA

2. _________ constitute a large domain or kingdom of prokaryotic microorganisms. Typically a few micrometres in length, _________ have a wide range of shapes, ranging from spheres to rods and spirals. _________ were among the first life forms to appear on Earth, and are present in most habitats on the planet.

   a. Bacterial conjugation
   b. Horizontal gene transfer
   c. Bacteria
   d. Calicheamicin

3. A _________ is a molecular unit of heredity of a living organism. It is widely accepted by the scientific community as a name given to some stretches of deoxyribonucleic acids (DNA) and ribonucleic acids (RNA) that code for a polypeptide or for an RNA chain that has a function in the organism, though there still are controversies about what plays the role of the genetic material. Living beings depend on _________s, as they specify all proteins and functional RNA chains.

   a. 23andMe
   b. BacMam
   c. Biodistribution
   d. Gene

4. _________s are non-protein coding transcripts longer than 200 nucleotides (Perkel 2013). This somewhat arbitrary limit distinguishes long ncRNAs from small regulatory RNAs such as microRNAs (miRNAs), short interfering RNAs (siRNAs), Piwi-interacting RNAs (piRNAs), small nucleolar RNAs (snoRNAs), and other short RNAs (Ma 2013).

   a. Chimeric RNA
   b. Circular RNA
   c. Cis-acting replication element
   d. Long non-coding RNA

5. _________ is, by MeSH definition, the degree of pathogenicity within a group or species of parasites as indicated by case fatality rates and/or the ability of the organism to invade the tissues of the host. The pathogenicity of an organism - its ability to cause disease - is determined by its _________ factors. The noun _________ derives from the adjective virulent.

   a. Branched DNA assay
   b. Capsid
   c. Capsomere
   d. Virulence

ANSWER KEY
18. Regulatory RNAs,

1. c
2. c
3. d
4. d
5. d

---

19. Gene Regulation in Development and Evolution,

CHAPTER OUTLINE: KEY TERMS, PEOPLE, PLACES, CONCEPTS

	Inner cell mass
	Steady state
	Cell
	Evolution
	Microtubule
	Cell surface receptor
	Signal transduction
	Secretion
	Signaling molecule
	Budding
	Morphogen
	Mating type
	Yeast
	Embryo
	Zinc finger
	Bacteria
	Hairless
	Neural tube
	Sonic hedgehog
	Syncytium
	Embryogenesis

19. Gene Regulation in Development and Evolution,

CHAPTER OUTLINE: KEY TERMS, PEOPLE, PLACES, CONCEPTS

- Toll
- Snail
- Insulator
- Form
- Nurse cell
- Oocyte
- Ferritin
- Gap gene
- Gene expression
- Pair-rule gene
- Gene
- Homeotic gene
- Bithorax complex
- Insect
- Appendage
- Limb
- Halteres
- Cellulose synthase
- Fibroblast growth factor
- Genome size
- Hox gene

19. Gene Regulation in Development and Evolution,

CHAPTER OUTLINE: KEY TERMS, PEOPLE, PLACES, CONCEPTS

Sea urchin

Synteny

CHAPTER HIGHLIGHTS & NOTES: KEY TERMS, PEOPLE, PLACES, CONCEPTS

Inner cell mass	In early embryogenesis of most eutherian mammals, the inner cell mass is the mass of cells inside the primordial embryo that will eventually give rise to the definitive structures of the fetus. This structure forms in the earliest steps of development, before implantation into the endometrium of the uterus has occurred. The Inner cell mass lies within the blastocoele (more correctly termed 'blastocyst cavity,' as it is not strictly homologous to the blastocoele of anamniote vertebrates) and is entirely surrounded by the single layer of cells called trophoblast.
Steady state	In ionic steady state, cells maintain different internal and external concentrations of various ionic species. The following is an inaccurate and unsupported statement, be warned: Cell membranes are permeable to potassium and various other ions, so in order to maintain a constant ionic concentration the cell must expend energy to actively transport these ions against the electrochemical gradient, out of the cell, at the same rate as they diffuse inward. Conversely, membranes are not permeable to sodium, so this ion must be actively pumped into the cell.
Cell	The cell is the basic structural, functional and biological unit of all known living organisms. Cells are the smallest unit of life that is classified as a living thing, and are often called the 'building blocks of life'. Cells consist of a protoplasm enclosed within a membrane, which contains many biomolecules such as proteins and nucleic acids.
Evolution	Evolution is a 2001 documentary series by the American broadcaster Public Broadcasting Service and WGBH on evolutionary biology. The spokespeople for the series were Jane Goodall (overall spokesperson), Kenneth R. Miller and Stephen Jay Gould (science spokespeople), Eugenie C. Scott (education spokesperson), Arthur Peacocke and Arnold Thomas (religious spokespeople).

Microtubule

Microtubules are a component of the cytoskeleton, found throughout the cytoplasm. These tubular polymers of tubulin can grow as long as 50 micrometres, with an average length of 25 µm and are highly dynamic. The outer diameter of a microtubule is about 25 nm while the inner diameter is about 12 nm.

Cell surface receptor

Cell surface receptors are specialized integral membrane proteins that take part in communication between the cell and the outside world. Extracellular signaling molecules (usually hormones, neurotransmitters, cytokines, growth factors or cell recognition molecules) attach to the receptor, triggering changes in the function of the cell. This process is called signal transduction: The binding initiates a chemical change on the intracellular side of the membrane.

Signal transduction

Signal transduction occurs when an extracellular signaling molecule activates a cell surface receptor. In turn, this receptor alters intracellular molecules creating a response. There are two stages in this process:•A signaling molecule activates a specific receptor protein on the cell membrane.•A second messenger transmits the signal into the cell, eliciting a physiological response.

In either step, the signal can be amplified.

Secretion

Secretion is the process of elaborating, releasing, and oozing chemicals, or a secreted chemical substance from a cell or gland. In contrast to excretion, the substance may have a certain function, rather than being a waste product. The classical mechanism of cell secretion is via secretory portals at the cell plasma membrane called porosomes.

Signaling molecule

A signaling molecule is a molecule involved in transmitting information between cells of a living multicellular organism, or between organisms of the same or different species.

Budding

Budding is a form of asexual reproduction in which a new organism develops from an outgrowth or bud on another one. The new organism remains attached as it grows, separating from the parent organism only when it is mature, leaving behind scar tissue. Since the reproduction is asexual, the newly created organism is a clone and is genetically identical to the parent organism.

Morphogen

A morphogen is a substance governing the pattern of tissue development in the process of morphogenesis, and the positions of the various specialized cell types within a tissue. More precisely, a morphogen is a signaling molecule that acts directly on cells to produce specific cellular responses depending on its local concentration.

Since morphogens diffuse through the tissues of an embryo during early development, concentration gradients are set up.

Mating type

Mating types are molecular mechanisms that regulate compatibility in sexually reproducing eukaryotes. They occur in isogamous and anisogamous species.

19. Gene Regulation in Development and Evolution,

CHAPTER HIGHLIGHTS & NOTES: KEY TERMS, PEOPLE, PLACES, CONCEPTS

Yeast	Yeasts are eukaryotic microorganisms classified in the kingdom Fungi, with 1,500 species currently described . Yeasts are unicellular, although some species with yeast forms may become multicellular through the formation of strings of connected budding cells known as pseudohyphae, or false hyphae, as seen in most molds. Yeast size can vary greatly depending on the species, typically measuring 3-4 µm in diameter, although some yeasts can reach over 40 µm.
Embryo	An embryo is a multicellular diploid eukaryote in its earliest stage of development, from the time of first cell division until birth, hatching, or germination. In humans, it is called an embryo until about eight weeks after fertilization (i.e. ten weeks after the last menstrual period or LMP), and from then it is instead called a fetus. The development of the embryo is called embryogenesis.
Zinc finger	A zinc finger is a small protein structural motif that is characterized by the coordination of one or more zinc ions in order to stabilize the fold. Originally coined to describe the finger-like appearance of a hypothesized structure from Xenopus laevis transcription factor IIIA, the zinc finger name has now come to encompass a wide variety of differing protein structures. Proteins that contain zinc fingers (zinc finger proteins) are classified into several different structural families.
Bacteria	Bacteria constitute a large domain or kingdom of prokaryotic microorganisms. Typically a few micrometres in length, bacteria have a wide range of shapes, ranging from spheres to rods and spirals. Bacteria were among the first life forms to appear on Earth, and are present in most habitats on the planet.
Hairless	Hairless, also known as H, is a well-characterized Drosophila gene. Many mutations to hairless are embryonic lethal; however, there are several viable hairless mutants. Hairless is involved in the Notch signaling pathway in Drosophila, acting as a suppressor of Notch signaling.
Neural tube	In the developing chordate, the neural tube is the embryo's precursor to the central nervous system, which comprises the brain and spinal cord. The neural groove gradually deepens as the neural folds become elevated, and ultimately the folds meet and coalesce in the middle line and convert the groove into a closed tube, the neural tube or neural canal (which strictly speaking is the center of the neural tube), the ectodermal wall of which forms the rudiment of the nervous system.
Sonic hedgehog	Sonic hedgehog is a protein that in humans is encoded by the SHH (sonic hedgehog) gene. Sonic hedgehog is one of three proteins in the mammalian signaling pathway family called hedgehog, the others being desert hedgehog and Indian hedgehog (IHH). SHH is the best studied ligand of the hedgehog signaling pathway.

Syncytium

A syncytium (; plural syncytia; from Greek: s?? = 'together' + ??t?? (kytos) = 'box, i.e. cell') is a multinucleate cell which can result from multiple cell fusions of uninuclear cells (i.e. cells with a single nucleus), in contrast to a coenocyte which can result from multiple nuclear divisions without accompanying cytokinesis. A classic example of a syncytium is the formation of skeletal muscle. The term may also refer to cells that are interconnected by specialized membrane with gap junctions, as seen in the heart muscle cells and certain smooth muscle cells, which are synchronized electrically in an action potential.

Embryogenesis

Embryogenesis is the process by which the embryo forms and develops. In mammals, the term refers chiefly to early stages of prenatal development, whereas the terms fetus and fetal development describe later stages.

Embryogenesis always starts with the fertilization of the ovum (or egg) by sperm.

Toll

The Toll genes encode members of the Toll-like receptor class of proteins. 'Toll' is German for 'amazing' or 'great'. Mutants in the Toll gene were originally identified by 1995 Nobel Laureates Christiane Nüsslein-Volhard and Eric Wieschaus and colleagues in the fruit fly Drosophila melanogaster in 1985, and cloned by the laboratory of Kathryn Anderson in 1988. Since then, eleven mammalian Toll genes have been identified.

Snail

Snail is a common name that is applied most often to land snails, terrestrial pulmonate gastropod molluscs. However, the common name 'snail' is also applied to most of the members of the molluscan class Gastropoda that have a coiled shell that is large enough for the animal to retract completely into. When the word 'snail' is used in this most general sense, it includes not just land snails but also thousands of species of sea snails and freshwater snails.

Insulator

An insulator is a genetic boundary element that blocks the interaction between enhancers and promoters. Insulators therefore determine the set of genes an enhancer can influence. The need for them arises where two adjacent genes on a chromosome have very different transcription patterns, and it is critical that the inducing or repressing mechanisms of one do not interfere with the neighbouring gene.

Form

In botanical nomenclature, a form is one of the 'secondary' taxonomic ranks, below that of variety, which in turn is below that of species; it is an infraspecific taxon. If more than three ranks are listed in describing a taxon, the 'classification' is being specified, but only three parts make up the 'name' of the taxon: a genus name, a specific epithet, and an infraspecific epithet.

The abbreviation 'f.' or the full 'forma' should be put before the infraspecific epithet to indicate the rank.

Nurse cell

The term nurse cell is used in several unrelated ways in different scientific fields:

19. Gene Regulation in Development and Evolution,

Oocyte

An oocyte, oöcyte, ovocyte, or rarely ocyte, is a female gametocyte or germ cell involved in reproduction. In other words, it is an immature ovum, or egg cell. An oocyte is produced in the ovary during female gametogenesis.

Ferritin

Ferritin is a ubiquitous intracellular protein that stores iron and releases it in a controlled fashion. The amount of ferritin stored reflects the amount of iron stored. The protein is produced by almost all living organisms, including algae, bacteria, higher plants, and animals.

Gap gene

A gap gene is a type of gene involved in the development of the segmented embryos of some arthropods. Gap genes are defined by the effect of a mutation in that gene, which causes the loss of contiguous body segments, resembling a gap in the normal body plan. Each gap gene, therefore, is necessary for the development of a section of the organism.

Gene expression

Gene expression is the process by which information from a gene is used in the synthesis of a functional gene product. These products are often proteins, but in non-protein coding genes such as ribosomal RNA (rRNA), transfer RNA (tRNA) or small nuclear RNA (snRNA) genes, the product is a functional RNA. The process of gene expression is used by all known life - eukaryotes (including multicellular organisms), prokaryotes (bacteria and archaea), possibly induced by viruses - to generate the macromolecular machinery for life. Several steps in the gene expression process may be modulated, including the transcription, RNA splicing, translation, and post-translational modification of a protein.

Pair-rule gene

A pair-rule gene is a type of gene involved in the development of the segmented embryos of insects. Pair-rule genes are defined by the effect of a mutation in that gene, which causes the loss of the normal developmental pattern in alternating segments.

Pair-rule genes were first described by Christiane Nüsslein-Volhard and Eric Wieschaus in 1980. They used a genetic screen to identify genes required for embryonic development in the fruit fly Drosophila melanogaster.

Gene

A gene is a molecular unit of heredity of a living organism. It is widely accepted by the scientific community as a name given to some stretches of deoxyribonucleic acids (DNA) and ribonucleic acids (RNA) that code for a polypeptide or for an RNA chain that has a function in the organism, though there still are controversies about what plays the role of the genetic material. Living beings depend on genes, as they specify all proteins and functional RNA chains.

Homeotic gene

Homeotic genes cause the development of specific structures in plants and animals. They include many of the Hox and ParaHox genes which are important for segmentation, They also include the MADS-box-containing genes involved the ABC model of flower development. It is important to note that not all homeotic genes are Hox genes; the MADS- box genes are homeotic but not Hox genes.

Bithorax complex

The Bithorax complex is a group of homeotic genes in Drosophila melanogaster which are believed to control the differentiation of the abdominal and posterior thoracic segments, located on chromosome III. When these genes are mutated, the third thoracic segment becomes a repeat of the second thoracic segment, creating what is essentially a second thorax. This can result in a second pair of wings, a second stomach, and duplicated thoracic features in varying degrees.

The complex includes Ultrabithorax (Ubx).

Insect

Insects (from Latin insectum, a calque of Greek ??t?µ?? [éntomon], 'cut into sections') are a class of invertebrates within the arthropod phylum that have a chitinous exoskeleton, a three-part body, three pairs of jointed legs, compound eyes and one pair of antennae. They are among the most diverse groups of animals on the planet, including more than a million described species and representing more than half of all known living organisms. The number of extant species is estimated at between six and ten million, and potentially represent over 90% of the differing animal life forms on Earth.

Appendage

In invertebrate biology, an appendage is an external body part, or natural prolongation, that protrudes from an organism's body (in vertebrate biology, an example would be a vertebrate's limbs). It is a general term that covers any of the homologous body parts that may extend from a body segment. These include antennae, mouthparts (including mandibles, maxillae and maxillipeds), wings, elytra, gills, walking legs (pereiopods), swimming legs (pleopods), sexual organs (gonopods), and parts of the tail (uropods).

Limb

A limb, or extremity, is a jointed, or prehensile (as octopus tentacles or new world monkey tails), appendage of the human or other animal body. In the human body, the upper and lower limbs are commonly called the arms and the legs.

Most animals use limbs for locomotion, such as walking, running, or climbing.

Halteres

Halteres are small knobbed structures modified from the hindwings (or forewings in the case of Strepsiptera) in some two-winged insects. They are flapped rapidly and function as gyroscopes, informing the insect about rotation of the body during flight. The word 'halter' comes from Greek ?? t??, a double knobbed device used in Ancient Greece by athletes during training in jumping.

Cellulose synthase

In enzymology, a cellulose synthase is an enzyme that catalyzes the chemical reactionGDP-glucose + (1,4-beta-D-glucosyl)n $\rightleftharpoons$ GDP + (1,4-beta-D-glucosyl)n^{+}1

Thus, the two substrates of this enzyme are GDP-glucose and (1,4-beta-D-glucosyl)n, whereas its two products are GDP and (1,4-beta-D-glucosyl)n+1.

This enzyme belongs to the family of glycosyltransferases, specifically the hexosyltransferases.

19. Gene Regulation in Development and Evolution,

CHAPTER HIGHLIGHTS & NOTES: KEY TERMS, PEOPLE, PLACES, CONCEPTS

Fibroblast growth factor

Fibroblast growth factors, or Fibroblast growth factors, are a family of growth factors, with members involved in angiogenesis, wound healing, embryonic development and various endocrine signaling pathways. The Fibroblast growth factors are heparin-binding proteins and interactions with cell-surface-associated heparan sulfate proteoglycans have been shown to be essential for Fibroblast growth factor signal transduction. Fibroblast growth factors are key players in the processes of proliferation and differentiation of wide variety of cells and tissues.

Genome size

Genome size is the total amount of DNA contained within one copy of a single genome. It is typically measured in terms of mass in picograms (trillionths (10^{-12}) of a gram, abbreviated pg) or less frequently in Daltons or as the total number of nucleotide base pairs typically in megabases (millions of base pairs, abbreviated Mb or Mbp). One picogram equals 978 megabases.

Hox gene

Hox genes are a group of related genes that control the body plan of the embryo along the anterior-posterior (head-tail) axis. After the embryonic segments have formed, the Hox proteins determine the type of segment structures (e.g. legs, antennae, and wings in fruit flies or the different vertebrate ribs in humans) that will form on a given segment. Hox proteins thus confer segmental identity, but do not form the actual segments themselves

Hox genes are defined as having the following properties:•their protein product is a transcription factor•they contain a DNA sequence known as the homeobox•in many animals, the organization of the Hox genes on the chromosome is the same as the order of their expression along the anterior-posterior axis of the developing animal, and are thus said to display colinearity..

Sea urchin

Sea urchins or urchins, sometimes called sea hedgehogs, are small, spiny, globular animals which, with their close kin, such as sand dollars, constitute the class Echinoidea of the echinoderm phylum. There are c. 950 species of echinoids inhabiting all oceans from the intertidal to 5000 meters deep. Their shell, or 'test', is round and spiny, typically from 3 to 10 cm (1.2 to 3.9 in) across.

Synteny

In classical genetics, synteny describes the physical co-localization of genetic loci on the same chromosome within an individual or species. Today, however, biologists usually refer to synteny as the conservation of blocks of order within two sets of chromosomes that are being compared with each other. This concept can also be referred to as shared synteny.

1. _________ constitute a large domain or kingdom of prokaryotic microorganisms. Typically a few micrometres in length, _________ have a wide range of shapes, ranging from spheres to rods and spirals. _________ were among the first life forms to appear on Earth, and are present in most habitats on the planet.

a. Bacterial conjugation
b. Horizontal gene transfer
c. Bacteria
d. Calicheamicin

2. _________ is a common name that is applied most often to land _________s, terrestrial pulmonate gastropod molluscs. However, the common name '_________' is also applied to most of the members of the molluscan class Gastropoda that have a coiled shell that is large enough for the animal to retract completely into. When the word '_________' is used in this most general sense, it includes not just land _________s but also thousands of species of sea _________s and freshwater _________s.

a. Caenogastropoda
b. Snail
c. Cocculinoidea
d. Cycloneritimorpha

3. _________s are a group of related genes that control the body plan of the embryo along the anterior-posterior (head-tail) axis. After the embryonic segments have formed, the Hox proteins determine the type of segment structures (e.g. legs, antennae, and wings in fruit flies or the different vertebrate ribs in humans) that will form on a given segment. Hox proteins thus confer segmental identity, but do not form the actual segments themselves

_________s are defined as having the following properties:•their protein product is a transcription factor•they contain a DNA sequence known as the homeobox•in many animals, the organization of the _________s on the chromosome is the same as the order of their expression along the anterior-posterior axis of the developing animal, and are thus said to display colinearity..

a. BMPR2
b. Bone morphogenetic protein 1
c. Hox gene
d. Bone morphogenetic protein 15

4. . _________s are specialized integral membrane proteins that take part in communication between the cell and the outside world. Extracellular signaling molecules (usually hormones, neurotransmitters, cytokines, growth factors or cell recognition molecules) attach to the receptor, triggering changes in the function of the cell. This process is called signal transduction: The binding initiates a chemical change on the intracellular side of the membrane.

a. BCKDHA
b. Cell surface receptor
c. BCKDK

5. _________ are small knobbed structures modified from the hindwings (or forewings in the case of Strepsiptera) in some two-winged insects. They are flapped rapidly and function as gyroscopes, informing the insect about rotation of the body during flight. The word 'halter' comes from Greek ??t??, a double knobbed device used in Ancient Greece by athletes during training in jumping.

a. Bacteriome
b. Biological screw joint
c. Calypter
d. Halteres

ANSWER KEY
19. Gene Regulation in Development and Evolution,

1. c
2. b
3. c
4. b
5. d

---

20. Systems Biology,

CHAPTER OUTLINE: KEY TERMS, PEOPLE, PLACES, CONCEPTS

- Synthetic biology
- Systems biology
- Candida albicans
- Chromosome segregation
- Gene
- Gene expression
- Robustness
- Steady state
- Inversion
- Embryogenesis
- Protein
- Repressilator
- Caenorhabditis elegans
- Cold Spring Harbor Laboratory
- Luria
- Model organism
- Phage group
- Choice
- Prophage
- Bacteriophage
- Experiment

20. Systems Biology,

CHAPTER OUTLINE: KEY TERMS, PEOPLE, PLACES, CONCEPTS

- Genome
- Latent period
- Recombinant DNA
- Complementation
- Prediction
- Transduction
- Bacteria
- Bacterial growth
- Jacob
- Evolution
- Insect
- Lactose
- Lactose permease
- Assay
- Chromosome
- Cloning
- Cloning vector
- Hot spot
- Insertional mutagenesis
- Limb
- Molecular biology

20. Systems Biology,

CHAPTER OUTLINE: KEY TERMS, PEOPLE, PLACES, CONCEPTS

- Martha
- Analysis
- Genetic code
- Cistron
- Saccharomyces
- Saccharomyces cerevisiae
- Genetic analysis
- Genome size
- Transformation
- Yeast
- Dormancy
- Elongation factor
- Endosperm
- Gamete
- Gametophyte
- Hermaphrodite
- Sporophyte
- Heterochromatin
- RNA interference
- Retinitis pigmentosa
- Ti plasmid

20. Systems Biology,

CHAPTER OUTLINE: KEY TERMS, PEOPLE, PLACES, CONCEPTS

_______ Transfer DNA

_______ Reverse genetics

_______ Ribosome

_______ Forward genetics

_______ Imprinting

_______ MicroRNA

_______ Mutagenesis

_______ Genetics

_______ Growth factor

_______ Immunoprecipitation

_______ Methylation

_______ Transcription

_______ Environment

_______ Pattern formation

_______ Stress

_______ Vernalization

_______ Epigenetics

_______ Plant

_______ White

_______ Body plan

_______ Apoptosis

20. Systems Biology,

CHAPTER OUTLINE: KEY TERMS, PEOPLE, PLACES, CONCEPTS

Cell

Drosophila melanogaster

Morgan

Mutation

Polytene chromosome

Balancer chromosome

Balancer

Engrailed

Promoter

Escherichia coli

Mouse

Blastocyst

Inner cell mass

Morula

Primitive streak

Synteny

Primitive

Germline

Homologous recombination

Microinjection

Gene knockout

20. Systems Biology,

CHAPTER OUTLINE: KEY TERMS, PEOPLE, PLACES, CONCEPTS

Stem cell

Kinase

Tetraloop

Torsion

Angle

Cysteine

CHAPTER HIGHLIGHTS & NOTES: KEY TERMS, PEOPLE, PLACES, CONCEPTS

Synthetic biology	Synthetic biology is the design and construction of biological devices and systems for useful purposes. It is an area of biological research and technology that combines biology and engineering, thus often overlapping with bioengineering and biomedical engineering. It encompasses a variety of different approaches, methodologies, and disciplines with a focus on engineering biology and biotechnology.
Systems biology	Systems biology is an emerging approach applied to biomedical and biological scientific research. Systems biology is a biology-based inter-disciplinary field of study that focuses on complex interactions within biological systems, using a more holistic perspective (holism instead of the more traditional reductionism) approach to biological and biomedical research. Particularly from year 2000 onwards, the concept has been used widely in the biosciences in a variety of contexts.
Candida albicans	Candida albicans is a diploid fungus that grows both as yeast and filamentous cells and a causal agent of opportunistic oral and genital infections in humans. RNA-binding protein Slr1 was recently discovered to play a role in instigating the hyphal formation and virulence in C. albicans. Systemic fungal infections (fungemias) including those by C. albicans have emerged as important causes of morbidity and mortality in immunocompromised patients (e.g., AIDS, cancer chemotherapy, organ or bone marrow transplantation).
Chromosome segregation	Chromosome segregation is a step in cell reproduction or division, where chromosomes pair off with their similar homologous chromosome. In mitosis, a complete copy of each one is made.

Gene	A gene is a molecular unit of heredity of a living organism. It is widely accepted by the scientific community as a name given to some stretches of deoxyribonucleic acids (DNA) and ribonucleic acids (RNA) that code for a polypeptide or for an RNA chain that has a function in the organism, though there still are controversies about what plays the role of the genetic material. Living beings depend on genes, as they specify all proteins and functional RNA chains.
Gene expression	Gene expression is the process by which information from a gene is used in the synthesis of a functional gene product. These products are often proteins, but in non-protein coding genes such as ribosomal RNA (rRNA), transfer RNA (tRNA) or small nuclear RNA (snRNA) genes, the product is a functional RNA. The process of gene expression is used by all known life - eukaryotes (including multicellular organisms), prokaryotes (bacteria and archaea), possibly induced by viruses - to generate the macromolecular machinery for life. Several steps in the gene expression process may be modulated, including the transcription, RNA splicing, translation, and post-translational modification of a protein.
Robustness	In biology, robustness is used to describe a species with a morphology based on strength and a heavy build. The alternative morphology is the gracile body type. For example, comparing similar species, rats have robust body types while mice are gracile.
Steady state	In ionic steady state, cells maintain different internal and external concentrations of various ionic species. The following is an inaccurate and unsupported statement, be warned: Cell membranes are permeable to potassium and various other ions, so in order to maintain a constant ionic concentration the cell must expend energy to actively transport these ions against the electrochemical gradient, out of the cell, at the same rate as they diffuse inward. Conversely, membranes are not permeable to sodium, so this ion must be actively pumped into the cell.
Inversion	In evolutionary developmental biology, inversion refers to the hypothesis that during the course of animal evolution, the structures along the dorsoventral axis have taken on an orientation opposite that of the ancestral form. In the early 19th century, the French naturalist Étienne Geoffroy Saint-Hilaire noted that the organization of dorsal and ventral structures in arthropods is opposite that of mammals. Decades later, in light of Darwin's theory of “descent with modification,” Anton Dohrn proposed that these groups arose from a common ancestor which possessed a body plan similar to that of modern annelids with a ventral nerve cord and dorsal heart.
Embryogenesis	Embryogenesis is the process by which the embryo forms and develops. In mammals, the term refers chiefly to early stages of prenatal development, whereas the terms fetus and fetal development describe later stages.

20. Systems Biology,

CHAPTER HIGHLIGHTS & NOTES: KEY TERMS, PEOPLE, PLACES, CONCEPTS

Protein	Proteins are large biological molecules consisting of one or more chains of amino acids. Proteins perform a vast array of functions within living organisms, including catalyzing metabolic reactions, replicating DNA, responding to stimuli, and transporting molecules from one location to another. Proteins differ from one another primarily in their sequence of amino acids, which is dictated by the nucleotide sequence of their genes, and which usually results in folding of the protein into a specific three-dimensional structure that determines its activity.
Repressilator	The repressilator is a synthetic genetic regulatory network reported in a paper by Michael Elowitz and Stanislas Leibler. This network was designed from scratch to exhibit a stable oscillation which is reported via the expression of green fluorescent protein, and hence acts like an electrical oscillator system with fixed time periods. The network was implemented in Escherichia coli using standard molecular biology methods and observations were performed that verify that the engineered colonies do indeed exhibit the desired oscillatory behavior.
Caenorhabditis elegans	Caenorhabditis elegans is a free-living, transparent nematode, about 1 mm in length, that lives in temperate soil environments. The name is a blend of Greek (caeno- = new, recent + rhabditis = rod -like) and Latin (elegans = elegant). In 1900, Maupas initially named it Rhabditis elegans, Osche placed in the subgenus Caenorhabditis in 1952, and Dougherty raised it to generic status in 1955. In 1974, Sydney Brenner began research into the molecular and developmental biology of C. elegans, which has since been extensively used as a model organism.
Cold Spring Harbor Laboratory	The Cold Spring Harbor Laboratory is a private, non-profit institution with research programs focusing on cancer, neurobiology, plant genetics, genomics and bioinformatics. The Laboratory has a broad educational mission, including the Watson School of Biological Sciences (founded in 1998). It currently employs over 400 scientists.
Luria	Luria is a genus of sea snails, marine gastropod mollusks in the family Cypraeidae, the cowries.
Model organism	A model organism is a non-human species that is extensively studied to understand particular biological phenomena, with the expectation that discoveries made in the organism model will provide insight into the workings of other organisms. Model organisms are in vivo models and are widely used to research human disease when human experimentation would be unfeasible or unethical. This strategy is made possible by the common descent of all living organisms, and the conservation of metabolic and developmental pathways and genetic material over the course of evolution.
Phage group	The phage group was an informal network of biologists centered around Max Delbrück that contributed heavily to bacterial genetics and the origins of molecular biology in the mid-20th century. The phage group takes its name from bacteriophages, the bacteria-infecting viruses that the group used as experimental model organisms. In addition to Delbrück, important scientists associated with the phage group include: Salvador Luria, Alfred Hershey, Seymour Benzer, Gunther Stent, James D.

Choice	Choice consists of the mental process of judging the merits of multiple options and selecting one or more of them. While a choice can be made between imagined options , often a choice is made between real options and followed by the corresponding action. For example, a route for a journey is chosen based on the preference of arriving at a given destination as soon as possible.
Prophage	A prophage is a phage genome inserted and integrated into the circular bacterial DNA chromosome or existing as an extrachromosomal plasmid. This is a latent form of a bacteriophage, in which the viral genes are present in the bacterium without causing disruption of the bacterial cell. Upon detection of host cell damage, such as UV light or certain chemicals, the prophage is excised from the bacterial chromosome in a process called prophage induction.
Bacteriophage	A bacteriophage is a virus that infects and replicates within bacteria. The term is derived from 'bacteria' and the Greek fa?e?? phagein 'to devour'. Bacteriophages are composed of proteins that encapsulate a DNA or RNA genome, and may have relatively simple or elaborate structures.
Experiment	The Experiment was an early nineteenth century boat powered by horses and incorporated the then novel idea of a screw propeller.
Genome	In modern molecular biology and genetics, the genome is the entirety of an organism's hereditary information. It is encoded either in DNA or, for many types of viruses, in RNA. The genome includes both the genes and the non-coding sequences of the DNA/RNA.
Latent period	Latent period is the time elapsed from virus entry into the cell until the first progeny are released. Latent period can also refer to the time delay between muscle stimulation and the beginning of contraction.
Recombinant DNA	Recombinant DNA molecules are DNA molecules formed by laboratory methods of genetic recombination (such as molecular cloning) to bring together genetic material from multiple sources, creating sequences that would not otherwise be found in biological organisms. Recombinant DNA is possible because DNA molecules from all organisms share the same chemical structure; they differ only in the sequence of nucleotides within that identical overall structure. Consequently, when DNA from a foreign source is linked to host sequences that can drive DNA replication and then introduced into a host organism, the foreign DNA is replicated along with the host DNA.
Complementation	In genetics, complementation occurs when two strains of an organism with different homozygous recessive mutations that produce the same phenotype produce offspring with the wild-type phenotype when mated or crossed. Complementation will occur only if the mutations are in different genes. In this case, each strain's genome supplies the wild-type allele to 'complement' the mutated allele of the other strain's genome.

20. Systems Biology,

CHAPTER HIGHLIGHTS & NOTES: KEY TERMS, PEOPLE, PLACES, CONCEPTS

Prediction	A prediction or forecast is a statement about the way things will happen in the future, often but not always based on experience or knowledge. While there is much overlap between prediction and forecast, a prediction may be a statement that some outcome is expected, while a forecast is more specific, and may cover a range of possible outcomes. Although guaranteed information about the future is in many cases impossible, prediction is necessary to allow plans to be made about possible developments; Howard H. Stevenson writes that prediction in business '... is at least two things: Important and hard.'
Transduction	Transduction is the process by which DNA is transferred from one bacterium to another by a virus. It also refers to the process whereby foreign DNA is introduced into another cell via a viral vector. Transduction does not require physical contact between the cell donating the DNA and the cell receiving the DNA (which occurs in conjugation), and it is DNAase resistant (transformation is susceptible to DNAase).
Bacteria	Bacteria constitute a large domain or kingdom of prokaryotic microorganisms. Typically a few micrometres in length, bacteria have a wide range of shapes, ranging from spheres to rods and spirals. Bacteria were among the first life forms to appear on Earth, and are present in most habitats on the planet.
Bacterial growth	Bacterial growth is the division of one piece of bacteria into two daughter cells in a process called binary fission. Providing no mutational event occurs the resulting daughter cells are genetically identical to the original cell. Hence, 'local doubling' of the bacterial population occurs.
Jacob	The Jacob sheep is a rare breed of small, piebald, polycerate (multi-horned) sheep. Jacobs may have from two to six horns, but most commonly have four. The most common color is black and white.
Evolution	Evolution is a 2001 documentary series by the American broadcaster Public Broadcasting Service and WGBH on evolutionary biology. The spokespeople for the series were Jane Goodall (overall spokesperson), Kenneth R. Miller and Stephen Jay Gould (science spokespeople), Eugenie C. Scott (education spokesperson), Arthur Peacocke and Arnold Thomas (religious spokespeople). The series was narrated by the Irish actor Liam Neeson.
Insect	Insects (from Latin insectum, a calque of Greek ??t?µ?? [éntomon], 'cut into sections') are a class of invertebrates within the arthropod phylum that have a chitinous exoskeleton, a three-part body, three pairs of jointed legs, compound eyes and one pair of antennae. They are among the most diverse groups of animals on the planet, including more than a million described species and representing more than half of all known living organisms.

Lactose

Lactose is a disaccharide sugar derived from galactose and glucose that is found in milk. Lactose makes up around 0~8% of milk (by weight), although the amount varies among species and individuals. It is extracted from sweet or sour whey.

Lactose permease

Lactose permease is a membrane protein which is a member of the major facilitator superfamily. Lactose permease can be classified as a symporter, which uses the gradient of H+ towards the cell to transport lactose in the same direction into the cell.

The protein has twelve transmembrane helices and exhibits an internal two-fold symmetry, relating the N-terminal six helices onto the C-terminal helices.

Assay

An assay is an investigative procedure in laboratory medicine, pharmacology, environmental biology, and molecular biology for qualitatively assessing or quantitatively measuring the presence or amount or the functional activity of a target entity (the analyte), which can be a drug or biochemical substance or a cell in an organism or organic sample. The measured entity is generally called the analyte, or the measurand or the target of the assay. The assay usually aims to measure an intensive property of the analyte and express it in the relevant measurement unit (e.g. molarity, density, functional activity in enzyme international units, degree of some effect in comparison to a standard, etc)..

Chromosome

A chromosome is an organized structure of DNA, protein, and RNA found in cells. It is a single piece of coiled DNA containing many genes, regulatory elements and other nucleotide sequences. Chromosomes also contain DNA-bound proteins, which serve to package the DNA and control its functions.

Cloning

In biology, cloning is the process of producing similar populations of genetically identical individuals that occurs in nature when organisms such as bacteria, insects or plants reproduce asexually. Cloning in biotechnology refers to processes used to create copies of DNA fragments (molecular cloning), cells (cell cloning), or organisms. The term also refers to the production of multiple copies of a product such as digital media or software.

Cloning vector

A cloning vector is a small piece of DNA, taken from a virus, a plasmid, or the cell of a higher organism, that can be stably maintained in an organism, and into which a foreign DNA fragment can be inserted for cloning purposes. The vector therefore contains features that allow for the convenient insertion or removal of DNA fragment in or out of the vector, for example by treating the vector and the foreign DNA with a restriction enzyme that creates the same overhang, then ligating the fragments together. After a DNA fragment has been cloned into a cloning vector, it may be further subcloned into another vector designed for more specific use.

Hot spot	In veterinary medicine, a 'hot spot' (or acute pyoderma, acute moist pyotraumatic dermatitis) is one of the many names for a raw, painful, irritated skin lesion that results in and worsens from a pet (such as a dog or a cat) constantly biting, scratching, chewing, and licking an area of its skin that is irritated or itchy. If it is covered by the dog's hair, the hair holds in the moisture and further irritates it. It is a patch that appears suddenly and is often bright red, hairless, and scaly looking.
Insertional mutagenesis	Insertional mutagenesis is mutagenesis of DNA by the insertion of one or more bases. Insertional mutations can occur naturally, mediated by virus or transposon, or can be artificially created for research purposes in the lab.
Limb	A limb, or extremity, is a jointed, or prehensile (as octopus tentacles or new world monkey tails), appendage of the human or other animal body. In the human body, the upper and lower limbs are commonly called the arms and the legs. Most animals use limbs for locomotion, such as walking, running, or climbing.
Molecular biology	Molecular biology is the branch of biology that deals with the molecular basis of biological activity. This field overlaps with other areas of biology and chemistry, particularly genetics and biochemistry. Molecular biology chiefly concerns itself with understanding the interactions between the various systems of a cell, including the interactions between the different types of DNA, RNA and protein biosynthesis as well as learning how these interactions are regulated.
Martha	Martha was the last known living Passenger Pigeon; she was named 'Martha' in honor of Martha Washington.
Analysis	Analysis is the process of breaking a complex topic or substance into smaller parts to gain a better understanding of it. The technique has been applied in the study of mathematics and logic since before Aristotle (384-322 B.C)., though analysis as a formal concept is a relatively recent development. The word comes from the Ancient Greek ?????s?? (analusis, 'a breaking up', from ana- 'up, throughout' and lysis 'a loosening').
Genetic code	The genetic code is the set of rules by which information encoded within genetic material is translated into proteins by living cells. Biological decoding is accomplished by the ribosome, which links amino acids in an order specified by mRNA, using transfer RNA (tRNA) molecules to carry amino acids and to read the mRNA three nucleotides at a time. The genetic code is highly similar among all organisms and can be expressed in a simple table with 64 entries.

Cistron	A cistron is a gene. The term cistron is used to emphasize that genes exhibit a specific behavior in a cis-trans test; distinct positions (or loci) within a genome are cistronic For example, suppose a mutation at a chromosome position x is responsible for a recessive trait in a diploid organism (where chromosomes come in pairs). We say that the mutation is recessive because the organism will exhibit the wild type phenotype (ordinary trait) unless both chromosomes of a pair have the mutation (homozygous mutation).
Saccharomyces	Saccharomyces is a genus in the kingdom of fungi that includes many species of yeast. Saccharomyces is from Greek s???a? (sugar) and μ???? (mushroom) and means sugar fungus. Many members of this genus are considered very important in food production.
Saccharomyces cerevisiae	Saccharomyces cerevisiae is a species of yeast. It is perhaps the most useful yeast, having been instrumental to winemaking, baking and brewing since ancient times. It is believed that it was originally isolated from the skin of grapes .
Genetic analysis	Genetic analysis is the overall process of studying and researching in fields of science that involve genetics and molecular biology. There are a number of applications that are developed from this research and these are also considered parts of the process. The base system of analysis revolves around general genetics.
Genome size	Genome size is the total amount of DNA contained within one copy of a single genome. It is typically measured in terms of mass in picograms (trillionths (10^{-12}) of a gram, abbreviated pg) or less frequently in Daltons or as the total number of nucleotide base pairs typically in megabases (millions of base pairs, abbreviated Mb or Mbp). One picogram equals 978 megabases.
Transformation	In molecular biology, transformation is genetic alteration of a cell resulting from the direct uptake, incorporation and expression of exogenous genetic material from its surroundings and taken up through the cell membrane(s). Transformation occurs naturally in some species of bacteria, but it can also be effected by artificial means in other cells. For transformation to happen, bacteria must be in a state of competence, which might occur as a time-limited response to environmental conditions such as starvation and cell density.
Yeast	Yeasts are eukaryotic microorganisms classified in the kingdom Fungi, with 1,500 species currently described . Yeasts are unicellular, although some species with yeast forms may become multicellular through the formation of strings of connected budding cells known as pseudohyphae, or false hyphae, as seen in most molds. Yeast size can vary greatly depending on the species, typically measuring 3-4 μm in diameter, although some yeasts can reach over 40 μm.
Dormancy	Dormancy is a period in an organism's life cycle when growth, development, and physical activity are temporarily stopped. This minimizes metabolic activity and therefore helps an organism to conserve energy.

20. Systems Biology,

CHAPTER HIGHLIGHTS & NOTES: KEY TERMS, PEOPLE, PLACES, CONCEPTS

Elongation factor	Elongation factors are a set of proteins that are used in protein synthesis in the cell. In the ribosome, they facilitate translational elongation, from the formation of the first peptide bond to the formation of the last one. Elongation is the most rapid step in translation:•in prokaryotes it proceeds at a rate of 15 to 20 amino acids added per second (about 60 nucleotides per second)•in eukaryotes the rate is about two amino acids per second. Elongation factors play a role in orchestrating the events of this process, and in ensuring the 99.99% accuracy of translation at this speed.
Endosperm	Endosperm is the tissue produced inside the seeds of most flowering plants around the time of fertilization. It surrounds the embryo and provides nutrition in the form of starch, though it can also contain oils and protein. This can make endosperm a source of nutrition in human diet.
Gamete	A gamete is a cell that fuses with another cell during fertilization in organisms that reproduce sexually. In species that produce two morphologically distinct types of gametes, and in which each individual produces only one type, a female is any individual that produces the larger type of gamete--called an ovum (or egg)--and a male produces the smaller tadpole-like type--called a sperm. This is an example of anisogamy or heterogamy, the condition in where females and males produce gametes of different sizes (this is the case in humans; the human ovum has approximately 100,000 times the volume of a single human sperm cell).
Gametophyte	A gametophyte is a haploid multicellular adult stage in the alternation of generations during the life cycle of land plants and algae. It produces haploid gametes. It is produced from mitotic cell division of spores, which are produced by meiosis in sporophytes.
Hermaphrodite	In biology, a hermaphrodite is an organism that has reproductive organs normally associated with both male and female sexes. Many taxonomic groups of animals do not have separate sexes. In these groups, hermaphroditism is a normal condition, enabling a form of sexual reproduction in which both partners can act as the 'female' or 'male'.
Sporophyte	A sporophyte is the diploid multicellular stage in the life cycle of a plant or alga. It develops from the zygote produced when a haploid egg cell is fertilized by a haploid sperm and each cell therefore has a double set of chromosomes, one set from each parent. All land plants, and most multicellular algae, have life cycles in which a multicellular diploid sporophyte phase alternates with a multicellular haploid gametophyte phase.
Heterochromatin	Heterochromatin is a tightly packed form of DNA, which comes in different varieties.

These varieties lie on a continuum between the two extremes of constitutive and facultative heterochromatin. Both play a role in the expression of genes, where constitutive heterochromatin can affect the genes near them (position-effect variegation) and where facultative heterochromatin is the result of genes that are silenced through a mechanism such as histone methylation or siRNA through RNAi.

RNA interference

RNA interference also called post transcriptional gene silencing (PTGS), is a biological process in which RNA molecules inhibit gene expression, typically by causing the destruction of specific mRNA molecules. Historically, it was known by other names, including co-suppression, post transcriptional gene silencing (PTGS), and quelling. Only after these apparently unrelated processes were fully understood did it become clear that they all described the RNAi phenomenon.

Retinitis pigmentosa

Retinitis pigmentosa is an inherited, degenerative eye disease that causes severe vision impairment and often blindness. The progress of RP is not consistent. Some people will exhibit symptoms from infancy, others may not notice symptoms until later in life.

Ti plasmid

A Ti or tumour inducing plasmid is a circular plasmid that often, but not always, is a part of the genetic equipment that Agrobacterium tumefaciens and Agrobacterium rhizogenes use to transduce its genetic material to plants. The Ti plasmid is lost when Agrobacterium is grown above 28°C. Such cured bacteria do not induce crown galls, i.e. they become avirulent. pTi and pRi share little sequence homology but are functionally rather similar.

Transfer DNA

The transfer DNA is the transferred DNA of the tumor-inducing (Ti) plasmid of some species of bacteria such as Agrobacterium tumefaciens and Agrobacterium rhizogenes. It derives its name from the fact that the bacterium transfers this DNA fragment into the host plant's nuclear DNA genome. The T-DNA is bordered by 25-base-pair repeats on each end.

Reverse genetics

Reverse genetics is an approach to discover the function of a gene by analyzing the phenotypic effects of specific gene sequences obtained by DNA sequencing. This investigative process proceeds in the opposite direction of so-called forward genetic screens of classical genetics. Simply put, while forward genetics seeks to find the genetic basis of a phenotype or trait, reverse genetics seeks to find what phenotypes arise as a result of particular genetic sequences.

Ribosome

The ribosome is a large and complex molecular machine, found within all living cells, that serves as the primary site of biological protein synthesis (translation). Ribosomes link amino acids together in the order specified by messenger RNA (mRNA) molecules. Ribosomes consist of two major subunits--the small ribosomal subunit reads the mRNA, while the large subunit joins amino acids to form a polypeptide chain.

Forward genetics

Forward genetics encompasses several means of identifying the genotype that is responsible for a phenotype. Initially, this was done by generating random mutations in an organism, often with radiation or insertional mutagenesis (ex.

20. Systems Biology,

Imprinting	Imprinting is the term used in psychology and ethology to describe any kind of phase-sensitive learning that is rapid and apparently independent of the consequences of behavior. It was first used to describe situations in which an animal or person learns the characteristics of some stimulus, which is therefore said to be 'imprinted' onto the subject. Imprinting is hypothesized to have a critical period.
MicroRNA	A microRNA is a small non-coding RNA molecule (ca. 22 nucleotides) found in plants and animals, which functions in transcriptional and post-transcriptional regulation of gene expression. Encoded by eukaryotic nuclear DNA, miRNAs function via base-pairing with complementary sequences within mRNA molecules, usually resulting in gene silencing via translational repression or target degradation. The human genome may encode over 1000 miRNAs, which may target about 60% of mammalian genes and are abundant in many human cell types.
Mutagenesis	Mutagenesis in the laboratory is an important technique whereby DNA mutations are deliberately engineered to produce mutant genes, proteins, strains of bacteria, or other genetically-modified organisms. Various constituents of a gene, such as its control elements and its gene product, may be mutated so that the functioning of a gene or protein can be examined in detail. The mutation may also produce mutant proteins with interesting properties, or enhanced or novel functions that may be of commercial use.
Genetics	Genetics, a discipline of biology, is the science of genes, heredity, and variation in living organisms. Genetics concerns the process of trait inheritance from parents to offspring, including the molecular structure and function of genes, gene behavior in the context of a cell or organism (e.g. dominance and epigenetics), gene distribution, and variation and change in populations (such as through Genome-Wide Association Studies). Given that genes are universal to living organisms, genetics can be applied to the study of all living systems; including bacteria, plants, animals, and humans.
Growth factor	A growth factor is a naturally occurring substance capable of stimulating cellular growth, proliferation and cellular differentiation. Usually it is a protein or a steroid hormone. Growth factors are important for regulating a variety of cellular processes.
Immunoprecipitation	Immunoprecipitation is the technique of precipitating a protein antigen out of solution using an antibody that specifically binds to that particular protein. This process can be used to isolate and concentrate a particular protein from a sample containing many thousands of different proteins. Immunoprecipitation requires that the antibody be coupled to a solid substrate at some point in the procedure.
Methylation	In the chemical sciences, methylation denotes the addition of a methyl group to a substrate or the substitution of an atom or group by a methyl group. Methylation is a form of alkylation with a methyl group, rather than a larger carbon chain, replacing a hydrogen atom.

Transcription

Transcription is the first step of gene expression, in which a particular segment of DNA is copied into RNA by the enzyme, RNA polymerase. Both RNA and DNA are nucleic acids, which use base pairs of nucleotides as a complementary language that can be converted back and forth from DNA to RNA by the action of the correct enzymes. During transcription, a DNA sequence is read by an RNA polymerase, which produces a complementary, antiparallel RNA strand.

Environment

The biophysical environment is the biotic and abiotic surrounding of an organism or population, and includes particularly the factors that have an influence in their survival, development and evolution. The naked term environment can make reference to different concepts, but it is often used as a short form for the biophysical environment. This practice is common, for instance, among governments, that usually name their departments and agencies dealing with the biophysical environment with denominations like Environment Agency.

Pattern formation

The science of pattern formation deals with the visible, orderly outcomes of self-organization and the common principles behind similar patterns in nature.

In developmental biology, pattern formation refers to the generation of complex organizations of cell fates in space and time. Pattern formation is controlled by genes.

Stress

Stress is a person's response to a stressor such as an environmental condition or a stimulus. Stress is a body's way to react to a challenge. According to the stressful event, the body's way to respond to stress is by sympathetic nervous system activation which results in the fight-or-flight response.

Vernalization

Vernalization is the acquisition of a plant's ability to flower in the spring by exposure to the prolonged cold of winter. After vernalization, plants have acquired the ability to flower, but they may require additional seasonal cues or weeks of growth before they will actually flower.

Many plants grown in temperate climates require vernalization and must experience a period of low winter temperature to initiate or accelerate the flowering process.

Epigenetics

In biology, and specifically genetics, epigenetics is the study of mitotically or meiotically heritable changes in gene expression or cellular phenotype, caused by mechanisms other than changes in the underlying DNA sequence--hence the name epi- -genetics.

The term also refers to the changes themselves: functionally relevant changes to the genome that do not involve a change in the nucleotide sequence. Examples of mechanisms that produce such changes are DNA methylation and histone modification, each of which alters how genes are expressed without altering the underlying DNA sequence.

Plant

Plants, also called green plants (Viridiplantae in Latin), are living multicellular organisms of the kingdom Plantae.

They form a clade that includes the flowering plants, conifers and other gymnosperms, ferns, clubmosses, hornworts, liverworts and mosses, as well as, depending on definition, the green algae. Plants exclude the red and brown seaweeds such as kelp, the fungi, Archaea and bacteria.

White

White Gene, abbreviated w, was the first sex-linked mutation ever discovered in the fruit fly Drosophila melanogaster. In 1910 Thomas Hunt Morgan and Lilian Vaughan Morgan collected a single male white-eyed mutant from a population of Drosophila melanogaster fruit flies, which usually have dark brick red eyes. Upon crossing this male with wild-type female flies, they found that the offspring did not conform to the expectations of Mendelian inheritance.

Body plan

A body plan, baupläne, ground plan, ground pattern, or bodyplan, is 'an assemblage of morphological features shared among many members of a phylum-level group'.

This term, usually applied to animals, envisages a 'blueprint' encompassing aspects such as symmetry, segmentation and limb disposition. Body plans have historically been considered to have evolved in a flash in the Cambrian Explosion, but a more nuanced understanding of animal evolution suggests the gradual development of body plans throughout the early Palaeozoic.

Apoptosis

Apoptosis is the process of programmed cell death (PCD) that may occur in multicellular organisms. Biochemical events lead to characteristic cell changes (morphology) and death. These changes include blebbing, cell shrinkage, nuclear fragmentation, chromatin condensation, and chromosomal DNA fragmentation.

Cell

The cell is the basic structural, functional and biological unit of all known living organisms. Cells are the smallest unit of life that is classified as a living thing, and are often called the 'building blocks of life'.

Cells consist of a protoplasm enclosed within a membrane, which contains many biomolecules such as proteins and nucleic acids.

Drosophila melanogaster

Drosophila melanogaster is a species of Fly (the taxonomic order Diptera) in the family Drosophilidae. The species is known generally as the common fruit fly or vinegar fly. Starting with Charles W. Woodworth's proposal of the use of this species as a model organism, D. melanogaster continues to be widely used for biological research in studies of genetics, physiology, microbial pathogenesis and life history evolution.

Morgan

Morgan is a lone female orca that was rescued in the Wadden Sea, off the northwestern coast of the Netherlands in June 2010. She lived several months in the Dolfinarium Harderwijk in the Netherlands. After a legal battle she was transported to the Loro Parque in Spain.

Mutation

In genetics, a mutation is a change of the nucleotide sequence of the genome of an organism, virus, or extrachromosomal genetic element.

	Mutations result from unrepaired damage to DNA or to RNA genomes (typically caused by radiation or chemical mutagens), errors in the process of replication, or from the insertion or deletion of segments of DNA by mobile genetic elements. Mutations may or may not produce discernible changes in the observable characteristics (phenotype) of an organism.
Polytene chromosome	Polytene chromosomes are over-sized chromosomes which have developed from standard chromosomes and are commonly found in the salivary glands of Drosophila melanogaster. Specialized cells undergo repeated rounds of DNA replication without cell division (endomitosis), to increase cell volume, forming a giant polytene chromosome. Polytene chromosomes form when multiple rounds of replication produce many sister chromatids that remain synapsed together.
Balancer chromosome	Balancer chromosomes are special, modified chromosomes used for genetically screening a population of organisms to select for heterozygotes. Balancer chromosomes can be used as a genetic tool to prevent crossing over (genetic recombination) between homologous chromosomes during meiosis. Balancers are most often used in Drosophila melanogaster (fruit fly) genetics to allow populations of flies carrying heterozygous mutations to be maintained without constantly screening for the mutations but can also be used in mice.
Balancer	Balancer are a hybrid breed of beef cattle, a combination of Gelbvieh and Angus. These cattle are bred for their hybrid vigour, resulting in a higher growth rate and better quality meat.
Engrailed	Engrailed is a homeodomain transcription factor involved in many aspects of multicellular development. First known for its role in arthropod embryological development, working in consort with the Hox genes, engrailed has been found to be important in other areas of development. It has been identified in many bilaterians, including the vertebrates, echinoderms, molluscs, nematodes, brachiopods, and polychaetes.
Promoter	In genetics, a promoter is a region of DNA that initiates transcription of a particular gene. Promoters are located near the genes they transcribe, on the same strand and upstream on the DNA (towards the 3' region of the anti-sense strand, also called template strand and non-coding strand). Promoters can be about 100-1000 base pairs long.
Escherichia coli	Escherichia coli is a Gram-negative, facultative anaerobic, rod-shaped bacterium that is commonly found in the lower intestine of warm-blooded organisms (endotherms). Most E. coli strains are harmless, but some serotypes can cause serious food poisoning in humans, and are occasionally responsible for product recalls due to food contamination. The harmless strains are part of the normal flora of the gut, and can benefit their hosts by producing vitamin K_2, and by preventing the establishment of pathogenic bacteria within the intestine.
Mouse	A mouse is a small mammal belonging to the order of rodents, characteristically having a pointed snout, small rounded ears, and a long naked or almost hairless tail. The best known mouse species is the common house mouse.

20. Systems Biology,

Blastocyst	The blastocyst is a structure formed in the early gestation of vertebrates. It is preceded by the morula. It possesses an inner cell mass (ICM), or embryoblast, which subsequently forms the embryo, and an outer layer of cells, or trophoblast, surrounding the inner cell mass and a fluid-filled cavity known as the blastocoele.
Inner cell mass	In early embryogenesis of most eutherian mammals, the inner cell mass is the mass of cells inside the primordial embryo that will eventually give rise to the definitive structures of the fetus. This structure forms in the earliest steps of development, before implantation into the endometrium of the uterus has occurred. The Inner cell mass lies within the blastocoele (more correctly termed 'blastocyst cavity,' as it is not strictly homologous to the blastocoele of anamniote vertebrates) and is entirely surrounded by the single layer of cells called trophoblast.
Morula	A morula is an embryo at an early stage of embryonic development, consisting of cells (called blastomeres) in a solid ball contained within the zona pellucida. The morula is produced by squad embryonic cleavage, the rapid division of the zygote. Once the zygote has divided into 32 cells, it begins to resemble a mulberry, hence the name morula.
Primitive streak	The primitive streak is a structure that forms in the blastula during the early stages of avian, reptilian and mammalian embryonic development. The presence of the primitive streak will establish bilateral symmetry, determine the site of gastrulation and initiate germ layer formation. To form the streak, reptiles, birds and mammals arrange mesenchymal cells along the prospective midline, establishing the second embryonic axis, as well as the place where cells will ingress and migrate during the process of gastrulation and germ layer formation.
Synteny	In classical genetics, synteny describes the physical co-localization of genetic loci on the same chromosome within an individual or species. Today, however, biologists usually refer to synteny as the conservation of blocks of order within two sets of chromosomes that are being compared with each other. This concept can also be referred to as shared synteny.
Primitive	Primitive in the sense most relevant to phylogenetics means resembling evolutionary ancestors of living things and in particular resembling them in the nature of their anatomy and behaviour. For example, one might regard a flatworm, which has no legs, wings, or image-forming eyes, as more primitive than a beetle, that in its more advanced morphology has all these things. The term 'primitive' might suggest simplicity, but need not strictly imply it; many 'advanced' organisms have lost complex structures that were present in some of their ancestral forms.
Germline	In biology and genetics, the germline of a mature or developing individual is the line of germ cells that have genetic material that may be passed to a child.

For example, gametes such as the sperm or the egg are part of the germline. So are the cells that divide to produce the gametes, called gametocytes, the cells that produce those, called gametogonia, and all the way back to the zygote, the cell from which the individual developed.

Homologous recombination

Homologous recombination is a type of genetic recombination in which nucleotide sequences are exchanged between two similar or identical molecules of DNA. It is most widely used by cells to accurately repair harmful breaks that occur on both strands of DNA, known as double-strand breaks. Homologous recombination also produces new combinations of DNA sequences during meiosis, the process by which eukaryotes make gamete cells, like sperm and egg cells in animals. These new combinations of DNA represent genetic variation in offspring, which in turn enables populations to adapt during the course of evolution.

Microinjection

Microinjection refers to the process of using a glass micropipette to inject a liquid substance at a microscopic or borderline macroscopic level. The target is often a living cell but may also include intercellular space. Microinjection is a simple mechanical process usually involving an inverted microscope with a magnification power of around 200x (though sometimes it is performed using a dissecting stereo microscope at 40-50x or a traditional compound upright microscope at similar power to an inverted model).

Gene knockout

A gene knockout is a genetic technique in which one of an organism's genes are made inoperative ('knocked out' of the organism). Also known as knockout organisms or simply knockouts, they are used in learning about a gene that has been sequenced, but which has an unknown or incompletely known function. Researchers draw inferences from the difference between the knockout organism and normal individuals.

Stem cell

Stem cells are undifferentiated biological cells, that can differentiate into specialized cells and can divide to produce more stem cells. They are found in multicellular organisms. In mammals, there are two broad types of stem cells: embryonic stem cells, which are isolated from the inner cell mass of blastocysts, and adult stem cells, which are found in various tissues.

Kinase

In enzymology, a [tyrosine 3-monooxygenase] kinase is an enzyme that catalyzes the chemical reactionATP + [tyrosine-3-monooxygenase] $\rightleftharpoons$ ADP + phospho-[tyrosine-3-monooxygenase]

Thus, the two substrates of this enzyme are ATP and tyrosine-3-monooxygenase, whereas its two products are ADP and [[phospho-[tyrosine-3-monooxygenase]]].

This enzyme belongs to the family of transferases, specifically those transferring a phosphate group to the sidechain oxygen atom of serine or threonine residues in proteins (protein-serine/threonine kinases). The systematic name of this enzyme class is ATP:[tyrosine-3-monoxygenase] phosphotransferase.

20. Systems Biology,

CHAPTER HIGHLIGHTS & NOTES: KEY TERMS, PEOPLE, PLACES, CONCEPTS

Tetraloop

Tetraloops are a type of four-base hairpin loop motifs in RNA secondary structure that cap many double helices. Three types of tetraloops are common in ribosomal RNA: GNRA, UNCG and CUUG. The GNRA tetraloop has a guanine-adenine base-pair where the guanine is 5' to the helix and the adenine is 3' to the helix.

Torsion

Torsion is an anatomical event which takes place during the very early part of the life of snails and slugs of all kinds. In other words, torsion is a gastropod synapomorphy which occurs in all gastropods during larval development. Torsion is the rotation of the visceral mass, mantle, and shell 180° with respect to the head and foot of the gastropod.

Angle

The angle of a rib (costal angle) may both refer to the bending part of it, and a prominent line in this area, a little in front of the tubercle.

This line is directed downward and laterally; this gives attachment to a tendon of the iliocostalis muscle.

At this point the rib is bent in two directions, and at the same time twisted on its long axis.

Cysteine

Cysteine is an a-amino acid with the chemical formula $HO_2CCH(NH_2)CH_2SH$. It is a semi-essential amino acid, which means that it can be biosynthesized in humans. The thiol side chain in cysteine often participates in enzymatic reactions, serving as a nucleophile. The thiol is susceptible to oxidization to give the disulfide derivative cystine, which serves an important structural role in many proteins.

CHAPTER QUIZ: KEY TERMS, PEOPLE, PLACES, CONCEPTS

1. The _________ is a synthetic genetic regulatory network reported in a paper by Michael Elowitz and Stanislas Leibler. This network was designed from scratch to exhibit a stable oscillation which is reported via the expression of green fluorescent protein, and hence acts like an electrical oscillator system with fixed time periods. The network was implemented in Escherichia coli using standard molecular biology methods and observations were performed that verify that the engineered colonies do indeed exhibit the desired oscillatory behavior.

   a. Repressilator
   b. Blood substitute
   c. Mycoplasma laboratorium
   d. Playing God

2. . In evolutionary developmental biology, _________ refers to the hypothesis that during the course of animal evolution, the structures along the dorsoventral axis have taken on an orientation opposite that of the ancestral form.

In the early 19th century, the French naturalist Étienne Geoffroy Saint-Hilaire noted that the organization of dorsal and ventral structures in arthropods is opposite that of mammals. Decades later, in light of Darwin's theory of "descent with modification," Anton Dohrn proposed that these groups arose from a common ancestor which possessed a body plan similar to that of modern annelids with a ventral nerve cord and dorsal heart.

a. Baldwin effect
b. Bateson-Dobzhansky-Muller Model
c. Inversion
d. Character displacement

3. _________ is a species of Fly (the taxonomic order Diptera) in the family Drosophilidae. The species is known generally as the common fruit fly or vinegar fly. Starting with Charles W. Woodworth's proposal of the use of this species as a model organism, D. melanogaster continues to be widely used for biological research in studies of genetics, physiology, microbial pathogenesis and life history evolution.

a. Barley
b. Bifidobacterium longum
c. Drosophila melanogaster
d. Botryllus schlosseri

4. In genetics, a _________ is a change of the nucleotide sequence of the genome of an organism, virus, or extrachromosomal genetic element. _________s result from unrepaired damage to DNA or to RNA genomes (typically caused by radiation or chemical mutagens), errors in the process of replication, or from the insertion or deletion of segments of DNA by mobile genetic elements. _________s may or may not produce discernible changes in the observable characteristics (phenotype) of an organism.

a. 2q37 monosomy
b. Mutation
c. B chromosome
d. Backcrossing

5. . _________, a discipline of biology, is the science of genes, heredity, and variation in living organisms.

_________ concerns the process of trait inheritance from parents to offspring, including the molecular structure and function of genes, gene behavior in the context of a cell or organism (e.g. dominance and epi_________), gene distribution, and variation and change in populations (such as through Genome-Wide Association Studies). Given that genes are universal to living organisms, _________ can be applied to the study of all living systems; including bacteria, plants, animals, and humans.

a. Gordo
b. Genetics
c. Laika

ANSWER KEY
20. Systems Biology,

1. a
2. c
3. c
4. b
5. b

Other Facts101 e-Books and Tests